THE BULKIES: POLICE AND CRIME
BELFAST, 1800–1865

IN THIS SERIES

ALSO AVAILABLE

The Bulkies:
Police and Crime in Belfast, 1800–1865

BRIAN GRIFFIN

IRISH ACADEMIC PRESS

in association with

THE IRISH LEGAL HISTORY SOCIETY

First published in 1998 by
IRISH ACADEMIC PRESS
44, Northumberland Road, Dublin 4, Ireland,
and in North America for
IRISH ACADEMIC PRESS
c/o ISBS, 5804 NE Hassalo Street, Portland, OR 97213.

A catalogue record for this book
is available from the British Library.

ISBN 0–7165–2670–0 Cloth
0–7165–2695–6 Paper

Typeset in 11 pt on 12 pt Plantin by
Carrigboy Typesetting Services, Co. Cork.

Printed by ColourBooks Ltd, Dublin.

Preface

THE IDEA OF RESEARCHING the history of the nineteenth-century Belfast borough police – the force better known by their nickname of the Bulkies – first occurred to me while I was engaged in researching the social history of the Royal Irish Constabulary and Dublin Metropolitan Police for my Ph.D. When I read about the extensive Belfast riots of 1857 and 1864, I became aware for the first time that the Irish Constabulary were not the only police force in the Ulster city; that there had been, in fact, a separate police force in Belfast prior to 1865. This other force, I discovered when I tried to read more about its activities, has been almost entirely overlooked by historians, except for some who have examined its controversial role in the 1857 and 1864 riots. This book is an attempt to redress the neglect of historians and to rescue the Bulkies from their undeserved obscurity. The choice of title, too, has been dictated by just such considerations.

In researching and writing this book, I have incurred a debt of gratitude to the staff of a number of libraries, archives and other institutions. I would like above all to place on record my thanks to the friendly staff at Belfast City Hall who allowed me to examine the minute books of the Belfast police commissioners and police committee, and to the equally helpful staffs of the Linenhall Library, Belfast Central Library, the Public Record Office of Northern Ireland, the Royal Ulster Constabulary Museum, the Ulster Museum, the National Library of Ireland, the National Archives in Dublin, the British Library and the London Fire Brigade Library. For permission to quote from manuscripts in their possession I would like to thank the following: Mr Robin Sinclair, Curator of the Royal Ulster Constabulary Museum, Dr David Craig, Director of the National Archives, Dr A.P.W. Malcomson, Deputy Keeper of the Records, Public Record Office of Northern Ireland, and to Ms Priscilla Campbell-Allen, owner of Reverend A. McIntyre's diary (PRONI, D.1558/2/3). My editor, Professor W.N. Osborough, made painstaking efforts to ensure that the manuscript was fit for publication. I would also like to thank the Institute of Irish Studies at the Queen's University of Belfast, for granting me the Junior Research Fellowship which made my initial research into the Bulkies possible.

BRIAN GRIFFIN

Contents

List of Illustrations

Frontispiece: Pottinger's Entry: View towards Ann Street (1892) by Ernest Hanford. Photograph reproduced with the kind permission of the trustees of the Ulster Museum, Belfast.

Illustrations appear between p. 84 and p. 85.

1. Advertisement of reward for information about the culprits who dug up the body of a Yeoman in Friar's Bush graveyard on 9 January 1814. Source: *Belfast Newsletter*, 1 February 1814. Reproduced courtesy of Mike McComb, Head Librarian, *Belfast Newsletter*.

2. Advertisement of reward for information about the culprits who bombed the house of Francis Johnson, muslin manufacturer, of Peter's Hill, on 28 February 1816. Source: *Belfast Newsletter*, 1 March 1816. Reproduced courtesy of Mike McComb, Head Librarian, *Belfast Newsletter*.

3. Advertisement for recruits to the Belfast police, August 1816. Source: *Belfast Newsletter*, 27 August 1816. Reproduced courtesy of Mike McComb, Head Librarian, *Belfast Newsletter*.

4. Map of Belfast in 1822. Source: George Benn, *The history of the town of Belfast* (Belfast, 1823). Reproduced courtesy of the British Library.

5. The Long Bridge, 'haunt of beggars, thieves, and thieves' compeers', *c.*1822. Source: George Benn, *The history of the town of Belfast* (Belfast, 1823). Reproduced courtesy of the British Library.

6. High Street, *c.*1830. Reproduced by courtesy of the trustees of the Ulster Museum, Belfast.

7. Map of Belfast in *c.*1842. Source: *Belfast and its environs, with a tour to the Giant's Causeway* (Dublin, 1842). Reproduced courtesy of the British Library.

Abbreviations

B.D.M.	*Belfast Daily Mercury*
B.N.L.	*Belfast Newsletter*
D.M.P.	Dublin Metropolitan Police
EHR	*English Historical Review*
Ir Jur	*Irish Jurist*
NA	National Archives
NLI	National Library of Ireland
N.W.	*Northern Whig*
PRONI	Public Record Office of Northern Ireland
R.I.C.	Royal Irish Constabulary

CHAPTER ONE

The police in eighteenth and nineteenth-century Ireland

SINCE THE LATE EIGHTEENTH century, Irish society has been affected to an enormous extent by the presence and activity of various police forces. Today we take for granted, north and south of the border, the presence of full-time, professional, centralized police paid for by the two governments responsible for governing Ireland. The perception that government-appointed and controlled police are part of the fabric of everyday society was alien just over 200 years ago. Indeed, as one historian has pointed out, for most of the eighteenth century Ireland was, at least theoretically, a self-policing society. Towns and rural parishes were, according to law, required to appoint watchmen to patrol at night for several months of the year, but this requirement, if met at all, was met very unevenly, especially in rural parishes.[1] The best published study of an eighteenth-century Irish watch, Brian Henry's examination of the parish watch in Dublin, reveals a decentralized (each of Dublin's twenty-one Church of Ireland parishes appointed its own watch), inadequately and unevenly-funded 'system' notable mainly for its inefficiency.[2] The inability of the parish watch to suppress public disorder in the 1780s was one of the principal reasons for its replacement, in 1786, with a novel form of police: a centralized, uniformed, permanent watch with jurisdiction throughout the city of Dublin.[3] Stanley Palmer has argued strongly that it was this Dublin watch of 1786, rather than the better-known London Metropolitan Police instituted in 1829, which constitutes the first 'modern'—that is, supraparochial and professional—police force in either Ireland or Britain. Palmer does not, however, posit an unbroken line of suc-

1. S.J. Connolly, *Religion, law and power: the making of Protestant Ireland 1660–1760* (Oxford, 1992), pp.198–99. See also R.B. McDowell, *Ireland in the age of imperialism and revolution 1760–1801* (Oxford, 1979), p.67.

2. Brian Henry, *Dublin hanged: crime, law enforcement and punishment in late eighteenth-century Dublin* (Dublin, 1994), pp.118–36.

3. Ibid, pp.137–53; S.H. Palmer, *Police and protest in England and Ireland 1780–1850* (Cambridge, 1988), pp.92–100, 119–20.

cession between the Dublin police of 1786 and the police forces of twentieth-century Ireland. He shows that the force which was established in 1786 was eventually abolished in 1795 and replaced with a hybrid system consisting of fifty constables controlled by Dublin's corporation and 576 men, mainly watchmen, controlled by the parishes; that this force was in turn replaced by another centralized watch, controlled by Dublin Castle, in 1799; and that the 1799 force was further reformed in 1808, mainly by the inclusion of a 150-strong horse and foot patrol.[4] This watch was eventually replaced in 1838 by a carbon-copy of the London Metropolitan Police, the government-controlled Dublin Metropolitan Police (D.M.P.). Palmer is hazy on the genesis of the D.M.P. Nigel Cochrane, however, shows that it was introduced in response to criticism of the existing force, whose watchmen were considered by Dublin public and corporation alike as hopelessly unsuited to the task of policing the city.[5] The D.M.P. continued to police Dublin until it was absorbed into the Garda Síochána (established in 1922) in 1925.

For most of the hundred years down to 1922, most of Ireland outside of Dublin city was policed by a force which in 1867 became known as the Royal Irish Constabulary (R.I.C.). In 1922 the R.I.C. was abolished and replaced by the Garda Síochána in the Irish Free State and by the Royal Ulster Constabulary in Northern Ireland. Stanley Palmer's magisterial *Police and protest in England and Ireland 1780–1850* (1988) gives the best account of the origins of the R.I.C.[6] The first forerunner of the R.I.C. were the baronial police established in rural Ireland in 1773. Envisaged as a rural force to assist magistrates in executing warrants, collecting revenues and preserving the peace, these baronial police were not a success given their small numbers: in the 1780s there were only about 600 baronial

---

4. Ibid, pp.134–36, 148–57.

5. Ibid, pp.403–04; N.I. Cochrane, 'The policing of Dublin, 1830–46: a study in administration' (unpublished M.A. thesis, University College Dublin, 1984), p.12. For a discussion of the early years of the D.M.P. see N.I. Cochrane, 'Public reaction to the introduction of a new police force: Dublin 1838–45' in *Eire-Ireland*, xxii (1987), 72–85.

6. Previous works which examine the late eighteenth and early nineteenth-century precursors of the R.I.C., and which Palmer's book supersedes, are Tadhg Ó Ceallaigh, 'Peel and police reform in Ireland, 1814–18' in *Stud Hib*, no.6 (1966), 25–48; Galen Broeker, *Rural disorder and police reform in Ireland, 1812–36* (London, 1970); Kevin Boyle, 'Police in Ireland before the union: I' in *Ir Jur*, new series, vii (1972), 115–37; idem, 'Police in Ireland before the union: II' in *Ir Jur*, new series, viii (1973), 90–116; idem, 'Police in Ireland before the union: III' in *Ir Jur*, new series, viii (1973), 323–48.

police throughout all of Ireland.[7] In 1787 the government instituted what it hoped would be a more efficient body in combating disorder in the Irish countryside. The 1787 police act[8] allowed for up to sixteen sub-constables per barony who were appointed by the county grand jury, and these sub-constables were commanded by a chief constable, appointed by the government. This new force replaced the existing baronial police. In the event, however, the new baronial police, some 500 men in total, were established only in disturbed districts of counties Kerry, Kilkenny, Tipperary and Cork, where they were at least moderately effective in combating disorder.[9] The rural police presence was added to in 1792 by the establishment of yet another baronial police appointed by the grand jury—the so-called 'Barnies'. Little is known of the 1792 force, apart from the fact that it had a limited presence (although more widespread than the 1787 force) and that it was ineffective.[10]

Down to 1814, then, rural Ireland's police consisted of the inefficient 1792 baronial force, which maintained a not very active presence in, at most, twenty counties, and the 1787 force, which by 1814 was operating only in parts of Meath and Cork.[11] To combat the widespread agrarian disorder of the period the chief secretary for Ireland, Robert Peel, succeeded in establishing yet another police body, the Peace Preservation Force: these were the first 'Peelers'. The Dublin Castle-controlled 'Peelers' were essentially a mobile paramilitary force, whose main task was to patrol proclaimed districts until tranquillity had been restored. On the restoration of order the 'Peelers' were then transferred to other districts. Starting off with thirty-two officers and men commanded by a special magistrate in the disturbed Tipperary barony of Middlethird in 1814, the force grew to some 2,326 men and officers, under the direction of fifteen special magistrates, in sixteen counties by 1822. The latter year saw the beginning of the introduction of the County Constabulary in Ireland, and a subsequent decline in the strength of the Peace Preservation Force. By the end of 1829 there were only 109 officers and men, directed by two special magistrates, in the force and these were active only in the city and county of

7. Palmer, *Police and protest*, pp.75–76.
8. 27 Geo III, c.42.
9. Palmer, *Police and protest*, pp.111–12, 136–37. In 1795 they also operated in proclaimed districts of Cavan, Leitrim, Longford, Meath, Roscommon, Sligo and Westmeath: ibid, p.139.
10. Ibid, pp.137–38. The nickname of 'Barnies' derives from one Barny McKeown, the most well-known of the 1792 baronial police.
11. Palmer, *Police and protest*, p.198.

Limerick. The outbreak of the Tithe War in 1830, however, saw a gradual increase in the Peace Preservation Force's numbers, which rose to 1,179 superintending magistrates, officers and men in some ten counties in 1833. The force was eventually abolished in 1836, and many of its members were accepted into the Irish Constabulary.[12]

The most significant development in nineteenth-century Irish police history was the establishment in 1822 of the County Constabulary, the direct ancestor of the R.I.C. It was the first nation-wide, permanent Irish police force. Its creator, Chief Secretary Henry Goulburn, envisaged the County Constabulary as an efficient force which would replace the baronial forces of 1787 and 1792 and be totally under Dublin Castle's control. It differed from the Peace Preservation Force in that it was to be permanently based in the towns, villages and townlands of Ireland, rather than move from one proclaimed district to another as was the standard procedure with the Peace Preservation Force. Although the County Constabulary was not as firmly under government direction as Goulburn had wished (justices of the peace, for example, played a significant role in the appointment of sub-constables and in directing the activities of the force), the establishment of the constabulary nevertheless represented a massive step in the creation of a centralized police force for most of Ireland.[13]

One of the features which made the County Constabulary less centralized than its R.I.C. descendant was the fact that there was no overall commander of the force. Instead, the County Constabulary was controlled by four provincial inspectors. This, combined with local magistrates' involvement in the force's affairs, meant that the standards of recruitment and discipline between each province were uneven.[14] Although considerable efforts were made to achieve a standardized approach to recruitment, discipline and the general running of the force (by 1835, for instance, justices of the peace were no longer permitted to appoint to the police),[15] it was not until 1836, when the approximately 7,000-strong County Constabulary was reformed by Under Secretary Thomas Drummond, that the

12. Details from ibid, pp.199–205, 225, 329–30.

13. Ibid, pp.238–40; Broeker, *Rural disorder*, passim. The nickname of 'Peelers' was also applied to the County Constabulary. For the conflict between Dublin Castle and justices of the peace over magistrates' directing of the County Constabulary's activities, see Virginia Crossman, *Politics, law and order in nineteenth-century Ireland* (Dublin, 1996).

14. Palmer, *Police and protest*, pp.350–51.

15. Ibid, pp.342–45.

force was totally centralized and run on uniform lines. In 1836 the County Constabulary was reformed as the Irish Constabulary, under the overall command of a single officer, the inspector general. One of the most important achievements of the first inspector general, Colonel James Shaw-Kennedy, was the introduction in 1837 of a code of rules and regulations for the Irish Constabulary. Although added to and modified in later years, Shaw-Kennedy's code provided the basic guideline for the constabulary's approach to policing throughout Ireland down to 1922.[16]

In summary, the fifty years down to 1836 had seen a number of experiments with centralized police forces. Eventually, by 1836, one government-controlled, permanent force—the Irish Constabulary —was responsible for policing all of Ireland, with the exceptions of the cities of Dublin, Derry and Belfast. As has already been pointed out, Dublin remained outside of the constabulary's jurisdiction, receiving its own government-controlled police force, the D.M.P., in 1838, in place of the previous watch.[17] Derry had its own municipal police force, which still awaits its historian; it was not until 1870 that the Derry local force was abolished, following allegations of inefficiency and partisanship in the riots of 1869,[18] and the R.I.C. assumed sole responsibility for policing the city. It is with the policing of the third of the cities listed, Belfast, that this study deals. Although there was a constabulary presence in Belfast from December 1824, the bulk of the police work in the fifty years from 1816 to 1865 was performed by a municipally-appointed and controlled force. That force, nicknamed the 'Bulkies' by the late 1840s,[19] is the main focus of this work.

16. For an excellent discussion of Shaw-Kennedy's code see G.F. Fulham, 'James Shaw-Kennedy and the reformation of the Irish Constabulary, 1836–38' in *Eire-Ireland*, xvi (1981), 93–106.

17. The act which established the D.M.P., 6 & 7 Will IV, c.29, passed in July 1836; the first D.M.P. patrols appeared on the streets of Dublin in January 1838.

18. See *Report of the commissioners of inquiry, 1869, into the riots and disturbances in the city of Londonderry. With minutes of evidence and appendix*, H.C. 1870 (c.5), xxxii, 411.

19. The earliest example of the nickname's application to the Belfast police is in the 16 August 1849 issue of the Belfast satirical magazine, the *Comet*. The precise meaning and origin of the term are not clear: it has been suggested to me by Inspector David Hutchison of the Belfast Harbour Police that the nickname derived from the men's bulky appearance when they wore capes. The use of the term 'bulky' to refer to a policeman was, however, already current in Britain. The *Oxford English Dictionary*, 2nd ed. (Oxford, 1989), p.637, explains that 'bulky' was a slang term, of unknown origin, for policeman. It gives two literary references, one for 1827 and one for 1841. I am indebted to my editor, Professor W.N. Osborough, for this reference.

Eventually, in 1865, the Belfast local police was abolished by act of parliament and replaced by the Irish Constabulary.[20] Belfast's experience of policing prior to this might appear anomalous, in that the city bucked the trend of having a centralized, professional, 'new' police force, controlled by Dublin Castle, patrolling its streets. Instead, from 1816 Belfast maintained its own municipal force out of local taxation, with, from December 1824, a contingent of constabulary patrolling the outskirts of the city and playing a supportive role in times of large-scale public disorder. Although Belfast remained largely unaffected by the development and consolidation of Dublin Castle's 'new', centralized police forces in the rest of Ireland, its distinctive local force still shared the major characteristics of the 'new' police which developed in this period, both in Ireland and, somewhat later, in Britain. For instance, the Belfast local force operated throughout those parts of the city which paid rates in return for lighting, paving, scavenging and other services. It was, in other words, a centralized force whose remit was far greater than that of a mere eighteenth-century-style parish watch. It was also under a single authority: the police board consisting of police commissioners and committee down to January 1844, and a police committee of Belfast Town Council after January 1844. This supervision of the Belfast force by elected civilian committees anticipates the mode of supervision later adopted by the 'new' professional, supraparochial police established in English boroughs from 1835.[21] Another feature which distinguishes the Belfast force from the feeble, and largely stationary eighteenth-century watch is that the typical 'Bulky' was an active, able-bodied man who patrolled Belfast's streets, at first at night and then, with the development of a day contingent, on a round-the-clock basis.

This book presents a detailed account of the activities of this body of men down to 1865. The topic of the Belfast local police has been ignored by historians despite the existence of readily available sources. An examination of the minutes of the municipal bodies charged with maintaining and supervising the local force, supplemented by material gleaned from a close reading of Belfast newspapers and from such sources as travellers' accounts, reminiscences of contemporaries, guide books and parliamentary papers has allowed the construction of a reasonably substantive portrait of these hitherto neglected figures. The emphasis in this work is on

20. 28 & 29 Vict, c.70.

21. For a discussion of the administration of the reformed English borough police after 1835 see Jenifer Hart, 'Reform of the borough police, 1835–1856' in *EHR*, lxx (1955), 411–27.

the social history of the police, on the 'Bulky' as a working man: hence topics which are of obvious importance to any working man, such as pay, the duties expected of the employee, pensions and benefits, disciplinary procedures and the hazards faced on the job are all explored. Considerable attention is also devoted to the topic of crime in Belfast down to 1865; it would, after all, be a strange history of the police which overlooked that which the policeman was supposed to dedicate his efforts to prevent! What emerges from this study, more clearly than hitherto, is the existence of a seamy underside to the so-called 'Athens of the North'. Pickpockets, prostitutes and juvenile offenders were as much a part of Belfast's story in this period as booming linen mills. Their activities are described in the pages below, as are the changes introduced to Belfast's policing system in response to the problems posed by the city's unprecedented population, and attendant crime, growth.

The relations between the police and Belfast's non-criminal classes are also examined in detail. This work shows that the police were not merely agents for preventing and detecting such crimes as burglary and pocket-picking, but that they were also active in enforcing a host of bye-laws and imposing order on Belfast's lower classes. In particular, this involved the police in action against a wide range of working-class leisure activities, as a result of which the force was held in odium by many, and probably most, of the city's lower classes. The final chapters of this volume deal with the demise of the local force and its replacement by the Irish Constabulary. In discussing these topics, the alleged sectarian nature of the municipal police in the 1850s and 1860s is discussed, as are the fortunes of the Irish Constabulary after they took over sole responsibility for policing the city. It is hoped that the findings presented below not only throw light on the neglected history of the Belfast local police but that they also increase our understanding of the social history of Belfast.

CHAPTER TWO

The early years: 1800–1816

THE 1800 POLICE ACT

THE POLICE AUTHORITY in Belfast was created by one of the last acts of the Irish parliament before the Act of Union. The 1800 Belfast police act, which received the royal assent on 1 August, authorized a two-tiered police board for the town, which until then had had almost no police presence apart from a fleeting experiment with a twelve-man watch in the middle of the eighteenth century.[1] By the end of the eighteenth century there were no police in Belfast, which contrasts starkly with the situation in Dublin. In the 1790s the southern city (which by 1799 had a population of around 180,000)[2] had a police force of from 535 to 691 men depending on the time of year.[3] Belfast was slower off the mark in establishing a comparable force, although it should be borne in mind that in 1800 the relatively prosperous northern town had only about 19,000 inhabitants[4] and thus was considerably less affected by crime and public disorder than Dublin.[5] Nevertheless there are signs that by 1800 Belfast was beginning to experience a significant level of crime, which made the introduction of a police force a desirable step. The 1800 Belfast police act states that the town's increasing population, commerce and wealth were not secure without a night watch, whose duties should include 'protecting the persons and property of all his majesty's subjects … from fires, thefts, burglaries, assaults, violences, and other outrages and injuries during the night time'.[6]

1. J.P. Starr, 'The enforcing of law and order in eighteenth century Ireland: a study of Irish police and prisons from 1665 to 1800' (unpublished Ph.D. thesis, University of Dublin, 1968), p.65.
2. Palmer, *Police and protest*, p.150.
3. Ibid, pp.135, 149.
4. Jonathan Bardon, *Belfast: an illustrated history* (Belfast, 1984), p.66.
5. For a discussion of crime in Dublin at the end of the eighteenth century see Palmer, *Police and crime*, pp.122–24, and Henry, *Dublin hanged*, passim.
6. An act for paving, cleansing, lighting, and improving the several streets, squares, lanes, and passages within the town of Belfast, in the county of Antrim; and for removing and preventing all encroachments, obstructions, and annoyances therein; and also, for establishing and maintaining a nightly watch

The police act established a police board consisting of two bodies, the police commissioners and police committee. The sovereign of Belfast and the burgesses, appointed by the marquis of Donegall, were ex-officio commissioners for life. There were also twelve commissioners elected for life by the £1 parish ratepayers. The police committee was to assist the commissioners in executing the provisions of the police act. There were to be from nine to twenty-one committee members, elected annually at the parish vestry of Belfast by the £1 ratepayers. There was a substantial property qualification for membership of the police board. A commissioner had to own property worth at least £100 or have a personal estate of at least £2,000, or be a member of parliament or the heir of a peer; a committee member had to be a resident householder with a personal estate of at least £1,000.[7] The duties of the commissioners and committee went far beyond maintaining a police force in Belfast. They had such wide-ranging duties and powers that they almost entirely superseded the inefficient corporation of Belfast.[8] The police board was responsible for running most of the civic affairs of Belfast until the creation of Belfast Town Council in 1842. An examination of the minutes of the commissioners and committee shows that for the first sixteen years of the nineteenth century almost all of their efforts were devoted to providing a range of services taken for granted by modern city dwellers. Street paving, sewer construction, lighting and scavenging were attended to, all of which were funded by rates on property. This concentration by the police board on such a wide range of activities which, to the modern mind, do not appear to be the business of a police body, requires some explanation. In the mid to late eighteenth century the term 'police', in Britain and Ireland, had acquired a meaning much broader than the modern definition of a professional body geared to fighting crime. Instead, 'police' had connotations of keeping order in a civic polity: not just order in the sense of com-bating crime, but also in the sense of regulating various municipal services such as water and paving.[9] The Belfast Police Board was,

throughout the said town and the precincts thereof, and for other purposes (40 Geo III, c.37 (Irish statutes), preamble and s.46).

7. These provisions were modified later, but the principle of a high property qualification was retained.

8. For the inadequate performance of Belfast's corporation see Cornelius O'Leary, 'Belfast urban government in the age of reform' in David Harkness and Mary O'Dowd (ed.), *The town in Ireland* (Belfast, 1981), pp.191–92.

9. For a discussion of this definition of 'police' see Palmer, *Police and protest*, pp.69, 97. See also ibid, pp.69–71, for the growing acceptance of the narrower, modern definition of the term.

therefore, a civic governing body, for which the provision of what *we* regard as police—a crime-fighting body—was but one part of a broader 'policing' function.

The costs of street maintenance and of the various other responsibilities of the police board were so high that the board felt that the rating system could not fund a police force as well. The police board initially shirked its statutory obligation to provide a police force for the town and concentrated on its other responsibilities.[10] Instead of funding a watch the board periodically distributed hundreds of handbills which detailed the bye-laws and the penalties for infringing them, obviously in the hope that this would act as a deterrent against minor offences. The handbills listed such offences as failing to sweep pavements in front of houses (fine 1*s*.), shaking carpets in the street after 8 a.m. (fine 2*s*.8*d*.) and riding on carts or leading carts through the town at more than walking pace (fine one crown).[11] As there were only two inspectors of nuisances to see that these edicts were obeyed, they were largely ignored or poorly enforced.[12] The police board also frequently offered rewards for information leading to the conviction of offenders. In the earliest recorded example, in March 1803, the police committee offered a one-guinea reward for information about the people responsible for 'breaking up the streets' and stealing sewer grates.[13] The advertised rewards were often out of all proportion to the offences committed. For instance, £50 was offered in March 1808 for information leading to the conviction of those who broke a number of street lamps on St Patrick's night, and on several occasions rewards of from £20 to £50 were advertised in an effort to catch people who stole door knockers or smashed street lamps.[14] It is not clear how successful this reward policy was, but the fact that the

---

10. This emphasis was not entirely without support in Belfast. For example, the *Belfast Commercial Chronicle* in its issue of 1 March 1809 pointed out that as large towns were 'encircled with a margin of misery' the 'most useful part of the police, in a great town, is that which respects the health of the inhabitants'.

11. Belfast City Hall, Belfast police committee minutes, 27 Mar. 1803, 10 Nov. 1804, 23 Jan., 19 Mar. 1808.

12. One of the first inspectors of nuisances, John Jefferies, was dismissed in December 1806 for taking bribes to influence the police committee's selection of men and horses in its employment, and for selling the 'public dung' for his own profit: ibid, 20 Dec. 1806.

13. Ibid, 8 Jan. 1803.

14. Ibid, 19 Mar. 1808; Belfast City Hall, Belfast police commissioners' minutes, 21 Mar. 1808, 25 Sept. 1809, 4 Mar., 11 Dec. 1811, 14 Sept. 1814, 2 Aug. 1815. The instances of broken lamps were not all malicious. On 1 November

board's minutes do not mention a single instance of actually paying a reward suggests that it was a failure.

THE 1812 VOLUNTARY WATCH

Complaints from the public about the poor protection afforded by the police authorities indicates that the absence of a night watch irked many Belfast inhabitants. In January 1806 a brief attempt was made by some of the 'respectable' citizens to establish a voluntary night watch. Another short-lived association was formed in January 1810 for the purpose of detecting and prosecuting offenders. The *Belfast Newsletter* expressed the ill-founded hope that 'this society will follow up their measures with energy, for when bad men combine it is time for good men to associate, and to convince these offenders that the law is not dead, though it may sleep'.[15] Efforts at establishing a voluntary watch came to naught, however, until May 1812. What appeared to contemporaries to be an unacceptable number of robberies and attempted burglaries, as well as the obstreperous behaviour of the increasing number of prostitutes and their associates, prompted the formation of the watch. The alarming incidents included a woman blinding an Anne Street shopkeeper with treacle and absconding with a large cheese, several housebreakings by 'banditti' and an attempted burglary of a Telfair's Entry grocery which was foiled by the armed intervention of the owner and his assistant.[16]

Following representations from a number of worried householders the sovereign, Thomas Verner, organized a meeting of the 'principal inhabitants' at the Exchange on 16 May in order to organize a night watch. Some groups had already taken to patrolling the streets at night.[17] At the Exchange meeting twenty-six 'gentlemen' were selected to recruit respectable volunteers willing to serve as a night watch, and also to collect subscriptions to defray the

1806 the police committee requested Colonel Heyland, commander of the Belfast garrison, to order that 'all sergeants when marching along the footways, shall slope their pikes, in order to prevent the continual breaking of the globes, from want of that precaution'.

15. *Belfast Newsletter* (hereafter *B.N.L.*), 10, 14 Jan. 1806, 5 Jan. 1810; George Benn, *A history of the town of Belfast from 1799 till 1810 together with some incidental notices on local topics and biographies of many well-known families* (London, 1880), p.76.

16. *B.N.L.*, 17 Feb., 3 Mar., 1, 8, 15 May 1812. Telfair's Entry is now called Telfair Street.

17. *B.N.L.*, 15 May 1812.

costs of the scheme.[18] On 21 May Verner chaired another meeting at the Exchange, which agreed that four volunteers should be chosen to act as watch constables each night. The four were to elect one of their number as chief constable for the night, and he was to direct their activities as well as have charge of a military patrol which usually consisted of a sergeant and twelve men from the Derry and Dumfries militia regiments.[19] Although Thomas Verner chaired the two meetings which led to the start of the voluntary watch system, he did not do so in his capacity as police commissioner and the watch was not funded from the town rates. However, the police commissioners did agree to the watch committee's request to supply £150 for a lock-up for prisoners, after they found that a military guard room was an unsuitable place of confinement for prostitutes. The new lock-up, in Ferguson's Entry, was provided in September 1812.[20]

The lack of a suitable lock-up was a cause for concern mainly when drunk or disorderly prostitutes were arrested by night patrols. Few prisoners of any other kind were ever taken up. While the watch frequently encountered drunks on the streets, these were invariably escorted home rather than arrested. The patrols mainly concerned themselves with preserving order at night, and prostitutes proved to be the main disturbers of the peace. The watch entry for 4 July gives a good idea of the problems which prostitutes posed to the watch:

the only observation that it is thought necessary to make is on the shamefull & troublesome behaviour of the idle women who haunt the streets and assemble round the Exchange, they are a most disgracefull set and induce a number of drunken and profligate men & boys to come after them which makes it very unpleasant for the persons who have charge of the patrole it being a worse remedy to take them into custody than to let them ramble about.[21]

The abuse heaped on the watch by drunken, disorderly prostitutes undoubtedly had a detrimental effect on the morale of the civilian

---

18. Reports of the Belfast voluntary night watch, May-Nov. 1812, Feb.-May 1816, pp.5–6 (PRONI, D.46).

19. Ibid, p.355.

20. Ibid, pp.72, 373; Belfast police commissioners' minutes, 3, 17 June 1812; *B.N.L.*, 29 Sept. 1812.

21. Reports of the Belfast voluntary night watch, May-Nov. 1812, Feb.-May 1816, p.89. For other mentions of troublesome prostitutes see pp.42, 45, 53, 59, 71, 72, 73, 76, 83, 84, 92, 94, 123, 150, 172–73, 191, 225, 247, 267, 272, 314.

volunteers. Those whose occupations are listed in the watch minutes came from the professional or upper artisan classes: surgeons, attorneys, bankers and auctioneers feature most prominently, as do various shopkeepers and artisans such as shoemakers and watchmakers.[22] It is unlikely that they relished their encounters with the more unruly of Belfast's lower orders; even the soldiers in the patrol were dissatisfied with their lot, especially as all they received for their nightly endeavours was a halfpenny loaf and two naggins of bad beer.[23]

As early as 22 June it was recommended that the watch organizers should fine volunteers who failed to turn up for patrol duty. On 19 November the watch committee complained that the volunteers, especially 'those who are possessed of large property in the town', frequently refused to serve their turn in the watch while others reluctantly turned up, thus placing the future of the watch system in jeopardy. Ten days later the sovereign chaired another meeting at the Exchange to discuss the watch's position. The meeting declared that 'the nightly watch for the preservation of the peace and property has ceased, from the want of attendance on the part of the inhabitants'.[24] Following an attempted burglary at a Smithfield shop early in December 1812 the *Belfast Newsletter* appealed for another effort to maintain a voluntary watch, warning that

if ... the lives and properties of the citizens are left to the mercy of the demons of the night, they will soon make us feel the weight of their exertions; and if it shall go abroad that they can plunder here without fear of detection, the capital of the north will soon become a famed rendezvous for rogues and vagabonds, who may applaud our apathy, and exclaim 'Blest place! [N]o guards, no centinels [sic] are here!'[25]

The sovereign called a special meeting of the police commissioners to consider the idea of paying for a night watch out of the rates. He suggested a watch comprised of eleven constables, paid at 2s.2d. per night, and a chief constable, paid at 3s.3d. per night, to patrol the town from 20 December 1812 to 20 February 1813, at an estimated total cost of £120. The police commissioners, however, refused to finance the proposed watch out of the public funds.[26]

22. Ibid, pp.369, 370, 371, 372, 388, 393, 395, 396, 398, 406, 408, 410, 411.
23. Ibid, p.154.
24. Ibid, pp.68, 403–04; *B.N.L.*, 27 Oct., 24 Nov. 1812.
25. *B.N.L.*, 4 Dec. 1812.
26. Belfast police commissioners' minutes, 27 Nov., 2 Dec. 1812; J.J. Monaghan, 'A social and economic history of Belfast 1801–1825' (unpublished Ph.D. thesis, Queen's University of Belfast, 1940), p.84.

The worried citizens instead had to rely partly on the efforts of the sovereign, as chief magistrate, at tackling crime. The sovereign had some occasional successes. For example, in January 1814 his investigations were largely responsible for the arrest in Carrickfergus of Hamilton Purse, a watchmaker involved in selling rappers (door-knockers) stolen from hall doors in Belfast. The *Belfast Newsletter* commented hopefully that

It is by such prompt and energetic measures alone, that we can hope for the prevention or detection of those crimes which are so frequently per-petrated in this populous town, for when once the miscreant banditti perceive the magistrate vigilant, and the law enforced, they will stand appalled, and either cease from crimes or change their scene of action.[27]

Concerned individuals also offered rewards in the hope of enticing informers to help solve certain crimes. In February 1814 £50 was offered for information about a burglary in a High Street shop, and almost £400 was offered to convict those responsible for disinter-ring a yeoman's body in Friar's Bush graveyard.[28] But most people who were worried about the crime problem still pinned their hopes on the police board's instituting a permanent watch paid for out of the public funds. In November 1814 a public deputation went to the police commissioners with such a request, but the proposal foundered on the question of who was to pay for the watch. Too many rate-payers had a vested interest in maintaining the police tax at its present level: four Belfast houses paid nearly one sixth of the whole tax, while many householders and shopkeepers contributed as little as 10*d*. or half a crown and naturally opposed any increase in their tax assessment. The police commissioners, while acknowledging the necessity of a night watch, declined to sanction the expense of a police force under the existing unsatisfactory rating system.[29]

THE 1816 VOLUNTARY WATCH

Given the police commissioners' opinion that the Belfast rates were insufficient to pay for both a night watch and the myriad other services provided by the police board, and the reluctance of a large

---

27. *B.N.L.*, 11 Jan. 1814. The watchmaker pleaded 'the necessity of a young and numerous family as compelling him to the perpetration of the crime'.

28. *B.N.L.*, 1, 8 Feb. 1814.

29. Ibid, 5, 8, 18 Nov. 1814; Belfast police commissioners' minutes, 14 Nov. 1814.

body of property owners to pay more taxes, it is possible that Belfast might have waited many more years before a regular system of police was introduced. However, a series of outrages in late 1815 and early 1816 prompted a reappraisal of the attitudes of both the police commissioners and Belfast tax payers. A Belfast citizen commented on the unhappy state of affairs in early 1816:

At the commencement of last winter a dreadful change took place, and a spirit of outrage and disturbance pervaded the lower classes; the streets of the town were infested by midnight ruffians, who, lurking in lanes, rushed out on the peaceable inhabitants, and hardly a night passed but some person was abused and robbed.[30]

Early in February 1816 a series of 'depredations', including street robberies and assaults and several burglaries of shops, prompted the inhabitants of the Bridge Street neighbourhood to hire a number of watchmen at 13s. per week.[31] A few days later about 200 of the 'most respectable inhabitants of Belfast' resumed a voluntary night watch scheme, which was practically a carbon copy of the ill-fated 1812 watch. Starting on 19 February, four men from a list of volunteers were sworn in as constables each night by Cortland M. Skinner, JP, and patrolled the streets with a military guard to preserve order and (it was hoped) catch 'depredators' in the act. Eventually some 343 volunteers indicated their willingness to act as watchmen. Enrolment and subscription lists were kept in the various coffee shops of the town.[32]

The air of optimism which greeted the new night watch was quickly dispelled following an incendiary bomb attack on the Peter's Hill house of Francis Johnson, muslin manufacturer, at 4 a.m. on the morning of 28 February. The voluntary watch had passed Johnson's house shortly before the explosion but had noticed nothing amiss. The incident, which was part of a bitter dispute between employers and weavers, convinced Belfast's propertied classes of the need for a professional watch or police system. A public meeting of the 'principal inhabitants of Belfast' on 29 February offered a £2,000 reward for the capture of the bombers.[33] The

---

30. *B.N.L.*, 26 Mar. 1816.
31. Ibid, 6, 9, 12, 16 Feb. 1816.
32. Ibid, 20 Feb., 26 Mar. 1816; Reports of the Belfast voluntary night watch, May-Nov. 1812, Feb.-May 1816, pp.571–76.
33. *B.N.L.*, 1 Mar. 1816. Three weavers were eventually tried for the attack and hanged in what was to be the last public execution in Belfast: Bardon, *Belfast*, p.68.

meeting also sent a deputation to the police commissioners to request the establishment of a municipal night watch. The deputation was received sympathetically by the commissioners, but they nevertheless pointed out that 'the establishment of a nightly watch will amount, on the most economical plan to be effectual, to a sum of money nearly equal to all the taxes now levied off the town for every other purpose of police', and they once again felt unable to support a municipally-funded force under the existing system of rates. However a new Belfast police bill, promoted by the marquis of Donegall and aimed at facilitating the establishment of a Belfast watch by considerably altering the town's rating system, was already making its way through parliament and was supported by the police commissioners.[34] It received the royal assent on 20 June.

In the meantime, the voluntary watch continued to patrol the streets. It was meant as a temporary measure, to last 'so long as the prevailing disposition to attack persons and rob shops, offices &c continues'.[35] The inhabitants of Donegall Street, North Street, Church Street and Bridge Street also hired watchmen to protect their district at night.[36] Not all contemporaries were convinced of the efficiency of the voluntary night watch. When sentencing Sarah Kane and a soldier named James Holey for robbing a pocket book containing some valuables, Solicitor General Charles Kendal Bushe, the presiding judge at the Co. Antrim spring assizes in Carrickfergus (and future chief justice of King's Bench), expressed the wish that he could have them hanged as a deterrent to others, 'for the police of Belfast was in a most disgraceful state. The streets were worse than he had ever heard of London, and certainly more dangerous.' He sentenced the guilty pair to seven years' transportation, 'to make an example, because the lower orders evinced a degree of profligacy that had scarcely been equalled'.[37]

The 1816 watch's experiences with drunk and disorderly prostitutes were similar to those of its 1812 predecessor. The following incidents give a further insight into what conditions were like at night in Belfast at this period. On 5 April a patrol commanded by James Robinson reported encountering a party of young gentlemen in Graham's Entry, a small street between High Street and Rosemary Street, which was a known haunt of prostitutes. Robinson wrote

34. Belfast police commissioners' minutes, 6 Mar. 1816; *B.N.L.*, 8 Mar. 1816.

35. Reports of the Belfast voluntary night watch, May-Nov. 1812, Feb.-May 1816, p.571.

36. *B.N.L.*, 26 Mar. 1816.

37. Ibid, 22 Mar. 1816.

that 'from their situations in life he was surprised to find them flying for shame when they should have been setting an example of correct conduct to the lower orders of the community'. On 9 April a patrol found a drunken countryman seeking lodgings for the night. While assisting the rural shelter-seeker the patrol arrested a naked man who was terrifying his landlady in a John Street lodging house, and when they were escorting their prisoner to the guard room they took up 'a boy and girl both remarkably young who were caught in the act of cohabition' [sic] in Smithfield. The watch of 24 April lodged a drunken woman found lying in Bridge Street in the guard room. She lay down by the fire, and 'being in a stupid state, by some accident got most of the clothes burn[ed] off her back'. Another patrol on 30 April rescued a drunken negro from a crowd that was assaulting him in Rosemary Street. The final watch book entry, that of 19 May 1816—the 91st night of the voluntary watch —describes how a patrol found James Storey, a former Belfast bookseller, and a man named Cooke who claimed to be a chaplain in the American navy, lying drunk in Rosemary Street. When questioned by the patrol 'they denied to be subject to English law and swore vengeance against any man who would oppose them'.[38] As these incidents suggest, the volunteers are unlikely to have shed many tears when the patrols were discontinued that summer.

38. Reports of the Belfast voluntary night watch, May-Nov. 1812, Feb.-May 1816: entries for 5, 9, 24, 30 Apr., 19 May 1816.

CHAPTER THREE

The policeman's lot: duties and remuneration

DUTIES IN 1816

THE MAIN EFFECT of the 1816 Belfast police act[1] was to alter the town's rating system, thus making it easier for the police board to pay for a municipal watch. The act retained the principle of a two-tiered police board, but stipulated that the commissioners should be elected by the £4 ratepayers, while the £2 ratepayers elected the committee members. Apart from these provisions there was little difference between the 1800 and 1816 acts; and, as the 1816 act did not entirely supersede the earlier one, both acts provided the legal basis for the municipal night watch which first took to the streets of Belfast early in September 1816. It was at first intended that the watch should perform duty only for thirty-two weeks of every year,[2] but the force which subsequently developed was a permanent one, and there has been a permanent, professional police presence in Belfast since September 1816.

The first watch consisted of thirty officers and men, but the addition of ten watchmen in late September brought its strength up to forty. There were thirty-five night watchmen, who were paid 8s.4d. per week (£21 13s.4d. per year), four officers or night constables paid at 11s.4d. per week (£29 11s.6d. per year) and a head constable (later designated chief constable) paid at 15s.6d. weekly (£40 6s. per year). On 16 October 1816 the police committee, who were responsible for hiring the force, appointed William H. Ferrar to the post of superintendent of police at a salary of £200 per annum. The superintendent's main duty was to serve as a stipendiary magistrate for Belfast.

The watch at first consisted of men who performed night duty, from 9 p.m. to 6 a.m. They were supplied with 'a long grey garment not unlike a soldier's greatcoat, confined at the waist by a belt,

1. An act to explain and amend an act of his present majesty for paving, cleansing, lighting and otherways improving the town of Belfast, in the county of Antrim; and for better effecting those purposes (56 Geo III, c.57).

2. Belfast police commissioners' minutes, 26 Aug. 1816.

suspended to which was an enormous craik or rattle'.[3] The rattle, a small version of which was a popular toy with Belfast children, was used to summon aid. Instead of a truncheon the men were armed with a long pike or halberd with a hook at the end, similar to the weapons carried by the Dublin watch. The hook was to be used for catching runaway offenders.[4] An observer in 1826 reported that the Belfast watchmen were

arm'd, like Chactaws, with huge tomahawks,
Or murderers that have deeds of death on hand.[5]

Although both the Belfast and Dublin forces were primarily night watches, it is important to distinguish between the two forces. By the 1830s the Dublin force consisted mainly of stationary watchmen described as 'decrepit, worn out, old men', selected 'for their age and infirmities and not required to be awake except at their meals'. They were 'in many cases' senile, and at least one was blind in both eyes and had to be brought to and from work by his wife. Instead of patrolling the streets they sat in sentry boxes and were supposed to watch over a street or stretch of street at night, but they often fell asleep in their snug shelters.[6] The Dublin men were, then, 'watchmen' in a very loose sense of the term.

The Belfast force was a much more active body of men.[7] In fact, they performed the uniformed beat or 'preventive patrol' which was characteristic of the 'new police' introduced later in Britain by Sir

3. Notes of a talk given by 'an octogenarian' to the Belfast Naturalists Field Club, 1868 or 1869 (PRONI, D.3361/3).

4. Ibid; Belfast police commissioners' minutes, 28 Aug. 1816. For the weapons of the Dublin watch see W.R. Le Fanu, *Seventy years of Irish life, being anecdotes and reminiscences* (London, 1893), p.81.

5. Anonymous, *The 'Northern Athens'; or, life in the emerald isle* (Belfast, 1826), p.45.

6. *Minutes of evidence taken before the select committee of the House of Lords appointed to enquire into the state of Ireland since the year 1835, in respect of crime and outrage, which have rendered life and property insecure in that part of the empire, and to report to the house,* H.L. 1839, 486–I; 486–II, xi.1.423, p.1002; account by Acting Inspector R. Thompson, D.M.P., 16 Sept. 1857 (NLI, Larcom papers, MS 7600); Le Fanu, *Seventy years,* pp.81–82; G.L. Lampson, *A consideration of the state of Ireland in the nineteenth century* (London, 1907), p.248; E.P. Blythe, 'The D.M.P.' in *Dublin Historical Record,* xx (1965), 117.

7. There are no statistics available of the ages of the first recruits, but the first advertisement stipulated that they should bring letters certifying their ability as well as their conduct: *B.N.L.,* 27 Aug. 1816.

Robert Peel.[8] Some contemporaries felt that the Belfast force would be more effective if it adopted the stationary watch system in streets, 'instead of the very doubtful one of a patrol establishment'.[9] The police board turned down the idea, and significantly the 'great expence' [sic] of a stationary watch compared to a mobile one was 'the only reason' that the former system was not preferred.[10] Proposals to provide the watchmen with sentry boxes were turned down, despite the *Belfast Newsletter*'s plea that the men's health was 'greatly injured' by exposure to inclement weather.[11] The idea of employing at least some of the force as a stationary watch was resurrected by a Belfast magistrate in September 1834 and the police committee agreed with the proposal on the grounds that it had been 'tried in several large towns with satisfaction to the public', but the police commissioners blocked the plan as 'most injudicious'.[12] This was only one of several differences of opinion between the two police bodies. The policy of a mobile watch at least had the merit, as one observer pointed out, that the men were (theoretically) less likely to fall asleep on the job:

The knaves [are] without a lantern or a box—
Hence there is small facility to drowse.[13]

The history of the force, however, shows that in practice the men proved adept at finding opportunities to sleep when out on the beat.

The surviving evidence suggests that the night watch's initial performance met with exaggerated approval from Belfast's propertied classes. The first recorded example of the force in action involved a hat-snatching incident in Bridge Street on the night of 7 September 1816. After a customer emerged from a hatter's shop in Bridge Street his hat was snatched from his head but a nearby watchman gave immediate chase to the culprit and managed to catch him. That such a trifling incident was deemed worthy of report in several newspapers, including a Dublin publication, is indicative of the relief felt at the presence of a professional police in Belfast.[14] The

8. P.J. Stead, 'The new police' in D.H. Bayley (ed.), *Police and society* (London, 1977), p.78.
9. *Belfast Commercial Chronicle*, 4, 7 Sept. 1816.
10. *B.N.L.*, 3 Sept. 1816.
11. Belfast police commissioners' minutes, 2 Dec. 1818; *B.N.L.*, 12 Feb. 1819.
12. Belfast police committee minutes, 16, 17 Sept. 1834.
13. '*Northern Athens*', pp.45–46.
14. The incident was reported in *Belfast Commercial Chronicle*, 14 Sept. 1816; *B.N.L.*, 13 Sept. 1816; and *Freeman's Journal*, 17 Sept. 1816.

Belfast Commercial Chronicle in the same month recorded its satisfaction with the night watch's patrols. It claimed that 'the bands of ruffians who have infested this town for some time have already taken alarm at being thus hindered in many of their well-laid schemes of depredation', and that 'since the watch was appointed no midnight robbery has been effected'.[15]

The *Belfast Newsletter* also commented upon the watch in favourable terms:

The advantages of our new police establishment becomes [sic] every day more apparent. The nest of hornets which has long infested this town, has been broken in upon; and several of these noxious insects have been committed to the county jail; among these [are] James Shannon, Mary Clokey, Ed Morrison, alias Waterloo, all of these accused of housebreaking; and Sarah Gibson for shop-lifting. They are noted characters, who, perhaps, in the course of the winter would have levied greater tribute off the town than would have paid the whole expence [sic] of the nightly watch. We applaud the vigilance of the police, and we hope they will persevere.[16]

Other favourable early accounts of the night watch include a description of a party of watchmen under Chief Constable Henry arresting a 'most dangerous gang of coiners' in Nelson Street on 19 September. On 20 September Watchman Todd discovered a 'respectable' Co. Down man lying intoxicated in Hudson's Entry. Todd scared away some men who managed to rob the drunk of his hat and shoes but they had not enough time to steal the £7 in his wallet, due to the watchman's appearance. Todd later recognised one of the robbers and arrested him while he was in possession of the stolen hat and shoes; it also turned out that he had pawned a watch which was stolen from an old bootseller in Charlemont Row. In another incident a watchman successfully used his pike to defend himself when attacked by three drunken men near Chapel Lane, and on 24 September another watchman arrested Rose McDonnell alias Liddy, 'a notorious character and old offender' about four miles from Belfast on the Lisburn Road after she stole some clothing from a man.[17]

The *Belfast Newsletter* felt that

The vigilance evinced by our police establishment is highly commendable, and promises to effect the complete deliverance of this town from the gang

15. *Belfast Commercial Chronicle*, 11, 14 Sept. 1816.

16. *B.N.L.*, 11 Oct. 1816. 'Waterloo' was described in the 19 September edition as 'very young, but quite adept in every species of thievery'.

17. *B.N.L.*, 24, 27 Sept., 1 Oct. 1816.

of vagabonds which have [sic] so long been the pest of the inhabitants, and the despoilers of their property. We have also to remark that our streets are no longer infested by those dissolute females, who were so offensive to decency and good morals.[18]

The duties performed by the night watch in 1816 were similar to those carried out later in the century by urban police forces in other parts of Ireland and Britain. The 1800 Belfast police act stated that the watch should detain 'all persons breaking the peace, or brawling, quarrelling in the street, or disturbing the inhabitants, or attempting to commit any burglary, felony, or other offence'.[19] The familiar formula of the 'prevention and detection of crime' does not quite summarise the duties expected of the force, as they were also required to enforce the various bye-laws designed primarily to bring some order to Belfast's social and commercial life. The 1800 and 1816 Belfast police acts enumerated a wide variety of offences for which the watchmen had to be on the alert. For example, people throwing dirt, ashes, dung or 'other noisome or offensive articles' on the streets, or who obstructed the pavements with baskets, caskets, carts, wagons, building materials or by obtrusively displaying meat, fish or other wares for sale which could damage the clothing of passers-by, were liable to fines, as were people who emptied privies or shook their carpets in the street or failed to sweep their pavement after certain specified hours. Wandering swine were to be seized and killed, and given to the Belfast Charitable Society. The watchmen also had to arrest 'furious drivers' and carters who rode on their carts rather than walking through the town and holding their horse's reins. They were also authorised to kill any dog within fifty yards of a public road which had not got a block of wood weighing at least five pounds fastened round its neck, and its owner was liable to a 10s. fine.[20] Following a rabies scare in Carrickfergus, Kilroot and Eden in 1819, in which three people died after being bitten by rabid dogs, the watch were ordered to be strict in killing stray dogs, especially in hot weather as it was erroneously believed that hot weather sparked off rabies in dogs. This remained a feature of Belfast police activity until the end of the period.[21]

18. Ibid, 11 Oct. 1816. The newspaper was rather premature in announcing the disappearance of prostitutes from Belfast's streets.

19. 40 Geo III, c.37 (Irish statutes), s.46.

20. Details from the 1800 and 1816 Belfast police acts, and *B.N.L.*, 28 Sept., 29 Oct. 1816; *Northern Whig* (hereafter *N.W.*), 13 Jan. 1825.

21. For police activity against stray or unmuzzled dogs see *B.N.L.*, 18 June 1819, 14 May 1858, 31 May 1860; *N.W.*, 29 July 1824, 19 May 1825; Belfast police commissioners' minutes, 15 May 1825, 12 June 1829; Belfast police committee minutes, 12 June 1829, 24 May 1832.

DUTIES DOWN TO 1865

The main features of Belfast police duty altered little between 1816 and 1865, although, as we shall see, there were some changes in these fifty years. The early watchmen carried out some tasks which the police of the later period were not expected to perform. For instance, from June 1818 ten to twelve watchmen were required to operate fire engines, at the rate of 10s. for each time they performed the duty (which payment was actually higher than the watchman's usual weekly wage).[22] By 1843 it was less necessary for members of the force to serve as fire-fighters, as by that year various insurance companies were also operating fire engines in the town.[23] From September 1844 twelve watchmen were required to operate the police fire engine on Saturdays only, until they were finally relieved of that duty on 10 October 1848. After that date the superintendent of the police remained in command of the police fire engine, but he had to hire labourers to operate it at the rate of a mere sixpence per duty performed.[24] Members of the force were still obliged, as before, to immediately attend at the scene of a fire,[25] and on one occasion in March 1857 they even helped to pull the fire brigade to the scene of a fire in Barrack Street 'as a horse could not be procured in time'.[26] Another unusual instance of police duty occurred during the cholera outbreak of 1832, when the force was used by the Board of Health to enforce quarantine restrictions on infected areas of the town.[27] There was a slight parallel to this in the early 1850s, when during a cholera scare a number of constables carried out a survey, under the supervision of health officers, of the sewerage and sanitation arrangements of every building in the borough.[28]

Generally speaking the duties performed by the police showed little variation in the period covered. The police board's 1843 description of the duties to be performed by their force as

22. Belfast police commissioners' minutes, 10 June 1818; also *B.N.L.*, 10 Oct. 1822.
23. *Vindicator* (Belfast), 8 Mar. 1843.
24. Town council committee on police affairs minutes, 25 Sept. 1844, 10 Oct. 1848.
25. *B.N.L.*, 13 Feb. 1818, 5 Apr. 1850, 22 Dec. 1860; Town council committee on police affairs minutes, 19 Mar. 1850.
26. *B.N.L.*, 3 Mar. 1857.
27. Ibid, 8 June 1832.
28. Ibid, 3 Nov. 1852, 3 Oct. 1853.

the affording [of] security to the persons and property of the inhabitants, the prevention and removal of all nuisances and obstructions in the streets and thoroughfares, the prosecution of all persons breaking ... any of the bye laws passed under the provisions of the Belfast police acts, the suppression of ordinary breaches of the peace and the general enforcement of good order in the town[29]

could equally have applied to police activities in 1816 or 1865. The 1856 Belfast police manual, which was closely modelled on that used by the London Metropolitan Police and the Dublin Metropolitan Police, lists in detail the offences to be prevented by the Belfast force. One of the aspects of 1850s' police duty which would have appeared novel to a man serving in the earlier decades was that the 1850s' men were required to compile annual lists of publicans, spirit grocers and beer sellers in each street, distinguishing those who kept 'singing saloons' and 'jig houses' and to comment on how their businesses were conducted. There were also lists of brothel keepers, prostitutes, marine stores and unlicensed theatres, and gambling houses to be made.[30] In the late 1850s the police were also ordered to inform the town clerk whenever people moved house, to assist the municipal tax collectors in keeping tabs on defaulters.[31]

DEVELOPMENT OF THE DAY POLICE

It soon became apparent to the police authorities that the manifold duties imposed on the force could not be satisfactorily performed without a day component: for instance, most of the offences listed in the Belfast police acts occurred during the day, whereas the night watchmen performed no duty between the hours of 6 a.m. and 9 p.m. The first day constables, Richard Hardy and John Magill, were appointed in October 1817 (until then they served as night

29. Belfast police commissioners' minutes, 20 Sept. 1843.

30. *Instructions to the Belfast police force, 1856* (Belfast, 1856), p.37 (hereafter *1856 police instructions*). There is little evidence that the Belfast force collected similar information before the 1850s. The only examples that the author has seen involved the watchmen in the 1820s recording the state of the lamps on their rounds each night, and in the 1840s reporting to the water commissioners instances of wasting water in the borough: Belfast police commissioners' minutes, 31 Mar. 1824; Belfast police committee minutes, 3 Dec. 1828; Town council committee on police affairs minutes, 23 June 1847.

31. *Report of the commissioners of inquiry into the origin and character of the riots in Belfast in July and September 1857; together with minutes of evidence and appendix,* H.C. 1857–58 [2309], xxvi, 1, p.174 (hereafter *1857 riots inquiry*).

watchmen). Before this the chief constable, Thomas Henry, performed duty in the day time, mainly searching for stolen goods and arresting suspects.[32] The day men's main duties initially were attending daily at the police office where the public could go if they required police assistance (the first police office was in Bridge Street), executing warrants and conveying prisoners to jail. They were paid £20 per annum, and in addition received emoluments for carrying out the duties detailed. A member of the force recalled later that when the day force was started 'the best men were chosen, both as regards personal appearance and education'.[33]

Their duties were spelled out in detail in a set of regulations printed especially for the day men by the police commissioners in 1822. The instructions show that the day men were involved in keeping the streets clear of the various 'nuisances' outlined in the police acts, ranging from children playing with marbles, hoops, spinning tops and balls to hawkers of herrings and careless cart drivers. To encourage their activity the day men were entitled, until 1825, to half of the fines imposed on offenders.[34] Their wages were increased to 10s. per week (£26 per annum) in 1831.[35] The day force by 1834 had risen to a strength of one chief constable and ten day constables, out of a total force of eighty full-time men and officers.[36] This rose to seventeen street constables, three house constables (in the police office), four head constables and a chief constable by 1843, out of a total full-time force of ninety-two men and officers. There were twenty-six street constables in 1851. The considerable extension of Belfast borough in 1853 necessitated a substantial increase in the size of the police force. In June 1858 the day men consisted of sixty-one policemen of all ranks, out of a total force strength of 165:[37] this was the maximum level of strength reached by the municipal police.

In summary, then, the day force increased in size until it eventually comprised more than one third of the total force strength. In the same years the police force more than quadrupled in size, from

32. *B.N.L.*, 25 Mar., 8 Apr., 11, 17 July, 1, 8 Aug. 1817.

33. Belfast police commissioners' minutes, 8 Oct. 1817; *B.N.L.*, 10 Mar. 1862.

34. Belfast police commissioners' minutes, 4 Nov., 11 Dec. 1822, 26 Mar. 1823, 10 Aug. 1825.

35. Belfast police committee minutes, 21 June 1831.

36. Ibid, 21 Oct. 1834.

37. Belfast police commissioners' minutes, 20 Sept. 1843; *The Belfast almanac, for the year of our lord 1851* (Belfast, 1851), pp.62–63; *Hansard, 3*, cl, col. 2152 (15 June 1858).

thirty-five men and officers in September 1816 to 160 men and officers at the end of the period.[38] Police strength kept pace with Belfast's population increase, as the town's population more than trebled from around 37,000 in 1821 to over 121,000 in 1861.[39] It is interesting to note that for most of the period the day force actually had no legal basis of existence. The 1800 and 1816 police acts make no mention of the police board's power of appointing day constables: they quite clearly specify that it could appoint a night watch only. This anomaly was not cleared up until after the creation of Belfast Town Council by the Irish Municipal Corporations Act of 1840. Its Committee on Police Affairs did not take over the duties of the police commissioners and police committee until January 1844, and it was not until July 1845 that the day police were given legal foundation, when the town council was empowered to select any number of *constables* it considered necessary. Unlike the old police acts, the 1845 act avoided the designation 'night watchman': henceforth, all Belfast policemen were called 'constables' (apart from the officers, of course) and the town council simply absorbed all serving policemen, night watchmen and day constables alike, into the officially-titled 'Police Force of Belfast'.[40]

SUPERNUMERARIES

In addition to full-time watchmen and constables, the police board from an early stage employed supernumerary policemen in their force. Although the first watchmen were sent on the streets without any preliminary training in police duties (which helps to account for the high attrition rate in their number, a topic to be discussed below), the fact that shortly thereafter the supernumeraries were introduced into the force suggests a comparatively 'modern' approach to policing on the part of the Belfast police authorities. The first supernumeraries, John Donaghy, John Moody, Jacob

38. *Minutes of evidence and appendix to the report of the commissioners of inquiry, 1864, respecting the borough of Belfast,* H.C. 1865 [3466–I], 27, pp.359–61 (hereafter *1864 Belfast borough inquiry*).

39. Bardon, *Belfast,* pp.66, 89.

40. Resident Magistrate Walter Molony, Belfast, to Under Secretary Edward Lucas, 1 Aug. 1843; draft copy of letter from Lord Lieutenant Earl de Grey to Inspector General Duncan McGregor, 29 Jan. 1844, on the legality of the Belfast police force (NA, C.S.O.R.P. 1844/I.15510); An act for the improvement of the borough of Belfast (8 & 9 Vict, c.142, ss. 7, 220); Town council committee on police affairs minutes, 27 Aug., 3 Sept. 1845.

Munson, Daniel Brown and Bernard Devlin, were employed as early as September 1819, when they replaced five watchmen who were dismissed for a variety of offences.[41]

It appears from the police board minutes, however, that not all appointees underwent a preliminary supernumerary stage, although this did become a progressively more common feature and was the rule by the end of the period. The police board maintained a list of supernumerary watchmen and constables and used it as a reserve to fill gaps in the ranks whenever the full-time men were sick or otherwise absent from duty. The supernumeraries could graduate to full-time status, but there was no guarantee of this. In 1837 supernumerary day constables were employed as night watchmen until vacancies arose in the day ranks, and were ordered in the meantime to devote their afternoons to learning the duties of day constables. When supernumeraries were appointed as day constables they were to be given one month's probation, at the end of which they were to be dismissed if deemed unfit for the duty.[42] Despite the uncertainties of the job there was no shortage of applications for the position of supernumerary: there were fifty applicants for twenty supernumerary watchman positions in 1835, for instance.[43] Even the fact that supernumeraries had to be 'ready at any time to be put on duty but … [in the] meantime do not receive pay' did not lessen the number of applicants. There were twenty-six supernumerary watchmen and fifty-eight full-time watchmen, and six supernumerary and seventeen street constables in 1843, and usually there was an average of from ten to twenty supernumeraries on the books in the latter years of the force.[44]

TENURE AND PAY

There were several aspects of Belfast police remuneration in the early nineteenth century which appeared attractive to prospective recruits. Firstly, once accepted as a full-time watchman or day constable, one was virtually assured of permanent employment if one obeyed the various rules and regulations and was diligent in one's duty. It is true that the police committee met each September

41. Belfast police committee minutes, 1 Sept. 1819.
42. Ibid, 28 Feb., 2 May, 12 Sept. 1837.
43. Ibid, 3 Feb. 1835.
44. Belfast police commissioners' minutes, 20 Sept. 1843; *1857 riots inquiry*, p.148; *1864 borough inquiry*, p.123.

to elect the watch for the following year, which the *Newsletter* described as 'a measure well calculated to secure the efficiency of this valuable establishment, by which means useful watchmen, etc will be retained, and those who are not qualified, or who misbehave, may be discharged'.[45] In practice the committee rarely opted not to renew a man's employment at the annual September ballot: the only exceptions were Watchman Henry Hughes in 1820 who failed to turn up for the election; Night Constable Robert Pettigrew in 1821, as his conduct had shown that he was not 'a proper person to fill his station'; and a constable and supernumerary constable in 1825 whose employment was discontinued for unstated reasons.[46]

Thereafter the annual revision became a formality, and was discontinued by the town council. Steady policemen, therefore, were virtually assured of their positions and had the prospect of round-the-year employment, an expectation which a large proportion of working men in the nineteenth century did not enjoy. The police wages were high enough to attract sufficient applicants for the force, and the police board was several times able to turn down petitions from the watchmen for more pay because the existing rates proved so attractive to recruits.[47] Pay increases were rare, then, in the first twenty-five years of the force's existence and they were generally awarded to the upper ranks. The chief night and day constables had their wages increased to £1 a week in 1824, 60 guineas a year in 1837 and to £100 a year in 1841.[48] At some time between 1840 and 1843 the superintendent's salary rose from £200 to £350 a year.[49] The remainder of the force had their first substantial pay increase since 1816 in January 1846: the night constables were raised from 8s.4d. to 10s. per week (£26 per annum) while the day constables were raised to 11s.6d. per week (£29 18s. per annum). The officers' wages, other than those of the chief constables, varied from 12s.6d. to 16s. weekly (£32 10s. to £41 12s. annually).[50] The chief night and day constables were raised to £120 a year in 1850, and in the following year the pay of the lowest officer grade, that of divisional night constable, was increased from 12s.6d. a week to

45. *B.N.L.*, 9 Sept. 1817.
46. Belfast police committee minutes, 14 Sept. 1820, 8 Sept. 1821, 3 Oct. 1825.
47. Ibid, 24 Oct. 1825, 19 Nov. 1833; Belfast police commissioners' minutes, 14 June, 26 July, 27 Dec. 1826, 9 May 1827, 20 Sept. 1843.
48. Belfast police committee minutes, 27 Mar. 1824; Belfast police commissioners' minutes, 7 June 1837.
49. Resident Magistrate Walter Molony, Belfast, to Under Secretary Lucas, 1 Aug. 1843 (NA, C.S.O.R.P. 1844/I.15510).
50. Town council committee on police affairs minutes, 14 Jan. 1846.

15s. (£39 a year).[51] In 1853 the day constables were boosted to 12s.6d. per week (£32 10s. per year) and the night constables to 11s. per week (£28 12s. per year).[52] Later requests for pay rises were turned down on the familiar grounds of the numerous applicants who were attracted by the existing wages.[53]

UNIFORMS

The wages of the police in real terms were actually higher than indicated in the outline above, as one needs to take into account the cost of the uniform with which they were provided. As we have already seen, the night watchmen under the police board received a grey greatcoat and, from 1838 onwards, a glazed hat.[54] The day constables received a blue uniform (in 1838 they were supplied with duck white trousers); from 1831 they received a glazed hat with the words 'Belfast Police' painted on it. In 1839 they were supplied with capes to help ward off the cold.[55] The uniforms probably provided only a modest protection for the police, to judge from one observer's comment in 1839 that the police authorities were so frugal in their expenditure on the force's livery that they were 'allowing their servants to appear in the streets like paupers'.[56] Under the auspices of the town council both the night and day force wore a dark blue uniform. The night men wore a long blue overcoat, trousers, round hat (a form of top hat) and were occasionally issued with a vest. In April 1848 they were supplied with leather collars to keep their necks warm, in place of the handkerchiefs of various colours which they used until then. In 1856 the town council followed the lead of other corporations in issuing oil capes to their men as protection against the rain. The day men's uniforms were similar, except that they wore a top coat instead of an overcoat.[57] In 1863 the force was also issued with shako hats.[58] The uniform, which was supplied free

51. Ibid, 12 Nov. 1850, 30 Dec. 1851.
52. Ibid, 24 May 1853.
53. Ibid, 21 Feb. 1854, 15 Mar. 1860; *B.N.L.*, 3 Jan. 1855, 2 Jan. 1857.
54. Belfast police committee minutes, 23 Jan. 1838.
55. Ibid, 8, 15 Nov. 1831, 29 May 1838, 26 Nov. 1839.
56. *B.N.L.*, 10 Oct. 1839.
57. Town council committee on police affairs minutes, 2 Apr., 8 Oct. 1845, 10 Apr. 1855, 30 Jan., 11 Sept. 1862; *B.N.L.*, 4 Apr. 1848, 2 Oct. 1856, 2 Feb. 1858; *1864 Belfast borough inquiry*, p.10.
58. Town council committee on police affairs minutes, 26 Mar. 1863.

of charge, was estimated to save a Belfast policeman more than £11 a year in the 1850s.[59]

REWARDS

There were other ways in which Belfast policemen's incomes differed from the wage rates indicated earlier. In 1818 a scheme was introduced whereby watchmen who served for three years without disciplinary action taken against them were entitled to a 10s. reward, which amounted to more than a week's wages.[60] Policemen were also allowed, on applying to the superintendent, to accept rewards from the public for apprehending offenders.[61] Rewards for exceptional police duty included the £1 given to Watchman Robert Clewlow who saved a woman from drowning 'at great risk to himself' in May's Dock in November 1822, and the £5 received by Constable Charles Noble from the government for arresting a forger, James Boyle, after his arrival from England in October 1826 with 3,000 counterfeit half crowns, shillings and sixpences in his possession.[62]

There were also rewards for more mundane services rendered. For example, in the 1820s the day constables were entitled to half of the proceeds from the sale of stolen goods unclaimed at the town clerk's office (the rest went to the House of Industry), and they also received half of the fines levied on publicans for selling at unauthorised hours on Sundays, as well as half the fines imposed on the owners of pigs found wandering on the streets.[63] This lucrative source of income was withdrawn in 1825 but was partly restored in 1838, in which year it was stated that constables and watchmen 'exerted themselves with much zeal' against erring retail spirit traders in the hope of receiving half of the penalties imposed for breaches of the licensing acts. When the police board withdrew this 'stimulation to increased vigilance' in 1839 there was a dramatic fall in the number of prosecutions.[64] From March 1824 day constables received 3s.4d. and night constables 2s.6d. per day simply for attending at

59. *B.N.L.*, 11 Feb. 1856.

60. Belfast police commissioners' minutes, 9 Sept. 1818. See also Belfast police committee minutes, 14 Sept. 1820, 8 Sept. 1821, 19 Sept. 1826.

61. Belfast police commissioners' minutes, 3 Mar. 1819.

62. Belfast police committee minutes, 23 Nov. 1822; J.P. Carroll, 'Notes for a history of police in Ireland', chapter 20, p.8 (NLI, MS 19486).

63. *B.N.L.*, 1 Oct., 15 Nov. 1822.

64. *N.W.*, 27 Oct. 1838, 15 Oct. 1839.

the Co. Antrim assizes.[65] In May 1837 the police commissioners permitted the Belfast magistrates to reward their men with any sum not exceeding £5 for the detection and successful prosecution of burglars or robbers; this led to a small number of instances in which Belfast policemen were rewarded with sums ranging from 5s. to 10s. for their efforts against thieves, street robbers and highway robbers.[66] In the 1850s grateful insurance companies paid generous rewards to Belfast policemen for prompt action when they discovered fires on their rounds. For example, Night Constable Arthur Whiteside received £1 1s. from both the National Insurance Company and the Sun Fire Insurance Company for discovering a fire in a Castle Place cabinet shop on 23 July 1858, and Night Constable Alexander Courtenay received £3 from an insurance company and the owners of a Waring Street shop for discovering a fire there on 3 September 1859.[67] The evidence suggests that monetary rewards were less common towards the end of the period than at its beginning, and that by the early 1860s good performance of police duty was more commonly recognised by the authorities' commendations than by cash awards.[68]

In addition to the official reward schemes, there might have been unofficial means by which Belfast policemen increased their income, judging by a disciplinary case in April 1839. In that month Day Constable Gracey was dismissed for drunkenness and for stating to Night Constable Courney that 'the night duty was preferable to the day duty inasmuch as more money could be made during the night from drunk men than during the day'.[69] It was sometimes alleged that British policemen were adept at robbing drunken prisoners,[70] and Day Constable Gracey's comments suggest that some Belfast policemen might have been similarly skilled. It might not be entirely coincidental that drunken Belfast prisoners used such epithets as 'robbers and pickpockets', 'a thief and a robber', 'midnight pickpocket', 'pickpocket and rascal' and 'a thief and a rogue' towards policemen arresting them.[71] When a blind news-vendor, James Corr, was arrested by a Constable Smith for disorderly

65. Belfast police committee minutes, 27 Mar. 1824.
66. Belfast police commissioners' minutes, 17 May 1837, 17 Apr. 1839, 3, 10, 17 June, 25 Nov. 1840, 17 Mar., 28 Apr. 1841.
67. *B.N.L.*, 7 Oct. 1858; *Belfast Daily Mercury*, 16 Sept. 1859 (hereafter *B.D.M.*).
68. J.A. Whiteside, 'Policing Belfast under Captain Shaw', in *Ulsterview* (Feb. 1966), p.19.
69. Belfast police commissioners' minutes, 24 Apr. 1839.
70. J.J. Tobias, *Crime and police in England 1700–1900* (Dublin, 1979), p.106.
71. *B.N.L.*, 14 Apr., 27 May 1856, 9, 19 Oct. 1858, 17 Aug. 1865.

conduct in Winetavern Street in August 1861 he cursed at the policeman and said he was 'a pickpocket, and that there had never been an honest blue-bottle in Belfast'.[72]

NIGHT WORK AND DAY WORK

There were other reasons, apart from Constable Gracey's crudely expressed opinion that night work was more lucrative than day work, why the night force was more popular than the day department. Firstly, the night hours were considerably shorter: the night men worked from 9 p.m. to 6 a.m. throughout the period, in contrast to the fifteen-hour day put in by the day constables.[73] The working hours were ideal for the night watchmen, for they enabled them to do their night-time police duty, catch some sleep afterwards and still have some time during the day for engaging in other occupations. For most of the period there was no rule to prohibit the men from working at other jobs in their spare time, unlike the regulations of the D.M.P. and Irish Constabulary. The Belfast regulations were closer to those of many English municipal police forces in this regard. Only a small number of spare-time occupations were considered unacceptable by the police authorities. For instance, in 1828 the men were forbidden to work as labourers.[74] Men who kept public houses were also threatened with dismissal if they did not cease their publican activity.[75]

With these exceptions the night men were free to occupy their day-time hours with whatever work they chose. The Belfast resident magistrate pointed out in 1843 that the watchmen 'when off duty exercise their trades & live where & how they please'.[76] The town council continued to allow their men to have jobs apart from police work, although they added keeping 'eating houses' to the list of prohibited occupations.[77] The night men's civilian occupations on occasion led to friction with members of the public. For example,

---

72. Ibid, 29 Aug. 1861.
73. For the hours worked see ibid, 11 Jan. 1820, 2 Apr. 1861; Resident Magistrate Molony, Belfast, to Under Secretary Lucas, 1 Aug. 1843 (NA, C.S.O.R.P. 1844/I.15510).
74. Belfast police committee minutes, 9 Dec. 1828.
75. Ibid, 10, 17 July 1832, 24 Mar. 1835; Town council committee on police affairs minutes, 29 Apr. 1846.
76. Resident Magistrate Molony, Belfast, to Under Secretary Lucas, 1 Aug. 1843.
77. Town council committee on police affairs minutes, 30 Sept., 11 Nov. 1846.

in May 1852 Constable McKnight leased land off the Falls Road. One day he found a man with a goat and a millworker exercising two dogs in his field. On McKnight's ordering the two trespassers to leave his land the men refused and became disorderly, and taunted the landholder to fight them instead. With the aid of Constable Sale McKnight managed to take one of the unruly trespassers prisoner, but this prompted a large crowd to gather, which rescued the prisoner with 'considerable violence'.[78] It was not until 1856 that the police authorities introduced a rule that a policeman should occupy his time with police work alone. Until then the night force was the most popular assignment for the police, as a day man, who might be out of his home from 5 a.m. to 10 p.m., 'never sees his children out of bed'. It is significant that the town council received three times as many applications for the night duty as they did for the day duty.[79] The new regulation did not entirely suppress the force's engaging in civilian occupations, however. Some policemen obeyed the letter, if not the spirit, of the law by having their wives run greengrocers' shops, boarding houses, pawnshops or second-hand clothes shops, while as late as March 1861 a member of the council's police committee stated that many of the night force still engaged in 'other business', and that he was 'glad to see them so industrious'.[80]

One should not suppose from the previous paragraphs that there were no drawbacks attached to night duty. Night work, despite the shorter hours, was physically more arduous than the day work, especially on account of the colder night temperatures and the greater risk of assault from drunk and disorderly prisoners. Sometimes night men were given a spell in the day force in order to recuperate their health, a sure sign that day work was not as physically demanding as night duty.[81] Day duty, as it involved greater contact with the public, was considered by the police authorities to require a more skilled and circumspect approach than the night work. Despite the longer working hours the police authorities considered it a promotion for a night man to get into the day force. Conversely, men transferred from the day to the night duty were deemed to have been punished by demotion. For example, Day Constable Humphrey

78. *B.N.L.*, 12 May 1852.

79. Ibid, 2 Dec. 1856, 2 Oct. 1857; *1856 police instructions*, p.4.

80. *1857 riots inquiry*, pp. 223, 239; Town council committee on police affairs minutes, 9, 30 Aug. 1860; *B.N.L.*, 2 Mar. 1861; *1864 Belfast borough inquiry*, pp. 332, 359–61; Andrew Boyd, *Holy war in Belfast* (2nd ed., Tralee, 1972), p.14.

81. Belfast police committee minutes, 27 July 1830; Town council committee on police affairs minutes, 12 Sept. 1848.

was removed from the police office in May 1835 and transferred to the night watch as a punishment for taking a bribe and not fully reporting the daily occurrences in the office, while Day Constable Bell was reduced to the night watch in November 1837 for drinking in a public house and 'standing on the street with a girl'.[82] In September 1848 Day Constable McWilliams was removed from the day to the night duty 'for being stupid and unintelligible when asked for information'.[83] The police authorities, because they considered the day department to be the superior section of their establishment, remunerated the day men more handsomely than the night men. It was not until 1861 that night constables received pay equal to that of the day men, but even after this the town council continued to view a transfer to the day work as a promotion for the night men.[84] It is open to question whether a night constable, with shorter working hours and more opportunities of supplementing his police wage with some spare-time employment, would have held a move to the day duty as an improvement in his lot.

SICK PAY, PENSIONS AND GRATUITIES

One should also include the various payments such as sick pay, gratuities and pensions when considering the monetary rewards available to the Belfast police. Sick payments were not overly generous in the early years, as the police board continued its frugal husbanding of the ratepayers' taxes. The board's early attitude can best be summarised by an incident in 1817 when Watchman John McMullan was incapacitated following an attack by a dog owned by Francis Huddleston of Ann Street. Rather than pay compensation to McMullan the police board ordered the superintendent to inform Huddleston that 'unless he pays the man's wages for the time he was unable to attend his duty in consequence of the hurt, the Commissioners will take steps to compel him'.[85] The police board's attitude towards compensating their men for injuries received on duty gradually softened, but never to the extent of allowing them full pay: in March 1822 Watchman Robert Boyce was paid 5s. per week, slightly more than half pay, after spraining his ankle when on duty, while in November 1823 Watchman Edward Martin,

---

82. Belfast police committee minutes, 19 May 1835, 14 Nov. 1837.

83. Town council committee on police affairs minutes, 5 Sept. 1848.

84. Ibid, 28 Mar. 1861; *1864 Belfast borough inquiry*, p.249.

85. Belfast police commissioners' minutes, 2 Apr. 1817.

who was absent from duty for fifteen weeks after sustaining a similar injury in similar circumstances, received only one month's pay for the time that he was off duty.[86] In 1839 the force was informed that because of the numerous applications for payment by injured police-men no sick payments would be made in future 'unless under very particular circumstances', and even then doctors' bills were to be deducted from the allowance. In 1843 the police authorities decided that half pay was adequate compensation for men who could not perform duty as a result of sickness or injury, and this remained the amount normally awarded (occasionally full pay was granted) so long as the patient was not on the sick list for more than four or five weeks. The town council's penny-pinching approach towards some of the injured men is illustrated by the case of Constable Hugh O'Hara in April 1845. O'Hara was granted one week's pay, and Inspectors Black and Hamilton were also ordered to have the policeman admitted to the Poor House for a number of weeks. In 1855 the men were warned that they would be dismissed if they spent more than three months on the sick list.[87]

There is no record of the police commissioners or police commit-tee paying gratuities or pensions to policemen obliged to retire from the force due to sickness or inability to continue duty. The first recorded gratuities occurred under the town council's regime. In December 1844 the town council's Committee on Police Affairs surveyed the force to remove from it such men who 'from age or other causes were incompetent to discharge their duties'. There were plenty of likely candidates for removal: a survey of the men's ages in 1843 showed that only eighteen of the ninety-three full-time members were aged thirty or less; another twenty-six were aged between thirty and forty years, thirty-two between forty and fifty years, and eighteen were older than fifty, three of whom were older than seventy. An observer stated that 'at least 5 years may be added to the ages of most of those stated ... as the return is on the authority of the men's own statement, and they look much older'. On New Year's Eve, 1844, the town council discharged eleven men, more than one eighth of their total force, on gratuity. The discharged

86. Belfast police committee minutes, 23 Feb. 1822; Belfast police commis-sioners' minutes, 12 Nov. 1823. The Bulkies were outside the scope of protec-tion afforded 'peace officers' by the malicious injuries clauses in the 1836 legislation on Irish grand juries. This remained the situation indeed for the R.I.C. in Belfast until 1898. See D.S. Greer, *Compensation for criminal injury* (Belfast, 1990), pp.10–11. I am grateful to Professor W.N. Osborough for this reference.

87. Belfast police commissioners' minutes, 17 Apr. 1839, 8 Mar. 1843; Town council committee on police affairs minutes, 2 Apr. 1845, 20 Feb., 5 June 1855; *B.N.L.*, 2 Aug. 1860.

men's ages ranged from thirty-nine to sixty-one, and their years of service from four to twenty-five. The highest gratuity awarded, one month's pay, was given to seven of the men.[88]

After March 1848, when 5% was deducted from the men's wages to establish a superannuation and relief fund (this was reduced to 2% of the wages in 1850), the amount of gratuity increased. A portion of the fines imposed by magistrates at the petty sessions was also diverted to the police superannuation fund.[89] In June 1850 Night Constable William Steen, who had served for two years, received a gratuity of £10 when he was discharged as an epileptic.[90] In September 1852 Detective Constable Stewart McWilliams was granted a gratuity of £25 on condition that he used it to help pay for his and his family's emigration to America. It appears that McWilliams, who was under suspension for some unknown transgression, was not incapacitated but was instead a source of embarrassment to the town council, and they were willing to pay handsomely to dispense with his services.[91] Other gratuities included £25 granted to Detective Constable John Kane in September 1852 when he was discharged as unfit after fifteen years' service, £15 awarded to Night Constable Thomas Greer in October 1852 after five years' service, and £17 granted after seventeen years' service to Constable Henry McLaverty in September 1856.[92] Night Constable John Irwen received the more modest sum of one week's wages in November 1859 when his health had broken down after one year's service, even though the regulations stipulated that no policeman with less than two years in the force was entitled to a gratuity.[93] In October 1860 Constable William Wright was granted £30 on his discharge as unfit after twenty years' service in the force, and Constable Hugh Heaney was given £20 in May 1863 after twenty-one years' service. Heaney was not incapacitated, but had simply resigned to emigrate to America.[94]

88. Resident Magistrate Molony, Belfast, to Under Secretary Lucas, 1 Aug. 1843 (NA, C.S.O.R.P. 1844/I.15510); Town council committee on police affairs minutes, 31 Dec. 1844; *N.W.*, 2 Jan. 1845.

89. Town council committee on police affairs minutes, 22 Mar. 1848; *B.N.L.*, 3 Mar. 1848, 2 Aug. 1850.

90. Town council committee on police affairs minutes, 4 June 1850.

91. Ibid, 10 Aug., 7 Sept. 1852.

92. Ibid, 28 Sept., 26 Oct. 1852, 29 Sept. 1856.

93. *1856 police instructions*, p.32; Town council committee on police affairs minutes, 3 Nov. 1859.

94. *B.N.L.*, 2 Oct. 1860, 2 June 1863.

The amounts awarded as pensions by the police authorities were as unpredictable as those awarded as gratuities. No pensions were granted by the police commissioners or police committee, but this is hardly surprising given the fact that by 1843 only four men had served for more than twenty years in the force.[95] The first pensions were awarded after the establishment of the superannuation and relief fund in 1848. There was no set amount of pension. The 226th section of the 1845 Belfast Improvement Act merely stated that the council might pension any policeman disabled in the discharge of his duty or worn out by length of service with any amount that it thought reasonable. Before a man received a pension he had to undergo a strict medical examination to verify that he was unable to perform further duty; also the chief night or day constable had to inform the police committee as to his conduct in the service, the number of his dependants and their occupations, and whether he owned any property or had any other means of support, before the amount of pension was decided.[96]

The first pensions were received in August 1848 by Constables Patrick Mallon, aged seventy-three, after seventeen years' service and John Clotworthy, aged sixty, after sixteen years' service. Both policemen were pensioned off at the rate of 3s.6d. per week (£9 2s. per year). Their pensions were to be paid out of the fines imposed at petty sessions, but were to be discontinued 'either upon future bad conduct or becoming chargeable on any public charity'.[97] This was not an idle threat: in January 1854 Pensioner Robert Gillespie, who joined the force in September 1833, lost his weekly pension of 3s.6d. for unspecified 'misconduct'.[98]

In the early years of the pension scheme 3s.6d. was the most common weekly pension awarded, but the council sometimes gave larger pensions as a mark of special esteem. For example Robert Campbell who served for thirty-five years with an 'unblemished character' was pensioned off at 7s.6d. weekly (£19 10s. annually) in June 1856.[99] In the same year Chief Night Constable William Armstrong resigned after more than twenty-six years' service. At first the council wanted to give him a weekly pension of 10s. but this was revised to 15s. (£39 annually). Armstrong, who was addicted to drink, was technically dismissed or required to resign, and thus

95. Resident Magistrate Molony, Belfast, to Under Secretary Lucas, 1 Aug. 1843.
96. *B.N.L.*, 3 Oct. 1848.
97. Town council committee on police affairs minutes, 22 Aug. 1848.
98. Ibid, 24 Jan. 1854.
99. Ibid, 10 June 1856.

ineligible for a pension. This was glossed over at the council meeting which decided on the amount of his pension. Reading between
the lines one feels that the council were glad to see the back of their
troublesome servant, but did not wish to be vindictive in withhold-
ing a pension from such a long-time employee.[100] It was probably
the unpredictable size of the pensions awarded which prompted a
councillor in 1860 to propose a fixed pension scale for policemen,
but his proposal was turned down.[101] The council insisted on
judging each case on its merits, unlike the system operating in the
Dublin Metropolitan Police and the Irish Constabulary, where
pension entitlements were minutely spelled out in the police regulations.[102] Thus one finds unusual pension awards throughout the
final years of the Belfast force's existence. For example in July 1860
Chief Day Constable Thomas Lindsay retired after thirty-six years
on a pension equal to his full pay, an unusual mark of esteem from
the council.[103] When Inspector Hugh McIlroy had to resign because
of ill health in November 1864 after about twenty years' service,
the council again bent the rules and awarded him a weekly pension
of fifteen shillings.[104]

The police authorities also occasionally granted pensions or gratuities to the widows and children of deceased policemen. The compensation scheme was as arbitrary as those for the men's pensions
and gratuities. The first widow's gratuity, of 27*s.* (just over three
weeks' pay), was made to the widow of Watchman Thomas McAuley,
who was found dead on the morning of February 1819; three years
later Mary Smith, widow of Watchman Miles Smith, was granted
10*s.* to enable her to return home to Monaghan after her husband's
death.[105] Constable Victor McClure's widow was granted a gratuity
of six weeks' pay in May 1839, 'he having received a severe cold in
our employ, which terminated in his death'.[106] The largest gratuity

100. Ibid, 25 Apr. 1854, 8 Jan., 4, 25 Mar. 1856; *B.N.L.*, 31 Mar., 2 Apr. 1856.

101. *B.N.L.*, 2 June 1860.

102. For the pension entitlements of R.I.C. and D.M.P. men and officers see
    Brian Griffin, 'The Irish police, 1836–1914: a social history' (unpublished
    Ph.D. thesis, Loyola University of Chicago, 1991), pp.189–205, 290–91.

103. The inspectors and constables of the day police also presented Lindsay with
    an oil portrait of himself, completed by Mr Robie of Arthur Street. *B.N.L.*,
    28 June, 3, 7 July 1860.

104. Ibid, 2 Nov. 1864.

105. Belfast police commissioners' minutes, 10 Feb. 1819; Belfast police commit-
    tee minutes, 23 Feb. 1822.

106. Belfast police commissioners' minutes, 22 May 1839.

awarded to a policeman's family was the £10 granted to the family of Constable Daniel Brown in April 1840 'as a testimony of our estimate of his faithful services during the period of 21 years'.[107]

The first pension awarded to a deceased policeman's relatives was given to the family of Constable John McBride, one of the men serving in the police office, who was killed on duty in July 1838. McBride was travelling by jaunting car to the Co. Antrim assizes at Carrickfergus to act as a witness against a person charged with uttering counterfeit money. His horse bolted and McBride was killed when he jumped clear of the car. He had served for fifteen years, during which time he was 'never known to be either in a passion or inebriated'. His death sparked off a public subscription for his wife and three children. The police board also granted his family a pension of 2s.6d. a week (£6 10s. a year).[108] When the town council superseded the police board a limit of £25 gratuity for deceased policemen's relatives was introduced.[109] The authorities' awards never came near to the £25 maximum allowed, however. Their thrifty principles are best illustrated by the £2 10s. granted to Jane Todd, the widow of Constable William Todd who died in April 1846, 'having been disabled in the execution of his duty and worn out by length of service'.[110] Todd had been in the force since 1823. Their largest gratuity award was £10. This was the amount given to the children of Day Constable Samuel Waring, who died in March 1858 after almost eleven years' service. In April 1864 the widows of Inspector James Hawkes and Constable Ferran were at first awarded £20 'compensation' on their husbands' deaths, but the frugal council whittled this down to £10.[111]

107. Ibid, 16 Sept. 1840.

108. *N.W.*, 24 July 1838; Belfast police commissioners' minutes, 27 Oct. 1841.

109. 8 & 9 Vict, c.142, s.227.

110. Town council committee on police affairs minutes, 22 Apr. 1846.

111. Ibid, 30 Mar. 1858, 7, 14 Apr. 1864.

CHAPTER FOUR

Discipline

THE ROLE OF THE POLICE BOARD AND THE TOWN COUNCIL

NO ACCOUNT OF the policeman's lot would be complete without a discussion of the disciplinary system of his force. An examination of the Belfast police's disciplinary system is complicated by the fact that from September 1816 to January 1844 the two departments of the police board, the police commissioners and police committee, had a role in enforcing the rules and regulations and they were often at loggerheads over their respective roles and responsibilities. The 1800 and 1816 Belfast police acts were partly to blame for the confusion which often existed. The 1800 act, for instance, gave the police committee the authority to frame 'such rules, orders, and regulations' for the night watch as it considered necessary, and to dismiss watchmen for 'neglect of duty, drunkenness, misbehaviour, or other cause whatever'; it gave similar powers to the police commissioners, however, without indicating how the dual roles of the two bodies were to be reconciled. It did state that the police committee were to assist the commissioners in executing the provisions of the act, but there was plenty of scope for confusion over the respective roles of the two bodies. The 1816 act further confused matters by giving the police commissioners the power to fine watchmen up to £1 for neglect of duty or misbehaviour, or to dismiss defaulters if they considered it necessary. The *Northern Whig* commented in September 1829:

Had the most subtle and mischievous ingenuity been directed to frame a law for the annoyance of the town, and the prevention of any thing like good order in its internal regulations, a more effectual plan could not have been devised than the police act[s], by which the local affairs of Belfast are managed. In every well ordered form of government, whether national or civic, the powers of the legislative and executive are carefully kept distinct, and the one is not suffered to interfere with the other. In the Belfast police act[s], the powers of the police commissioners and the police committee are so jumbled together, that the exact extent of the privileges of each of these bodies has never yet been wholly ascertained. The consequence is, that when the police committee wish to promote any public measure, or work which would promote the interest, or add to the accommodation of the inhabitants, the commissioners oppose it as an assumption of power on the part of the executive, which belongs entirely to themselves, as the legislative body. On the other hand, it cannot be denied that the committee, by way of resenting the arbitrary bearing of the commissioners, may sometimes exercise that power which the act gives them, and throw obstacles in the way of measures proposed by the board of commissioners.[1]

This extract, while dealing with the broader topic of clashes between the commissioners and committee over the running of Belfast's urban government, could equally have been written about their handling of the municipal police force.

The police board at first came to an arrangement whereby the police committee heard disciplinary cases at its weekly meetings and recommended the course of action to be taken. The police commissioners then reviewed the cases and usually agreed with the committee's decision, although they also occasionally decided disciplinary cases without involving the police committee. There were several acrimonious clashes between the two departments of the police board, and these often involved arguments about the police force. One of the longest-running contentious issues was the provision of a police office and watch house for the police establishment, which was to serve as a lock-up for prisoners, as a place where the public could go to for police assistance, and as a magistrates' court house.

The first police office was in Bridge Street,[2] but this was replaced in December 1818 by a house in Rosemary Street.[3] The Bridge Street office must have been a shambles, because the Rosemary Street watch house which replaced it was a very dilapidated building indeed. In July 1823 the Association for the Improvement of Prisons and Prison Discipline in Ireland complained to Thomas Verner, the sovereign of Belfast, that 'The black hole (justly so called) connected with the police office in the interior of the town, consists of a few gloomy cells without ventilation, more adapted for wild beasts than for the miserable human beings who are so often its inmates'.[4] The police committee agreed. In January 1826 it

---

1. *N.W.*, 17 Sept. 1829.

2. *Belfast Commercial Chronicle*, 21 Sept. 1816.

3. Belfast police commissioners' minutes, 2 Dec. 1818.

4. Ibid, 23 July 1823. Belfast Court House, where the quarter sessions were held, appears to have been in a similarly poor condition, judging from the complaint of the clerk of the court in May 1828 that 'I find it almost impossible to perform my duties in it, [with] rain falling on my papers & obliterating my notes as fast [as] I take them'.(NA, C.S.O.R.P. 1828/665).

complained of 'the very bad state of the present police office, as it is in so ruinous a condition as to be dangerous, besides which the sewer is choked up and the lower part of the concern [is] most disgustingly filthy in consequence', and unsuccessfully requested the Belfast House of Industry to accommodate the police. The *Belfast Newsletter* condemned the police commissioners' insistence on keeping the 'crazy, inconvenient, mouldering old building, in no way adequate to the purpose to which it is most preposterously appropriated ... At present it is dangerous, inconvenient, straitened in room, filthy and disgraceful not merely to Belfast but to humanity'. It hoped that 'some better place will promptly be chosen for a police office, than the wretched dung-pound, or hot-bed of putrescence, now occupied for that purpose in Rosemary Street'. It added that 'if it were ... offered in its present state as a stye for pigs, the angry hogs would curl their snouts with indignation, grunting refusal, and squeaking disdain'. On one occasion a prisoner escaped from the watch house simply by breaking down the rotten wall of his cell![5]

The police committee repeatedly petitioned the commissioners to move to better premises than the Rosemary Street office, but the commissioners, carefully husbanding the rate revenues of the town, refused to sanction the expense it would involve. The committee's accusations of dereliction of duty did not help to make the commissioners regard their requests in a more favourable light.[6] There was a temporary move to a Marquis Street premises, off Smithfield, in 1828[7] but the police commissioners did not agree to a permanent move from Rosemary Street until July 1833. A critic took an uncharitable view of their reluctance to leave Rosemary Street: 'like a colony of rats, long in possession of an old building, they were determined not to desert it as long as it could afford them shelter.'[8] Even the new premises in Poultry Square (later re-named Police Square) were unpleasantly reminiscent of the Rosemary Street watch house. In an article entitled 'Filth of the Belfast Police Office' the *Northern Whig* claimed in 1838 that

The dirty, loathsome, and unhealthy state of the police establishment of this town, is notorious. The building is in a dangerous state, and is

5. Belfast police committee minutes, 2 Jan. 1826; Belfast police commissioners' minutes, 11 Jan. 1826; *B.N.L.*, 17 Nov., 29 Dec. 1826.
6. Belfast police committee minutes, 27 Mar. 1824, 17 Oct. 1825, 8 Mar. 1826, 20 Feb., 20 Mar. 1827, 14 Aug., 2 Oct. 1827, 5 Feb. 1828, 18 May, 17 Aug. 1830, 2, 10 Aug., 16 Nov. 1831; Belfast police commissioners' minutes, 12 Jan. 1825, 15 Mar. 1826, 11 Aug., 9 Nov. 1831, 1 Feb. 1832.
7. *B.N.L.*, 2 May 1828.
8. Letter from 'Censor' in *N.W.*, 13 Sept. 1827.

insufficient for the required purposes; the cells are too few, too small, and not sufficiently ventilated; and the whole concern is so filthy, as to render it dangerous to the health of the officers employed, and the prisoners confined.[9]

The watch moved temporarily to the House of Correction in August 1838 because of the feared collapse of the gable walls,[10] but thereafter the Poultry Square premises remained the headquarters of the Belfast municipal police.[11]

The relations between the police committee and police commissioners, which were severely strained over the question of the police office, were further soured after several clashes involving the discipline of the police force. One of the major bones of contention between them concerned a policeman named Stewart Beggs. He first appears in the records as a night watchman elected in September 1817. He was promoted to day constable in June 1818 in place of John Magill, who was dismissed for being 'repeatedly drunk on his duty'. Beggs was dismissed from the force in February 1819 'for very improperly confining Mr Heagney in the black hole all night, along with felons'. Nevertheless, the police committee tried to re-appoint Beggs in April 1820, but the commissioners blocked this on the grounds that he had been previously dismissed. Beggs was mysteriously re-elected constable in May 1825, but was subsequently dismissed by the police committee in October 1832 for offering insults 'of the grossest kind' to a gentleman named Gilmer, both in Gilmer's office and in the street. The committee felt that 'such conduct is contrary to all discipline, and … if for a moment tolerated would bring the whole establishment into the utmost confusion, and render it a nuisance rather than a benefit'. Beggs appealed to the commissioners to be re-instated and they amazingly supported him. The committee announced its determination not to have Beggs re-accepted. One feels that their complaint that Beggs was 'not only gross to Mr Gilmer, but exceedingly insolent to the committee' only endeared Beggs to the police commissioners. The committee finally relinquished their opposition and re-appointed Beggs as day constable on 5 March 1833. The reason for the volte-face is not clear, but it is probable that the committee felt in a magnanimous mood following an agreement reached with the police commissioners on

9. Ibid, 18 Aug. 1838.
10. Belfast police commissioners' minutes, 15 Aug. 1838.
11. *Slater's national commercial directory of Ireland* (Manchester and London, 1846), p.417; Town council committee on police affairs minutes, 4 Aug. 1857; *1864 Belfast borough inquiry*, p.9. Poultry Square's name was later changed to Police Square; Police Square is now called Victoria Square.

26 February 1833 that in future 'the entire business of the establishment relating to officers and watchmen, was to devolve upon
the committee' and that the commissioners would not interfere in
the committee's decisions affecting the force.[12]

The commissioners initially stood by the terms of the agreement,
except to register a protest over the committee's dismissal of Day
Constable John Noble in November 1833. Noble first came to the
unfavourable attention of the committee by his evidence to the
1833 parliamentary commission of enquiry into the Irish municipal
corporations, where he alleged that the superintendent had had him
removed as magistrates' clerk in June 1833 so that he could appro-
priate the clerk's fees to himself. The police committee dismissed
Noble for altering several entries in the police books to injure Arthur
Skinner, son of the man who had had Noble removed from the clerk-
ship. The commissioners expressed their doubts as to the legality
of dismissing Noble without their consent, but the committee
simply reminded them of the February 1833 agreement and sacked
Noble.[13] The final major disagreement between the commissioners
and committee over disciplinary matters occurred in 1838. It was
precipitated by the police commissioners' dismissal in February
1838 of a watchman named Cochrane after they heard of his
'outrageous conduct' towards an old man on the Malone Road.
This was followed by a farcical turn of events, in which Cochrane
was alternately hired and dismissed by the two departments, both
of which claimed the authority of the Police Acts for their actions.
The fact that by this time most of the police committee were Tories
while most of the police commissioners were Whigs might have
added rancour to the struggle. Eventually Cochrane was restored
to his position, but the chagrined committee refused to have anything more to do with the disciplinary system of the force. From
July 1838 the committee looked after the recruitment, clothing and
equipment of the police while the commissioners deliberated on

12. Details of Beggs's case from Belfast police committee minutes, 6 Sept. 1817,
    13, 20 June 1818, 15 Apr. 1820, 23 May 1825, 2, 30 Oct. 1832, 5 Mar. 1833;
    Belfast police commissioners' minutes, 20 Feb. 1819, 19 Apr. 1820, 24 Oct.
    1832. The agreement is mentioned in the police committee minutes of 3 Dec.
    1833.

13. *First report of the commissioners appointed to inquire into the municipal corporations*
    in Ireland. Appendix, parts I and II: reports from the north-eastern circuit, H.C.
    1835 [27] [28], xxviii, 199, p.704; Belfast police committee minutes, 4, 12
    Nov., 3 Dec. 1833; Belfast police commissioners' minutes, 27 Nov. 1833;
    Northern Herald (Belfast), 11 Jan. 1834.

disciplinary matters.[14] This arrangement lasted until the end of January 1844, when the town council took over the duties and responsibilities of the police board. Thereafter the town council's Committee on Police Affairs, all of whose members were elected councillors, ran the police force and decided upon disciplinary matters.

Throughout the history of the force, then, elected civilian officials, be they members of the police board from 1816 to 1844 or members of the town council from 1844 to 1865, decided the disciplinary action to be taken against the Belfast police. There were only trivial exceptions to this general rule. For example, in 1837 the superintendent was empowered to fine day constables up to one shilling for slovenliness.[15] The chief night and day constables from April 1844 were allowed to suspend men found drunk on duty until their cases were brought before the disciplinary board, and in the following year the 1845 Belfast Improvement Act gave the mayor of Belfast the power to impose up to one month's imprisonment with or without hard labour on any constable found neglecting his duty,[16] although there is no record that the mayor ever actually exercised this power. In June 1860 the town council's police committee complained that 'their time was taken up in trying constables for petty offences, and much to their own inconvenience, rendering their meetings more prolonged than they need have been'; in an effort to cut down on the amount of time spent adjudicating on disciplinary matters they allowed the superintendent to fine up to 10s. in cases where he was convinced of a constable's guilt.[17] This power was briefly held by the last superintendent of the force, Captain Eyre Massey Shaw, who was in charge of it from June 1860 to August 1861.[18] In November 1863 Chief Constable Green, the most senior officer in the force in the absence of a super-

14. *N.W.*, 7 Nov. 1837; Belfast police commissioners' minutes, 21, 28 Feb., 7, 21, 28 Mar., 3 May 1838; Belfast police committee minutes, 6, 13, 27 Mar., 3, 10, 17 Apr., 3 May, 17 July 1838.

15. Belfast police committee minutes, 16 May 1837.

16. Town council committee on police affairs minutes, 3 Apr. 1844; 8 & 9 Vict, c.142, s.222.

17. Town council committee on police affairs minutes, 21 June 1860; *B.N.L.*, 3 July 1860.

18. Shaw resigned from the force to take up the post of superintendent of the London fire brigade in September 1861. A recent biography of Shaw devotes only two sketchy pages to his period as superintendent of the Belfast police. See Ronald Cox, *Oh, Captain Shaw: the life story of the first and most famous chief of the London fire brigade* (London, 1984), pp.30–31.

intendent, was allowed to deal with 'any trifling neglect of duty' on the part of the constables, but his decisions in these trivial cases were subject to appeal to, and ratification by, the police committee.[19]

Except in the minor and exceptional circumstances cited in the previous paragraph, the various elected civilian police bodies saw to the discipline of Belfast's police force. This was similar to the arrangement adopted by English municipal police forces after the Borough Police Act of 1835.[20] The Belfast police from at least as early as 1820 were subject to a printed set of rules and regulations.[21] Unfortunately none of the early copies have survived, but from reading the decisions made in disciplinary cases and the periodic orders issued by the police board it is possible to get a fairly complete idea of what the regulations involved. The evidence suggests that the early regulations differed very little from those in force in 1856, the only year for which a complete printed set of regulations has survived.

IMMORALITY AND CORRUPTION

We know that from an early date the police authorities expected high standards of behaviour from their force. Immoral conduct and corruption were particularly frowned upon. In January 1821 Watchman Patrick Smith was dismissed for 'deserting his lawful wife and confessedly cohabiting with another woman', while four months later Constable William Grey was dismissed for 'ill treating his wife'. The same punishment was visited upon Watchman Jacob Munson 'for having been in conversation with a prostitute on his station and afterwards being found without his pike'.[22] Consorting with prostitutes was a risky business for a Belfast policeman, as the police authorities usually dismissed men for that offence. For example, in December 1831 Watchman Michael McManus was discharged when he was found off station in a woman's company, his guilt being aggravated by the fact that he was 'in the practice of keeping company with bad women'. Watchman McGowan was

---

19. Town council committee on police affairs minutes, 12 Nov. 1863.

20. T.A. Critchley, *A history of police in England and Wales 900–1966* (London, 1967), p.63.

21. The regulations are mentioned in Belfast police commissioners' minutes, 2 Feb. 1820, 26 Nov., 3 Dec. 1828, 5 May 1830; Belfast police committee minutes, 16 Dec. 1828, 10 Feb. 1829, 26 Nov. 1837, 6 Oct. 1841.

22. Belfast police committee minutes, 11 Jan., 19, 26 May 1821.

dismissed in October 1832 for dallying five hours with a woman charged with robbing a man on the street, before taking her to the watch house.[23] Several other men were dismissed for keeping company with prostitutes, including a married man in February 1841 who spent a night in a Caddell's Entry brothel and Day Constable William McQuilty in September 1852 for kissing a prostitute in public when on duty.[24] It would appear from the relatively small number of cases involving policemen consorting with prostitutes that the authorities' strictures were usually obeyed. A Belfast councillor claimed in 1858 that because most municipal policemen were married they were less likely to stray from the path of virtue than members of the Irish Constabulary, who were not allowed to marry until they had served for at least seven years, and opined that 'a number of young men on the streets of Belfast at night would not be as efficient as married men in performing their duties in removing certain characters'.[25] Police avoidance of intimate relations with prostitutes is also borne out by the fact that only two policemen are mentioned in the police minutes as absent from duty due to venereal disease, both of whom were dismissed in 1862. One of the men was a Constable Robert Peel.[26]

There are occasional cases of corruption mentioned in the police board records. It seems to have been a greater problem in the earlier period than in later years. As early as May 1818 a watchman was dismissed for allowing a prisoner charged with robbery to leave the police office to conceal money: the watchman had apparently planned on receiving a portion of the loot.[27] Watchmen Michael Kennedy and John Knight and Constable Patterson were dismissed in December 1821 for 'extorting money to stop a prosecution for assault'.[28] The police authorities were highly embarrassed in 1822

23. Ibid, 27 Dec. 1831, 9 Oct. 1832.

24. Ibid, 3 Jan. 1837; Belfast police commissioners' minutes, 7 Aug. 1839, 24 Feb. 1841; Town council committee on police affairs minutes, 2 Sept. 1846, 7 Sept. 1852, 23 Dec. 1856.

25. *B.N.L.*, 13 July 1858. The topic of married men's and bachelors' experiences of life in the R.I.C. and D.M.P., including some men's availing of prostitutes' services, is discussed by Brian Griffin, 'The Irish police: love, sex and marriage in the nineteenth and early twentieth centuries' in Margaret Kelleher and James Murphy (ed.), *Gender perspectives in nineteenth-century Ireland: public and private spheres* (Dublin, 1997).

26. Town council committee on police affairs minutes, 30 Jan., 6 Mar. 1862.

27. Belfast police committee minutes, 2 May 1818.

28. Belfast police commissioners' minutes, 19 Dec. 1819.

when Constable Charles Mann was found guilty of receiving stolen goods and sentenced to eighteen months' imprisonment and to two public whippings. Mann's accomplice was a prostitute named Biddy Loughran, 'well known as a transgressor'. When plying her trade Loughran often managed to steal property from clients; she then either pawned the goods and informed Mann who bought them at a low price from the pawnbroker concerned, or Mann bought the goods directly from Loughran. At his trial the policeman produced as character witnesses brothel keepers and prostitutes, described by the presiding judge as 'a gang of rogues' whom Mann rewarded for committing crime.[29] It is perhaps not surprising that a Belfast resident alleged in July 1823 that the police 'connive at the practice of prostitution, or go smacks with the robbers of coals or hats out of halls'.[30] In the 1830s there were numerous instances of policemen accepting bribes from prisoners to release them or to drop prosecutions against them.[31] The most unusual corruption cases were probably those of Watchman McLarinon who was dismissed in August 1833 for keeping an army officers' dog and collar in his house for the purpose of extorting a reward for finding them, and Day Constable Humphries who was dismissed in October 1839 for assisting in the disposal of spirits stolen from Emerson's liquor store. His accomplice, Day Constable Kane, was less severely punished as he had merely helped to carry two bottles of the loot.[32] Instances of corruption appear considerably less frequently in the town council's records, and this might reflect a general improvement in police honesty. Chief Constable Thomas Lindsay claimed proudly in 1857 that no Belfast policeman was convicted of larceny in the previous thirty years. But not all contemporaries were as convinced of the upright behaviour of the municipal force. As late as 1856 Arthur Hill Thornton, head of a delegation of 103 ratepayers from Robert Street and the adjoining streets who wanted the brothels in the area suppressed, alleged that the police 'supplemented their pay' by taking bribes from the brothel keepers. He urged a pay increase of 2*s*.6*d*. per week for constables as 'Many of them were more in the service of persons who ought to be prosecuted than they were in the service of the ratepayers'.[33]

29. *B.N.L.*, 28 May, 2 Aug. 1822.
30. Letter from 'Discretion' in *Irishman* (Belfast), 4 July 1823.
31. See Belfast police committee minutes, 23 Aug. 1831, 30 Oct. 1832, 7 Aug. 1833, 12 Aug. 1834, 30 Aug. 1836, 24 Jan. 1837; and Belfast police commissioners' minutes, 1 Apr. 1840.
32. Belfast police committee minutes, 7 Aug. 1833; Belfast police commissioners' minutes, 30 Oct., 6 Nov. 1839.
33. *B.N.L.*, 2 Sept. 1856; *1857 riots inquiry*, p.45.

NEGLECT OF DUTY

As well as charges of corruption and improper behaviour, the police authorities were concerned about allegations that their force routinely neglected their duties. Such allegations became common once the initial enthusiasm which greeted the introduction of the force had waned. There were even complaints that the simplest of the watchmen's duties, that of calling the hour and weather and waking those inhabitants who requested an early morning call,[34] were inadequately performed. Critics suggested that the hours were called so incoherently that the watchmen might as well shout in High Dutch or Hebrew; it was not unknown for adjacent watchmen to shout conflicting hours.[35] Despite complaints that calling the hour unnecessarily advertised a watchman's presence to criminals at night the force continued the practice until June 1844.[36]

There were more serious criticisms concerning the disorderly scenes in Belfast's streets, despite the presence of the night watch. One resident described a midnight scene which he witnessed in April 1826:

[A]lmost every corner, the mouths of the different entries, as well as the more open parts of the streets, were literally swarming with drunken men, chiefly sailors, and unfortunate females on the watch for their prey. I observed, also, [that] several of the most popular taverns, which are so conveniently situated in the different entries and passages for the practice and accommodation of every species of debauchery and vice, were not only open and brilliantly illuminated at that unseasonable hour, but from the noise and bustle within, the sound of which was easily heard in the street, it evidently appeared that they were in full occupation, and reaping a rich harvest of emolument from the folly, dissipation and extravagance of their deluded or vicious inmates.[37]

The *Northern Whig* was a noted critic of police inaction against disorderly street scenes, especially in the vicinity of its premises. Cornmarket in particular was a scene of frequent brawls, 'blasphemous imprecations', and obstructions from women squatted 'like

34. *B.N.L.*, 18 Oct. 1816; Thomas Gaffikin, *Belfast fifty years ago* (Belfast, 1894), p.30. Gaffikin's work actually describes life in Belfast in the first three decades of the nineteenth century.
35. *B.N.L.*, 15 Feb. 1820, 19 Feb. 1822; *N.W.*, 5 Mar. 1829.
36. Belfast police committee minutes, 12 Jan. 1836, 10 Oct. 1837; Belfast police commissioners' minutes, 27 Sept. 1837; Town council committee on police affairs minutes, 19 June 1844.
37. Letter from 'Civis' in *B.N.L.*, 28 Apr. 1826.

Indian squaws' on the pavements while they sold herrings and vegetables.[38] It claimed in November 1824 that Cornmarket was 'a den of blackguards, an eternal bear-garden, where the pugilistic drunkard, and the expert pickpocket, reign undisputed', and warned that if the watch did not become more active Belfast would become proverbial 'for its inefficient police, and its muddy and nauseous streets'.[39]

ATTEMPTS TO TIGHTEN DISCIPLINE

While one should beware of accepting the special pleading of newspapers at face value, there is no doubt that their general point about the frequently poor performance of the early watch was valid. The police board knew that problems of poor discipline in their force led to a slack approach to duties. In September 1819 the commissioners admitted that 'many irregularities' had occurred, but explained that the insufficient number of constables meant that the watchmen could not be visited enough times at night to ensure their vigilance. They appointed a chief constable for the night watch in the following month at a salary of 15*s.* weekly. The first man appointed, John Lambert, proved an embarrassment: he was dismissed in August 1822 for 'a gross and violent assault upon a respectable inhabitant and for his general turbulent and improper conduct'.[40] No replacement was appointed until March 1829. In the absence of a chief constable, the police board depended upon the efforts of the day and night constables to ensure that the men conducted their duties diligently. The constables employed from 1817 to 1824 proved hopelessly inadequate for the task. None of the five constables in the force in September 1817 were still serving in 1824. From 1817 to 1824 some twenty-six different men were appointed to the five constable positions, and of these as many as seventeen were dismissed—nine for drunkenness, four for improper behaviour towards the public or prisoners, two for corruption, one for unknown reasons and one on account of his age.[41] The *Northern Whig* blamed the poor state of the watch department on the absence of a chief night constable, although it skimmed over the

38. *N.W.*, 5, 18 Aug. 1824, 19 July 1827, 14 May 1829.

39. Ibid, 18 Nov. 1824.

40. Belfast police commissioners' minutes, 29 Sept., 6, 30 Oct. 1819, 7 Aug. 1822.

41. Information taken from the Belfast police board minutes, 1817–24.

poor performance of John Lambert. The superintendent, William H. Ferrar, agreed, but also blamed the night constables, whom he considered 'totally unfit for the services required'.[42] At this stage the superintendent of the police force, despite his title, played no part in the disciplinary affairs of the force. After Ferrar died in December 1826 the police committee tried to have his successor, Cortland M.Skinner, JP, visit the men on the beat two nights weekly 'or oftener if convenient', in addition to attending to the daily magistrate's duty at the police office. Skinner protested that his predecessor never had to inspect the men at night, and the commissioners agreed that it was up to himself whether he visited the men or not.[43] He retired due to old age in 1833 and was replaced by his son, Captain Arthur Macgregor Skinner, RN, who held the position until July 1840. His successor, R.D. Coulson, was the first superintendent to concern himself with the day-to-day running of the force. Coulson's contract specified that he should ensure that each man had a copy of the rules and regulations; each night he was to check that the men were fit for duty and he was to visit the force at different hours both day and night.[44] Coulson resigned in June 1843 but his successor as superintendent, Thomas Verner, was appointed on the same understanding that he keep close tabs on the men's patrolling activity. His failure to fulfil the terms of his contract led to Verner's removal as superintendent by the police authorities in January 1849.[45]

In the early years, due to a lack of reliable officers and the non-involvement of the superintendent in the disciplinary affairs of the police, the police board had little choice but to impose a severe disciplinary regime on their force. From the start of 1818, the first year for which there are complete disciplinary returns, down to the end of 1824 the police board decided on the following punishments: three demotions, five suspensions, fifteen cautions or reprimands, nineteen fines and a massive 107 dismissals, the dismissals representing some 71.8% of the punishments.[46] The number of dismissals would probably have been even higher had the board carried out its threat to discharge any man whose lack of vigilance resulted in gas lamps on his beat being broken or damaged.[47]

42. *N.W.*, 18, 25 Nov. 1824.
43. Belfast police committee minutes, 29 Dec. 1826, 9 Jan. 1827; Belfast police commissioners' minutes, 10 Jan. 1827.
44. Belfast police commissioners' minutes, 18 Aug. 1840, 27 Jan. 1841.
45. Ibid, 7, 30 June 1843; Town council committee on police affairs minutes, 5 Oct. 1847; *N.W.*, 2 Nov. 1848; *B.N.L.*, 4 Jan. 1849.
46. Data taken from the Belfast police board minutes, 1818–24.
47. Belfast police commissioners' minutes, 10 Sept. 1823.

After 1824 the amount of dismissals as a proportion of the total punishments inflicted declined considerably. There are a number of possible reasons for this. Firstly, in March 1824 three of the five constables in the force were dismissed, 'Constable McMaster, on account of his age, and Constables McClenaghan and Garson, on account of their drunkenness'. The purge seems to have been the start of a new approach to officer selection by the police board. At the start of 1825 the board advertised for three new night constables at the increased pay of 14*s.* per week: the higher wages were designed to 'induce a better class of persons to offer themselves for the appointment' of constable.[48] The record of the fifteen constables recruited in the seven years from 1825 to 1831 is more impressive than that of the twenty-six employed from 1817 to 1824. Only five were dismissed: two for unknown reasons, one for improper treatment of civilians, one for corruption and one for failing to apprehend a robbery suspect.[49] The use of a more reliable constable seems to have had an improved effect on the discipline of the force. Undoubtedly a second reason for the improvement was the increased use of supernumeraries, although this was not immediately apparent. As late as December 1828 the committee was complaining that the constables were not visiting the supernumeraries and night watchmen enough times during the night.[50] Another important development was the permanent recruitment of a chief night constable, following repeated appeals by the police committee that the commissioners should sanction the appointment of a chief constable of a 'respectable class'. If the salary were high enough, the committee argued, they could obtain 'a man of character, judgment, activity and good temper, whose authority would be respected and obeyed'. The chief night constable's job would be to direct the activities and check on the conduct of the constables and watchmen, as well as take charge of prisoners and deliver them before the magistrates each morning. The first man appointed, in March 1829, was William Maxwell but he resigned in January 1830 because of ill-health. His replacement, Thomas Lindsay, proved ideal for the position. His four years' experience as a 'sergeant' in the Monaghan constabulary[51] proved an invaluable asset in the Belfast police, where he served as chief night and day constable until 1860.

The disciplinary records of the force show that after 1824 it was less necessary for the police board to have recourse to the ultimate

48. Ibid, 12 Jan. 1825.
49. Details from Belfast police board minutes, 1817–31.
50. Belfast police committee minutes, 16 Dec. 1828.
51. *B.N.L.*, 15 Sept. 1857; Gaffikin, *Belfast fifty years ago*, p.30.

sanction of dismissal. Less severe punishments such as fines, suspensions, demotions and reprimands increasingly constituted a larger share of the recorded disciplinary actions. In the next seven years, 1825 to 1831, eighty-two men of all ranks were dismissed: this constituted only 20.3% of the total punishments recorded.[52] In the final years of the police board's operation, 1832 to 1843, the 192 dismissals represented only 22% of the punishments.[53] It is more difficult to calculate what proportion of the force was dismissed annually, because the overall police strength is known for only a small number of years. The records show that 40.5% of the men and officers of the force in October 1817 were dismissed in the next three years, while only 18.8% of the men in the force in October 1825 were dismissed by the end of 1828.[54]

DRUNKENNESS, SLEEPING ON DUTY, ABSENCE WITHOUT LEAVE

The most common offences punished by the police authorities were drunkenness, sleeping on duty, and being absent without leave or being found off the beat. A comparison of the police minutes for the 1820s and 1850s shows very little variation in the types of offences decided upon by the disciplinary boards:

Table 1. Offences committed by Belfast police, 1820s and 1850s

Offences punished	1820–29	%	1850–59	%
Drunkenness	117	34.4	441	38.4
Sleeping on duty	85	25.0	174	15.2
Absent from duty	39	11.5	177	15.4
Total	241	70.9	1,147	69.0[55]

Source: Belfast police board minutes, 1820–29; Town council committee on police affairs minutes, 1850–59.

52. Data from Belfast police board minutes, 1825–31.
53. Data from Belfast police board minutes, 1832–43. No men were disciplined by the police board in January 1844, the final month of the board's existence.
54. Data taken from Belfast police board minutes, 1818–21, 1825–28.
55. I have treated those cases where men were recorded as being drunk and asleep on duty as cases of drunkenness.

Clearly drunkenness on duty was the single most pressing problem. There was nothing unusual in this, as drunkenness was the most common disciplinary problem affecting the Irish Constabulary and D.M.P.,[56] as well as British police forces. The police authorities tried to curb their men's drinking by punishing publicans who served policemen during their hours of duty. The early police acts made publicans who 'harboured' policemen liable to a fine of up to £2, which penalty was increased to £5 by the 1845 Belfast Improvement Act. The police board and the town council often had accounts of such cases published in the Belfast newspapers in the hope of deterring publicans from serving policemen,[57] but the persistent drink problem shows that the fines were not sufficient deterrents. Even on the force's last night on duty, 31 August 1865, Samuel Black, a member of the town council's police committee, addressed the men and told them to 'be particular to avoid intoxicating liquors'.[58] The police authorities' threats that they would dismiss every policeman found guilty of drunkenness[59] were not carried out. In fact, most fines also involved drunkenness cases, which suggests that the disciplinary board decided each case on its merits rather than impose an automatic dismissal for each offence. Some men avoided the ultimate sanction by promising to take the total abstinence pledge.[60] Sometimes the authorities accepted a policeman's excuse that his drunkenness arose from his taking drink for medicinal purposes, such as warding off cholera,[61] but such stories were not always believed. For instance, Night Constable George Singleton failed to convince the disciplinary board in January 1865 that he and Night Constable Thomas Pennington had a legitimate reason for drinking brandy in a Cromac Street public house when they were supposed to be on duty. (Since July 1834 policemen could enter a public house

56. For a discussion of drinking as a disciplinary problem in the R.I.C. and D.M.P. see Griffin, 'Irish police,' pp.517–33, 580–84, 596–602.

57. *B.N.L.*, 22 Oct. 1816, 7 Nov. 1817, 19 July 1825, 4 Aug. 1851, 2 June 1852, 2 June 1857, 6 Nov., 15 Dec. 1862; Belfast police committee minutes, 21 July 1829, 20 Nov. 1832, 13 May 1834; *Northern Herald*, 10 May 1834; Belfast police commissioners' minutes, 7 Mar., 28 Sept., 13 Nov., 26 Dec. 1839; Town council committee on police affairs minutes, 26 Oct. 1847, 5 May, 7 July 1857, 30 Oct. 1862.

58. *B.N.L.*, 1 Sept. 1865.

59. Belfast police commissioners' minutes, 26 Mar. 1823; Belfast police committee minutes, 28 Apr. 1829, 27 Jan. 1835; *1856 police instructions*, p.4.

60. Belfast police commissioners' minutes, 12 Feb. 1840, 10 Feb. 1841; Town council committee on police affairs minutes, 19 Mar. 1863.

61. Town council committee on police affairs minutes, 24 Nov. 1846, 26 Sept. 1854.

only when duty required it, but they were obviously still forbidden to drink on the premises.) Singleton claimed rather lamely that he had 'pains in his inside' and had induced his comrade to join him in a brandy cure. Both constables were dismissed.[62]

The impression one gets from the punishments recorded in the police minutes is that drunkenness was very much an occupational hazard for members of the Belfast force. Apart from the early years of the force, when an unusually severe disciplinary system was enforced, the police authorities seem to have accepted the inevitability of police drunkenness and that it would be impossible to dismiss men for just a single instance of inebriety on duty; to do this would have meant having no experienced policemen in the force. Much the same attitude was evident in the Irish Constabulary and D.M.P.: despite official warnings that drunkenness would be punished with automatic dismissal, more men in these forces were fined or demoted for drunkenness than were dismissed for it.[63] In Belfast the municipal authorities may not have been happy with their force's fondness for drink, and signalled their disapproval by dismissing repeat offenders, but they only fined or punished in other ways for most initial infringements. They suppressed the more overt instances of drink abuse, as for example the tradition of supernumerary constables and watchmen treating their comrades when they were permanently accepted in the force, a practice known as 'paying their footing',[64] but were unable to transform their subordinates into a force of tee-totallers. By the end of the period members of the police committee admitted that it was inevitable that their force, especially the night men, should drink on duty. In March 1862 Councillor Savage accounted for the frequent fines imposed on members of the night police for 'drunkenness and loitering in the shade' by the poor quality of their uniforms; apparently the night men routinely took drink in an effort to warm themselves, and this often led to drunkenness. Councillor Suffern explained that their coats 'would not keep out a shower of rain, and their hats only kept their heads wet'.[65]

As stated earlier, sleeping on duty and being absent from duty were the other main disciplinary problems. Both offences were commonly committed by the night men, who frequently yielded to the temptation to steal away from the rigours of their beat for a few hours' rest. The numerous empty or partly-constructed buildings in the ever-expanding town gave ample opportunities to work-shy

---

62. Belfast police committee minutes, 22 July 1834; *B.N.L.*, 12 Jan. 1865.
63. Griffin, 'Irish police,' pp.524–25, 529–32, 582.
64. Town council committee on police affairs minutes, 21 May 1845.
65. *B.N.L.*, 10 Mar. 1862.

policemen to take their ease. The police authorities gradually increased their sanctions in an effort to stamp out the irregularities. In March 1823 policemen who were absent from duty without leave were warned that they would be fined 1s.3d. for each offence; in July 1828 sleeping watchmen were threatened with demotion to the bottom of the supernumerary list, and finally in September 1832, following the dismissal of Watchmen McKenna and Carlin (Carlin was found asleep in a house, while McKenna acted as a lookout), men found in similar circumstances were threatened with dismissal.[66] As in the case of drunken policemen, however, the police authorities frequently dealt leniently with absent or drowsing men. For instance, when Watchman Dan McCarrol was found asleep on his station in September 1829 he was only fined 2s.6d. as it was his first offence in eleven years. Watchman O'Niele was only reprimanded for the same offence in November 1831 'in consequence of the state of his family's health', while in the following month Watchman James Kelly was merely fined one shilling, 'his family being in distress'. In December 1832 Watchman William Robinson was only suspended from duty rather than being dismissed, 'in consequence of having recently returned from the Cholera Hospital'. Watchman John Harrison who was found asleep on duty in June 1836 was merely fined one shilling on the paradoxical ground of his 'character for activity'![67] In August 1839 Watchman McGuickan was only reprimanded 'in consequence of his not receiving his natural rest from the illness of his child', and a similar punishment was imposed on Watchman Sutton in November 1840, who was obviously suffering under severe mental strain following three deaths and one birth in his family in the previous month.[68]

The next most common offence, at least in the 1820s and 1830s, was neglect of duty. This could in theory mean failure to carry out any part of a policeman's duty, as for example neglecting to watch over sewers, trenches or other excavations at night when ordered to do so by the police board[69] but in practice it usually meant a watchman's negligence making it easier for burglars to commit robberies. In every case of house breaking an investigation was held

---

66. Belfast police commissioners' minutes, 26 Mar. 1823, 23 Jan. 1828; Belfast police committee minutes, 18 Sept. 1832.

67. Belfast police committee minutes, 1 Sept. 1829, 8 Nov. 1831, 4 Dec. 1832, 7 June 1836.

68. Belfast police commissioners' minutes, 14 Aug. 1839, 4 Nov. 1840.

69. *Copy of the contract between the commissioners & committee of police, of the town of Belfast, and John and George Barlow, of the city of London* (Belfast, 1834), p.9; Belfast police committee minutes, 3 Nov. 1835, 7 June 1836.

to see if a watchman's carelessness was a contributing factor. The police board usually dismissed culpable policemen in such cases. An exception to the rule involved Watchman Miller in September 1824— he was only fined 10s. (more than a week's wages) following a robbery on his beat at Ekenhead's stores. The fact that the burglars gained entry by placing two logs against the wall of the premises was deemed a mitigating circumstance.[70] When the police commissioners became solely responsible for discipline in 1838 their decisions in neglect cases were less severe than in earlier years. If burglars entered premises from the rear or through the roof the watchman on the beat was merely cautioned; if they entered from the front, the watch-man was more likely to be dismissed.[71] An unusual decision in a neglect of duty case occurred in July 1841, involving a Constable Doran who neglected to arrest a person who attempted to throw a stone or brick at Superintendent Coulson. Doran was also insolent to his officer. He was ordered to make a 'satisfactory apology' to Coulson at the roll call of the day constables.[72] The fact that the police authorities felt that the prospect of losing the respect of one's peers had a useful disciplinary effect perhaps reflects a growing esprit de corps in the force. It is significant that from July 1847 the chief day and night constables read the sentences passed by the disciplinary board at roll call.[73]

OTHER OFFENCES

Apart from cases involving drunkenness, sleeping on duty, unauthorized absence or neglect of duty there were very few other cases of indiscipline recorded. Incivility to civilians or improper treatment of prisoners were occasionally the subjects of disciplinary hearings. The most serious case of improper behaviour occurred in February 1822, when Watchman James Dennis shot and killed a man[74] when attempting to quell a disturbance in Israel Lee's Quay Lane public house, a premises described as 'an irregular night house, where

---

70. Belfast police committee minutes, 11 Jan. 1821, 18 Sept. 1824, 24 Sept. 1833, 3 Oct. 1837; Belfast police commissioners' minutes, 30 Mar. 1825, 12 Apr., 25 Oct. 1826, 20 Feb. 1828.
71. Based on the cases of eight watchmen in Belfast police commissioners' minutes, 26 July 1838.
72. Ibid, 14 July 1841.
73. Town council committee on police affairs minutes, 7 July 1847.
74. Watchmen were supposed to be armed with pikes rather than firearms. See above, p.19.

spirits are sold without license, and gambling carried on'. Dennis was sentenced to death for murder.[75] This was, of course, an extreme example of improper behaviour by a policeman. Most cases involved using foul language to members of the public or roughly bringing drunks to the police office. To facilitate civilians who wished to make complaints about policemen the police board supplied their force with numbers for easier identification. It is not clear when this was first done. In March 1829 the police committee first instructed the watchmen to give their number when requested by a civilian (the numbers were originally painted on the back of the watchmen's coats, but from February 1838 were painted on their collars). By 1856 constables were warned that refusing to give their name or number or trying to conceal their number when requested were offences punishable by dismissal.[76]

75. *B.N.L.*, 5 Feb., 26 Mar. 1822.
76. Belfast police committee minutes, 10 Mar. 1829, 27 Feb. 1838; *1856 police instructions*, p.12.

CHAPTER FIVE

Crime in Belfast, 1816–1865

INTRODUCTION

IN 1814 WILLIAM DRENNAN wrote that visitors to Belfast were 'prepossessed with the exterior appearance' which it presented, and were unaware that 'there is more tinsel ornament than unalloyed gold in this town, which has been unaptly styled the Athens of Ireland'.[1] There is no doubt that visitors to the northern town generally sang its praises, and presented the picture of a thriving metropolis whose prosperity contrasted starkly with the condition of other Irish towns and cities.[2] Knowledgeable residents were aware that the idealized accounts glossed over or completely ignored the uglier realities of life in Belfast. John Gibson, the assistant barrister to Belfast quarter sessions, lamented to the grand jury in October 1840 'the enormous number of cases that were always found on the Belfast list' despite its reputation as the 'Athens of Ireland', and that 'though the calendar is always to such an amount, it attracts no attention— no observations are made about it—the public prints are silent on the subject'. Drawing attention to the unacceptable level of crime in Belfast was an unpopular activity. Some months later Gibson complained that the person who pointed to the reality behind the town's ornate facade 'calls down the condemnation and censure of certain sensitive individuals, who may conceive that any allusion to the state of crime in their town is a direct personal insult to themselves'.[3] Few people dared run the risk of being considered 'unpatriotic' for describing the actual state of Belfast society. One who did was an anonymous writer to the *Belfast Newsletter* at the end of the period:

1. Quoted in C.E.B. Brett, 'The Georgian town: Belfast about 1800' in J.C. Beckett and R.E. Glasscock (ed.), *Belfast: origin and growth of an industrial city* (London, 1967), p.76.
2. See for example S.C. Hall and A.M. Hall, *Ireland: its scenery, character &c* (3 vols., London, 1841–43), iii, 52–53; J.H. Smith, *Belfast and its environs, with a tour to the Giant's Causeway* (Dublin, 1853), p.17; J.B. Doyle, *Tours in Ulster: a hand-book to the antiquities and scenery of the north of Ireland* (Dublin, 1854), pp.2–3.
3. *N.W.*, 29 Oct. 1840; *B.N.L.*, 15 Jan. 1841.

Unless to a few clergymen, doctors, police, and occasionally, a heroic philanthropist, the district of the town lying between Hercules Street and Smithfield is absolutely unknown. The centre of its abominations is not more than two minutes' walk from the Ulster Club and the fashionable promenades of Donegall and Castle Place; yet our wealthy and comfortable classes that so frequently coast it never penetrate—never know anything about it. The stranger who visits Belfast passes down Donegall Place, enters Castle Place, with their gratifying evidences of industry and taste, and is all admiration at the aspect and progress of our town. He leaves us to commend in other circles what he has witnessed in Belfast. But the simple soul has but the outside and best side of the matter. He little imagines that while he was all aglow with admiration at the architecture of our leading streets that the great warehouses which stud them cast their shadows on scenes of filth, and squalor, and poverty, and vice, and crime—an eternal disgrace to the community in which they are allowed to exist.[4]

This chapter offers an alternative view of life in the town to that offered by most of the writers of travellers' guides, and discusses the problem of crime in Belfast down to 1865, the final year of the municipal force's existence.

VAGRANTS

One of the groups who were routinely arrested by Belfast policemen and who were popularly believed to be behind much of the town's crime was the population of vagrants and beggars.[5] Since 1809 a House of Industry had been in existence, with the aim of suppressing begging in Belfast's streets. It employed two constables dressed in blue coats and red capes and carrying long pointed staffs to arrest 'strollers and mendicants' found at large.[6] In March 1817, only a few months after the start of the municipal police force, the House of Industry in Smithfield requested the police committee to assist in arresting vagrants and conveying them to the workhouse.[7] The police board were amenable to the request, not only because of their desire to suppress vagrancy but because it considered that there was a direct link between vagrancy and criminal activity. In April 1820 the police commissioners blamed the 'alarming' increase in robberies and thefts in Belfast and its vicinity in the previous two to three

4. Letter from 'H' in *B.N.L.*, 22 Apr. 1865.
5. For claims that vagrants were criminals see *N.W.*, 25 Feb. 1833, 27 Sept. 1838; *B.N.L.*, 25 Apr. 1834, 1 Mar. 1850.
6. *Irishman*, 13 June 1823.
7. Belfast police committee minutes, 26 Mar. 1817.

years on the vagrant population.[8] The force was frequently reminded either to arrest beggars, especially children, or to protect the House of Industry constables in bringing vagrants to the workhouse.[9] While arresting beggars remained a routine part of the Belfast policeman's duty, there is no evidence to substantiate the claims that vagrants were involved in anything more illegal than begging.

PROSTITUTION AND ASSOCIATED CRIME

Some of the permanent residents of Belfast proved far more trouble-some to the police than the supposedly criminal vagrants. Certain areas of the town had unenviable reputations as centres of criminal activity throughout the period covered by this study. One of the most notorious of these areas was Caddell's Entry, between High Street and Rosemary Street. One gets an indication of its unsavoury reputation from the fact that when a man died of a fit in the entry in February 1819 it was generally believed that he had been murdered there.[10] It was no coincidence that two Edinburgh bodysnatchers named Feeny and Stewart used the disreputable street as their base of operations in 1823 when engaged in robbing bodies from Belfast graveyards and shipping them to Scotland. Only the accidental circumstance of an offensive smell from a barrel on a ship leaving Belfast led to the 'resurrectionists'' downfall.[11] Caddell's Entry's reputation had not changed much by the end of the period, when its shebeen houses and brothels regularly led to disorderly scenes and larcenies upon unwary customers.[12] The town council took no action against the brothels until pressured into doing so by public opinion in 1862. In May of that year at least nine brothel-keepers were cleared out on the charges of keeping lodging houses which were not properly licensed, and the street's name was subsequently changed to High Street Place, as if to erase from public memory

8. Belfast police commissioners' minutes, 12 Apr. 1820.

9. Ibid, 8 Feb. 1826, 11 Mar. 1835; Belfast police committee minutes, 28 July 1835; Town council committee on police affairs minutes, 2 Nov., 21 Dec. 1847; *B.N.L.*, 4 Jan. 1848; *1856 police instructions*, p.24.

10. *B.N.L.*, 12 Feb. 1819.

11. *Irishman*, 18 July 1823. Scottish bodysnatchers continued to visit Belfast graveyards until the late 1830s. See *B.N.L.*, 4, 8, Jan. 1828, 7 Feb. 1832; *N.W.*, 24 Sept., 1 Oct. 1829, 14 Sept. 1837.

12. *B.N.L.*, 25 Apr. 1853, 17, 19 Apr. 1854, 25 May 1855, 27, 31 Oct. 1856, 28 June 1858, 14 May, 17, 22 Sept., 19 Oct., 12 Dec. 1860, 10 June, 16 July, 6 Sept. 1861, 2 May 1862.

the scenes which had persisted in the area for decades.[13] The belated move against Caddell's Entry might have been a response to the establishment in May 1862 of a 'Midnight Meeting Movement' which stated its aim to be 'endeavouring to rescue fallen females'.[14]

Other streets which were mentioned as early centres of prostitution were Gordon Street, Mitchell's Entry, Millfield, Francis Street, Bluebell Entry, Miller's Lane off Berry Street, and Little Edward Street.[15] There were undoubtedly other early red-light districts, although contemporary newspapers are noticeably reticent about naming them. Other areas where passers-by had to be on their guard were Smithfield, where cudgel-wielding men were ready at 'the least alarm' to 'brain a Peeler, and to screech their joys'; and the Long Bridge, the 'haunt of beggars, thieves, and thieves' compeers'.[16] The latter locality was a favourite scene for a confidence trick known as 'ring-dropping', which was played on gullible countrymen visiting Belfast. It involved 'finding' a ring or other supposedly valuable object in the countryman's presence. Once the visitor was convinced that the worthless ring was valuable he was persuaded to buy it from the confidence tricksters at a bargain price. By the time he discovered that the item was either worthless or worth a mere fraction of what he had paid for it the culprits were far from the scene. The trick was played at the Long Bridge and other localities in the 1820s and early 1830s.[17] Another area with an unsavoury reputation, at least in the early 1830s, was High Street: young ladies who proceeded through the disorderly street in the evenings went

13. Town council committee on police affairs minutes, 22 May, 26 June 1862; *B.N.L.*, 2 June 1862. The device of changing the names of red-light districts and streets whose names had unsavoury connotations was also later adopted in Dublin. See J.V. O'Brien, *'Dear, dirty Dublin': a city in distress, 1899–1916* (Berkeley, 1982), pp.193–94 and W.N. Osborough, *Law and the emergence of modern Dublin: a litigation topography for a capital city* (Dublin, 1996), pp.46–55, 181–84.

14. *B.N.L.*, 16 May 1862.

15. Ibid, 20 Mar. 1818, 6 Apr. 1821, 21 May, 9 July, 1, 8 Oct., 19 Nov., 24 Dec. 1822. Mitchell's Entry and Bluebell Entry were two small streets between High Street and Waring Street.

16. 'Northern Athens', pp.18, 26.

17. *B.N.L.*, 19 Mar. 1823, 21, 28 Jan., 4 Feb., 18 Mar., 22 Apr. 1834; *N.W.*, 24 Mar. 1824, 12 Feb. 1829; *Northern Herald*, 18 Jan., 15, 22 Feb. 1834. The Long Bridge was demolished in 1841 and replaced with a larger structure: *Belfast and its environs, with a tour to the Giant's Causeway* (Dublin, 1842), pp.60–61; Peter O'Keeffe and Tom Simington, *Irish stone bridges: history and heritage* (Blackrock, Co. Dublin, 1991), pp.221–23.

in company 'for mutual protection', and watchmen were specially detailed to preserve order there at nights.[18]

As stated earlier, contemporary printed sources have little to say about disreputable areas of Belfast until the middle of the century. One of the first sources to break the veil of silence was Reverend William Murphy O'Hanlon's *Walks among the poor of Belfast* in 1853, which startled Belfast public opinion with its graphic descriptions of misery in the lower-class areas of the city. O'Hanlon's work was indicative of a changing trend in Belfast's publications in the 1850s and 1860s. The reading public were no longer treated to the myth of unblemished material and social progress; Belfast's portrait was given a few well deserved warts. The paucity of similar frank references in the earlier decades makes it difficult to compare social conditions in the 1820s with those of the 1850s, but it seems fair to assume that the distressed areas described by Reverend O'Hanlon had similar problems at the start of the period under examination.

For example Millfield, described as an area of prostitution in the 1820s, had changed little by 1853. Nearby Round Entry is described by O'Hanlon as

a place celebrated for its iniquity ... This entry harbours the most loath-some corruptions; and in these bawdy houses, under the cover of darkness, deeds of villainy are perpetrated which never come to light in our police court. Unwary youth are entrapped and drawn into these places as flies into a spider's web—inebriated, robbed, and then turned out guilty, ruined, stricken, with a sting in the conscience and a stain upon their character, which is seldom, if ever, removed .... [19]

The entry, which consisted of twenty-five houses off North Street, was a 'miserable alley of vice and crime'. A clergyman who visited the street in September 1853 considered it unsafe for a person to enter it alone.[20] Other unsavoury localities described by Reverend O'Hanlon included Plunket's Court, off Carrick Hill, 'the resort of miserable women and pickpockets, who find a fit asylum in its dark and filthy receptacles',[21] and Barrack Lane:

18. Belfast police committee minutes, 11 Sept. 1832; Revd N.G. Batt, 'Belfast sixty years ago: recollections of a septuagenarian' in *Ulster Journal of Archaeology*, ii (1896), 95.

19. Revd W.M. O'Hanlon, *Walks among the poor of Belfast* (Memston, 1971 reprint of the 1853 original), pp.21–22. Round Entry was a small street between Hercules Street and North Street.

20. *B.N.L.*, 24 Nov. 1852, 17 Jan., 23 Mar. 1853, 15 Jan., 13 Nov. 1855, 8 May 1860, 15 Oct. 1861; Revd A. McIntyre's diary of visits to the poor of Belfast, Aug. 1853-Aug. 1856: entry for 19 Sept. 1853 (PRONI, D.1558/2/3).

21. O'Hanlon, *Walks*, p.17.

here every kind of profligacy and crime is carried on, despite the police, who seem to be little terror to evil-doers in this quarter. Passers of base coin, thieves, and prostitutes, all herd here together in this place as in a common hell, and sounds of blasphemy, shouts of mad debauch, and cries of quarrel and blood, are frequently heard here through the livelong night, to the annoyance and terror of the neighbourhood ... It is the practice, as we were informed, of these miscreants to frequent the docks, and, having caught sailors, like unwary birds, in their toils [sic], to allure them to these pitfalls, where they are soon peeled and plundered.[22]

Had Reverend O'Hanlon visited Caxton Street, which ran from Robert Street to Little Edward Street, he would have been struck by its brothels and drunk and disorderly women brawling in the streets.[23] Other streets which were notorious both for their brothels and the larcenies practised within them included Long Lane with its 'schools of vice' off North Street,[24] Pottinger's Entry between High Street and Ann Street,[25] Green Street,[26] Dock Street[27] and Brown Street.[28]

The 'miserable region of Gregg's Row' was another area where unwary strangers were fleeced by brothel inmates. According to the *Belfast Newsletter* in 1853, the street was known 'not only over Belfast, but over the greater portion of Ulster ... as being a kennel for all sorts of impurity'.[29] Lodging-house keepers in Ritchie's Place harboured 'notoriously bad characters'; one house in particular, a 'den of infamy', was a place where stolen goods were purchased.[30] Walker's Lane, off Queen Street, was an especially noted red light district which became particularly unruly on Saturday nights,[31] while nearby Gibb's Entry was known as a resort of thieves.[32]

22. Ibid, p.16.
23. Revd McIntyre's diary, 21 Oct. 1853; see also *B.N.L.*, 28 Jan., 28 Mar., 16 Nov. 1858, 24 Jan. 1860, 15 Jan. 1861, 11 Nov. 1862, 8 Jan. 1863.
24. *B.N.L.*, 28 Mar. 1853, 25 June 1858, 1 Dec. 1860.
25. Ibid, 8 Jan. 1857.
26. *Ulsterman*, 26 Oct. 1857; *B.N.L.*, 4 Dec. 1862. Green Street ran between James Street (now southern part of Corporation Street) and Edward Street.
27. *B.N.L.*, 8 Oct. 1855.
28. Ibid, 13 June 1855.
29. Ibid, 31 Jan., 1 June 1853. Gregg's Row was between West Street and Samuel Street, off Millfield.
30. *B.D.M.*, 9 Feb. 1859; *B.N.L.*, 18 Feb. 1860. Ritchie's Place was off North Street.
31. *B.N.L.*, 16, 23 June, 25 Oct. 1852, 21 Mar. 1853, 8 Sept. 1854, 8 June, 17 Oct. 1855, 15 Oct. 1858, 17 Dec. 1860, 8 Oct. 1861, 17 June, 20, 28 Aug. 1862, 20 Jan., 2, 3 Feb. 1863; *B.D.M.*, 1 Dec. 1854.
32. *B.N.L.*, 10 Jan. 1853.

North Queen Street and its purlieus had numerous brothels and public houses which catered for the troops stationed in the infantry barracks.[33] Robert Street, between Hill Street and Academy Street, swarmed with prostitutes: landlords in the area preferred to rent their houses to prostitutes than to 'decent people', as they could afford to pay double the usual rent.[34] There were also unruly brothels in Meeting House Lane and Suffern's Entry,[35] May's Lane, a street described in 1851 as 'a wretched place',[36] Church Street,[37] Talbot Street,[38] Morrison's Court off Carrick Hill, described as 'the abode of wretched and abandoned women',[39] Thomas Street,[40] Allen's Court,[41] Grattan Street,[42] Hill Street,[43] Constabulary Lane[44] and Cotton Court.[45]

The two most notorious areas for prostitution and associated larcenies were Hudson's Entry, a small street of forty houses between North Street and Smithfield, and Anderson's Row, off Millfield. Of the two streets Hudson's Entry was probably the least desirable place in which to live. Its conditions shocked even Reverend A. McIntyre, who was used to the squalor of Belfast's back streets. He considered it a 'filthy place in every sense', and counted from sixteen to twenty brothels there with from four to seven prostitutes in each house in October 1853.[46] Reverend O'Hanlon described the street as 'a complete den of vice and uncleanness, probably unsurpassed in what is called the civilized world'.[47] Unwary passers-by were often lured into the 'nest of crime' by women who snatched their hats; once in the street they were robbed by waiting associates.

33. Ibid, 14 Feb. 1853; O'Hanlon, *Walks*, p.13.
34. *B.N.L.*, 20 July 1855, 2 Aug. 1858, 14 July 1860, 28 Feb., 4 Mar. 1862; *B.D.M.*, 11 Oct. 1859.
35. Revd McIntyre's diary, 23 Sept., 25 Oct. 1853. Suffern's Entry was a small street off North Street. Meeting House Lane was off William Street.
36. *B.N.L.*, 8 Oct. 1851, 28 Jan. 1857. May's Lane was off North Queen Street.
37. *B.N.L.*, 8 Oct. 1851, 10 May 1861.
38. Ibid, 4 July, 30 Sept. 1861.
39. O'Hanlon, *Walks*, p.18.
40. *B.N.L.*, 28 Aug. 1857.
41. Ibid, 29 Sept. 1858. Allen's Court was off Peter's Hill.
42. Ibid, 2 Sept. 1859. Grattan Street ran from Gordon Street to Talbot Street.
43. *B.N.L.*, 3 Jan. 1860.
44. Ibid, 6 Aug. 1861.
45. Ibid, 3 May 1862. Cotton Court was off Waring Street.
46. Revd McIntyre's diary, 21 Oct. 1853.
47. O'Hanlon, *Walks*, p.44.

Others were simply dragged in and robbed of their clothing and other possessions.[48] One gets an indication of the type of people that resided in the street from an incident which occurred there in January 1852, in which a customer in a public house was robbed of his watch: the victim was first rendered insensible with whiskey doctored with snuff.[49] Hudson's Entry was also the residence of professional thieves and pickpockets, some of them from as far away as Omagh and Dublin.[50] It is not surprising that in December 1863 the *Belfast Newsletter* described the street as 'the most horrible den of iniquity in the town', after four constables were assaulted there by drunks armed with knives and a poker.[51] Hudson's Entry also posed a formidable problem to the Irish Constabulary after they took over the policing of the town in September 1865. In 1867 the chairman of Antrim quarter sessions referred to 'an abominable locality known as Hudson's Entry in this town, and it has no parallel in the kingdom. Person or property has no protection in it. The owner of this locality should for the sake of public morality and justice take one stone from the top of the other and hurl it to the ground'.[52] Anderson's Row was Hudson's Entry's closest rival in notoriety. Consisting of just over a dozen houses, it was severely over-crowded. It was reported in 1853 that one of the houses had ten families residing in it, while its so-called 'lodging houses' were 'unfit, badly ventilated, and crowded'.[53] Julius Rodenberg, a German visitor to the street in the late 1850s, wrote that it was

a narrow, short cul-de-sac, which sends to meet the intruder the miasma of rotting straw, filthy rags, and rubbish of every description, with which the ground is covered instead of pavement. There are some twelve or fourteen houses—if these dens can be so called—in Anderson['s] Row, and in them dwell about two hundred beggars, thieves, and prostitutes. Often these dens are chokingly full of denizens—often some are empty, because their former inhabitants have migrated to prison.[54]

48. *B.N.L.*, 11 June 1850, 16 Jan., 22 Nov. 1852, 29 Sept. 1855, 17 May, 12 Dec. 1856, 15 Apr., 25 May 1857.

49. *N.W.*, 17 Jan. 1852.

50. *B.N.L.*, 2 Aug., 3 Dec. 1852, 9 Oct. 1855, 26 July 1856, 15 Jan., 25 May, 14 Oct. 1857, 24 Oct. 1861.

51. Ibid, 29 Dec. 1863.

52. Ibid, 14 Jan. 1867.

53. Ibid, 4 May 1853.

54. Julius Rodenberg, *A pilgrimage through Ireland, or the island of the saints* (London, 1860), p.313.

One of the houses, known as the Menagerie, held about 100 'wretches' when its usual inhabitants were not serving prison sentences. It had twenty-seven rooms filled with 'improper characters'. The street's motley inhabitants of child pickpockets, burglars and prostitutes paid rent three times weekly.[55]

The attitude of the Belfast police authorities towards the numerous prostitutes in the town was that they should be allowed to ply their trade in brothels so long as they conducted themselves peacefully. Those prostitutes who were arrested were invariably guilty of theft, 'rioting', drunkenness or importunately soliciting passers-by.[56] This was similar to the approach taken by police forces in nineteenth-century England.[57] Brothels were suppressed only following requests from nearby residents, and these were surprisingly few. The first recorded orders to the police to suppress a 'house of ill fame', concerning a premises in Queen Street, occurred as late as August 1850.[58] Private individuals occasionally showed their exasperation at police inaction against brothels. In August 1851 a mob attacked Susan Lee's brothel in Talbot Street in an effort to rid themselves of their unruly neighbours. The police intervened to prevent the mob from wrecking the house. An eye-witness recorded that 'When the outrage was at its height, some of the casual visitors of the place were seen scrambling like cats over the adjacent walls and roofs'.[59] In the same month a wealthy gentleman who had had £50 stolen from him in a Queen Street brothel, but had failed to substantiate the charge in court, prosecuted the proprietor, Elizabeth Smith of Ballinahinch, for keeping a brothel. According to the *Belfast Newsletter* the court house was 'more densely crowded than we ever remember to have seen it, unless upon the occasion of a contested election'. The prosecuting solicitor detailed some of the difficulties in bringing home a charge against a brothel-keeper:

He was at first disposed to summon a great number of persons who were known to be in the habit of visiting the house in question; but he had subsequently abandoned that intention, by the advice of gentlemen who

55. Ibid, p.315; *B.N.L.*, 18, 19, 24, 25 Jan. 1860. The name Anderson's Row was changed to Millfield Place in December 1860: *B.N.L.*, 3 Dec. 1860.

56. Belfast police commissioners' minutes, 23 Mar. 1825; Belfast police committee minutes, 18 July 1826; *1856 police instructions*, p.19.

57. Michael Pearson, *The age of consent: Victorian prostitution and its enemies* (Newton Abbot, 1972), p.25; R.D. Storch, 'Police control of street prostitution in Victorian London: a study in the contexts of police action' in D.H. Bayley (ed.), *Police and society* (London, 1977), pp.50–52.

58. Town council committee on police affairs minutes, 27 Aug. 1850.

59. *B.N.L.*, 27 Aug. 1851.

suggested to him that, as many of those parties moved in a highly-respectable sphere, the course would give rise to much unpleasantness and disgrace in families.[60]

Belfast's wealthier citizens were prepared to condone the existence of brothels (and occasionally to visit them) so long as they were not too near their own homes. People whose property values were lowered by the proximity of brothels brought prosecutions against their unwanted neighbours. August 1851 saw a number of prosecutions for this reason against premises in North Street, Long Lane and Back Lane. The excise authorities also wanted to shut down brothels as it was known that their owners sold expensive wines and spirits without licences.[61] A short-lived association for 'discountenancing vice' in the Robert Street and Talbot Street district was formed in August 1856. Its main (and unsuccessful) aim was to suppress the brothels there.[62] The police occasionally brought charges against brothel keepers if neighbours complained that their premises were unruly; sometimes they merely tried to dissuade clients from entering by posting a constable outside who either noted the names of the customers or shone a light into their faces as they went in.[63] However, police harassment of brothels was desultory and mainly a response to a temporary public outcry. Most brothels continued in business behind their 'lodging house' facades.[64]

JUVENILE CRIME

Prostitutes who stole from clients were only one of the groups who featured regularly in the criminal calendar. Juvenile delinquents were also responsible for a large share of Belfast's crime. They may have had their own special slang as early as 1816. In March of that year a Mr Cleland caught Bernard Woods, 'a young boy', stealing a basket of glassware from his shop. Cleland explained that when he was bringing the boy to the 'black hole' a crowd gathered around them, 'and from some cant words which the boy uttered he suspected he gave notice to some associates, for immediately he received

60. Ibid, 6 Aug. 1851.
61. Ibid, 8 Aug. 1851. Long Lane was between North Street and Church Street; Back Lane was off Peter's Hill.
62. *B.N.L.*, 25 Aug., 2 Sept. 1856.
63. Ibid, 22 Sept. 1856, 6, 7 Dec. 1860; *Ulsterman*, 16 Jan. 1857; *B.D.M.*, 17 Feb. 1859.
64. The censuses grossly underestimate the number of prostitutes in Belfast. The 1851 census records only 38 brothel keepers and prostitutes; that of 1861 records only twelve prostitutes.

a blow, and the boy was rescued'.[65] The *Belfast Newsletter* claimed in September 1816 that 'idle vagabonds' who regularly gathered at the markets and whiled away their time in gambling formed a 'nursery of crime, where young boys are initiated, and become completely depraved'.[66] Contemporaries regarded petty pilfering by children, such as stealing hay from carts in the pig market, with alarm as it 'habituates them to dishonest practices, vitiates their principles, and paves the way for more enormous crimes'. The quays, especially when sugar, rum or coal were being unloaded, and the pork market were particularly favourite targets for juvenile thieves.[67] The important role of youngsters in Belfast crime was commented upon in 1820:

The numerous depredations that are committed in this town, call loudly for some means of prevention more effectual than any which now exist. The cunning and dexterity which are evinced by the depredators prove them to be adepts in their line; but all these would cease to operate were it not for the encouragement they meet with from persons who are known to be receivers of stolen goods. Their system of concealment is so complete and so intricate, as in most cases to elude all detection. Little boys and girls are trained up in the mode of pilfering; they hand over the property to older associates, and it passes through a variety of hands until it reaches the depot of those persons who form the last link in the chain. They well know the mazes and windings which are calculated to shield them from responsibility, and thus the public are defrauded and property rendered insecure, while the first aggressors are mere children.[68]

Not all of these juveniles came from impoverished families. In May 1820 a watchman arrested fifteen-year old James McCartney, the son of a Berry Street shopkeeper. McCartney was a member of a gang 'who skulk about the hall doors and under the lamp posts, watching their opportunity, should a door be accidentally left open, or by means of skeleton latch keys, to enter and rob the houses'.[69] Some of the child criminals in the early period were of an astonishingly young age: in June 1826 John Cullen was sentenced to one year in prison with hard labour for stealing six silk shawls from a

65. *B.N.L.*, 22 Mar. 1816. The shopkeeper spotted Woods the next day and he was re-captured. He received seven years' transportation for the attempted theft.

66. *B.N.L.*, 3 Sept. 1816.

67. Ibid, 10 Apr. 1821; Belfast police committee minutes, 10 Jan. 1824; Belfast police commissioners' minutes, 22 Nov. 1826.

68. *B.N.L.*, 19 May 1820.

69. Ibid, 30 May 1820.

Bridge Street shop. He was only six years old, and was so small that he could not be seen in the dock during his trial.[70]

The problem of juvenile delinquency persisted into the 1830s. Philip Fogarty, the assistant barrister at Belfast quarter sessions, stated in April 1837 that 'there was a great state of demoralization among the youth of the town', and that 'much of this evil was to be attributed to the number of pawnbrokers in Belfast, who offered a ready receptacle for any goods that might be improperly come by'.[71] In November 1837 the *Northern Whig* advocated the provision of a special reformatory for young offenders similar to that established in Glasgow or run by a Captain Brenton of the Children's Friend Society in London. The newspaper claimed that 'it is a notorious, though melancholy fact, that youthful offenders of five, six, or seven years old, are so well drilled in the art of evasion, that it is almost impossible to ascertain their names, or the places where their parents, or those who receive and dispose of their plunder, are to be found'.[72] Some of the numerous young criminals in Belfast— one observer commented in January 1843 on the 'horde of juvenile thieves with which our town is infested'—were inducted into a life of crime by unscrupulous adults. One of these was Mary Quin, an itinerant beggarwoman who was prosecuted in September 1840 for kidnapping four Belfast children; three were from Forest Lane while the fourth was from McTier's Court, off North Lane. Quin travelled through Antrim pretending to be the widowed mother of the kidnapped children, who were forced to beg for her. She had on several occasions 'induced girls of very tender years to leave their homes, and, by introducing them to houses of ill-fame, brought them to a course of prostitution'. It is unlikely that the child who was taken from McTier's Court felt it an unusual hardship to beg for a living. Reverend O'Hanlon described in 1853 how the young subsisted there by breaking freestone for a pittance. He remarked, 'Of such stuff ... are our jailbirds made. Hulks, penal colonies, and the gallows will never ask in vain for prey so long as society nurtures such cockatrices' dens as these'.[73]

70. Ibid, 20 Jan. 1826. Belfast was not the only Irish city where crimes were committed by very young children. For references to extremely youthful accused in Cork and Dublin respectively, see R.B. McDowell, *The Irish administration, 1801–1914* (London and Toronto, 1964), p.162 and Griffin, 'The Irish police', pp.436–37.

71. *N.W.*, 11 Apr. 1837.

72. Ibid, 2 Nov. 1837. It was not until 1858 that legislation was passed to establish reformatory schools in Ireland. A reformatory for Protestant youths was established on the Malone Road. See below, p.78.

73. Ibid, 8 Sept. 1840, 7 Jan. 1843; O'Hanlon, *Walks*, p.21. Forest Lane ran between Ann Street and High Street. McTier's Court was off North Street.

More is known about the problem of child crime during the 1850s and 1860s, for the same reason that more is known about prostitution and the generally unsavoury areas of the town in the same period: contemporary sources, especially newspapers, became more forthright in providing such details to their readers. That there was a significant level of juvenile delinquency there can be no doubt. The *Belfast Newsletter* stated in March 1853 that 'small thieves and small thefts' occupied most of the criminal proceedings in Belfast's courts.[74] Many children of tender years had considerable criminal experience. A reporter at Belfast Police Office in January 1848 wrote that

Some of the lads who appeared at the bar were, even in their youthfulness, the most perfect specimens of depraved humanity that any locality could exhibit. The sinister eye, and repulsive features—the brutal head, and stubborn demeanour—were evidence sufficient to condemn them, of any offence against society, in any court in Britain.[75]

Some of the more experienced child criminals included John McLoughlin, 'a highly-distinguished member of the Lilliputian corps of thieves' who already had eleven previous convictions before being found guilty in April 1853 of stealing a coat; Patrick Corrigan, aged ten or eleven in June 1853, who had been to jail for sixteen months and twice whipped for picking pockets; John McClure, aged fourteen in August 1853, who had sixteen convictions for theft, served ten prison terms and was whipped six times; James Kennedy, a 'young scoundrel' with nine convictions for theft before 1854, who was so well-known to the police that he 'could not safely pursue his profession any longer in his customary garb, and had, therefore, donned the attire of a seaman'; twelve-year-old Robert Wilson, who by February 1856 had served twenty-two months in prison for theft and other offences; fifteen-year-old Robert Campbell of Carrick Hill, described in July 1856 as 'the leader of a gang of pickpockets and thieves'; fifteen-year-old Hugh Tierney, a 'professional thief' with seventeen convictions, forty months in jail and five whippings on his record by July 1856, and Bernard McLoughlin, fourteen years old in December 1856, who had twenty-three convictions for theft, suffered five whippings and spent over three years in prison.[76]

74. *B.N.L.*, 25 Mar. 1853.

75. Ibid, 21 Jan. 1848.

76. Ibid, 4 Apr., 20 June, 24 Aug. 1853, 11 Oct. 1854, 9 Feb., 30 June, 1, 9 July, 13 Dec. 1856.

Other veteran juvenile criminals included fourteen-year-old Arthur Murphy, who had fifteen previous convictions for theft and spent three years in jail before his October 1855 appearance in court, charged with stealing a bottle of spirits from a High Street shop. He was sentenced to three months' imprisonment and a whipping for the latter offence.[77] Other frequent appearers in the dock were Catherine Brown, aged thirteen or fourteen in January 1857, 'whose countenance bore the expression of hardened guilt'. She had eleven convictions and had served fifteen months before being charged with a burglary in that month. The young offenders also included 'a very small girl' named Ellen Brown, with six jail terms served before her May 1858 conviction for stealing a piece of printed calico from a shop; John Morrison, 'a young lad of fourteen years, but an old thief' who was sentenced to three months for stealing a loaf of bread from a Massereene Street shop in August 1858; Henry Chapman, aged eleven or twelve, who already had seventeen convictions for stealing by the same month; and Letitia Loughran, 'a very little girl' with thirteen prison sentences for theft and other offences by November 1858.[78]

Juveniles drifted into crime for a variety of reasons, but it is fair to say that the grinding poverty of many lower class districts was a principal factor. The death of a parent often meant that the only alternatives facing youngsters were crime or the workhouse. For example, two 'little boys' named Corrigan and Johnston respectively were caught stealing a waistcoat in a High Street shop in January 1853. Corrigan's father was dead, and his mother tried to make a living by occasionally selling fish; Johnston's mother was dead, and his father had re-married and refused to support him.[79] Daniel Montgomery, another 'little boy' who was caught stealing delph in February 1855, avoided a prison sentence when he explained that his mother was dead and his father was 'away at the wars', leaving him without any means of support.[80] Twelve-year-old John McManus of West Street, who had already spent four months in prison before his court appearance in October 1859 on a charge of stealing a pair of socks and assaulting Constable McKnight in the police office, explained that his father was dead and that he was the sole support

---

77. Ibid, 22 Oct. 1855. He clocked up nineteen jail terms totalling forty-nine months altogether and five whippings by December 1857, in which month he was charged with stealing clothes from a house: *B.N.L.*, 9 Dec. 1857.

78. Ibid, 23 Jan. 1857, 26 May, 10, 17 Aug., 16 Nov. 1858.

79. Ibid, 14 Jan. 1853.

80. Ibid, 9 Feb. 1855.

of his sick mother and his little brother.[81] It is reasonable to assume that these youngsters and many others like them would not have got into trouble with the authorities had their families' economic circumstances been more favourable. This was recognized by the *Belfast Newsletter* in May 1858:

There is no class more sinned against by the community than the class of juvenile criminals; and they repay the community with fearful interest ... The Arabs of the city, like the Arabs of the wilderness, have their hands against every man ... Many a young family, left by the death or desertion of parents, homeless and friendless, drift into offences against the law, hardly in their cases crimes, and once stepped into the polluting stream, find it impossible to return, doubly impossible to cleanse themselves from the dark stains that cover them.[82]

Other youngsters were unfortunate enough to be born into families with criminal tendencies.[83] For example, Daniel Gribben, 'a hard-faced young rogue' of fourteen years in June 1851 with fifteen convictions, thirty-five months in prison and eight whippings behind him, was actually born in jail, where his mother was serving a sentence for larceny: 'Nursed in crime, his apprenticeship to pilfering commenced almost as soon as he was able to walk; and he is now accounted one of the most expert of his profession'.[84] A mother and child pickpocket team was arrested in High Street in December 1853.[85] Anne McConaghy, aged about nine years old in November 1859, was 'addicted to theft'; she had been corrupted into a life of crime by some members of her own family.[86]

Sometimes neglect rather than bad example was sufficient to force children into criminal activity. The Society for the Reformation of Juvenile Offenders pointed out in February 1857 that many of Belfast's delinquents were orphans, but 'many more [were] the children of depraved and profligate parents, who, unwilling to bear the burden of their support, send them from their homes, to gain a subsistence as best they may'.[87] Some children were forced by their parents to beg, and then often drifted into a life of crime.[88]

81. *B.D.M.*, 27, 29 Oct. 1859.
82. *B.N.L.*, 1 May 1858.
83. Ibid, 29 Oct. 1852.
84. Ibid, 6 June, 1 Sept. 1851.
85. Ibid, 12 Dec. 1853.
86. *B.D.M.*, 8 Nov. 1859.
87. *B.N.L.*, 3 Feb. 1857. For more on the Society for the Reformation of Juvenile Offenders, see below, p.78.
88. *N.W.*, 13 Feb. 1838; *B.N.L.*, 25 Mar. 1853, 3 Dec. 1860; *B.D.M.*, 8 Nov. 1859.

But frequently neither adverse economic circumstances nor parental neglect accounted for juvenile criminal activity. Simple rebellion against parental authority was also a factor. The *Belfast Daily Mercury* in September 1857 blamed not poverty but prosperity:

of late years a great labouring population has centred in Belfast, composed, for the most part, of people foreign to the town, who have been attracted by various inducements, and have brought with them half-civilized habits. These persons, receiving high wages and constant work, have become inflated with a bastard independence. They are ignorant and turbulent to such a degree that no town in the empire could equal them as being more brutal in passion, more savage in their party animosities, or more thoroughly demoralised as regards all that constitutes a civilization based on moral and religious culture.

The very manufacturing and commercial enterprise that has made our town the industrial capital of Ireland, has also accumulated this vicious population to an extent that is really fearful to contemplate. It is not that the heads of families are ignorant and brutal—the evil pervades all the social relations of the masses. There is scarcely any opportunity afforded for the cultivation of the domestic feelings—household ties are scarcely formed ere they are broken asunder. Children at an early age become independent of their parents—work is so plenty, and wages are so tempting, that the great mass of children become perfectly independent of parental control by their twelfth year. They do not remain at school. They crowd into our mills and factories, and, in a short time, any good that they received at school is obliterated. They are emancipated from all control just at the time when control, if wisely exercised, would be most valuable to them, and the result of all this is to be observed in the class of crimes which, for the most part, occupy our police court. Fathers beating children, children rebelling against their parents, husbands assaulting wives, and sons beating mothers—prosecutions for drunkenness, common assaults and petty thefts, and the use of obscene and profane language—such are the crimes with which the police sheet is daily crowded.[89]

While the newspaper might have exaggerated the consequences for family life of Belfast's industrialization, there is no doubt that part of the juvenile crime problem had its roots in rebellion against parental authority. For instance, Mary Jane McAnulty, a thirteen-year-old girl, was the despair of her mother in 1858. Mary Jane repeatedly stole from her mother and pawned the goods, and had 'fallen into the companionship of improper women' in Hudson's Entry, where she went to reside in a house of ill fame. Mrs McAnulty, who blamed the bad example of Smithfield theatre shows for her daughter's behaviour, lost her job in an Academy Street shop because

89. *B.D.M.*, 25 Sept. 1857.

of Mary Jane's delinquency.[90] It emerged from the trial for theft of fourteen-year-old Mary Cushlahan, fifteen-year-old William Hawthorn, and Mary Crawford, aged around sixteen years, in December 1859 that they had 'long since set their parents at defiance, and in fact had left their homes, and were frequenting the worst haunts of vice in Belfast'.[91] The despairing parents of a thirteen-year-old boy explained at his trial in August 1860 that they had deprived him of his clothes to keep him indoors, and on one occasion had tied him to his bed for a week in a vain attempt to dissuade their kleptomaniac son from thieving.[92] At the November 1862 trial of Mary White, a 'young girl', for assaulting her mother, Eleanor, in Millfield Place, her mother explained that she had repeatedly removed Mary from 'bad houses, but she won't stay away from the accursed dens, and she so very young ... she says that she will live and die walking the streets, if it were only to vex me'.[93]

Professional crooks were only too happy to entice juveniles into crime. The *Belfast Newsletter* complained in April 1849 that 'There are few towns which are more infested with young thieves than Belfast. These are mostly mere children, under twelve years of age, and many of them have been allured, by evil companions, from respectable homes to those haunts of villainy, the purlieus of Smithfield, North Street, and similar localities'.[94] One of these 'evil companions' was Thomas Corrigan, a member of a family of thieves. Just fourteen years old in 1851, it was stated that 'he has frequently in his pay lads even younger than himself, whom he rewards at the rate of two-pence a day' for stealing on the quays. According to the *Belfast Newsletter*, 'Families are known to depend for subsistence solely upon the proceeds of river-side theft, perpetrated by very little boys and girls, some of whom are regularly hired or supported by "Fagins" of the lowest grade'.[95] In 1852 the *Newsletter*, commenting on the case of John Curell, 'a mere sprouting lettuce' who was caught stealing coals on the quays, stated that 'the greater portion of our town thieves make their debuts on Queen's Quay'.[96] It is no surprise to read of the 'unfortunate juveniles who are harboured for crime in Hudson's Entry'; in 1852 it was stated that they 'stroll

90. *B.N.L.*, 12 Oct. 1858.
91. *B.D.M.*, 29 Dec. 1859.
92. *B.N.L.*, 25 Aug. 1860.
93. Ibid, 28 Nov. 1862.
94. Ibid, 13 Apr. 1849.
95. Ibid, 16 June 1851.
96. Ibid, 11 Aug. 1852.

about the town pilfering from shops or picking pockets'.[97] One of the youngsters raised to crime there was a boy named William John Riddell. He lived with a woman named Anne Quinn and, in his own words, 'I robbed the world for her'.[98] In August 1855 the mayor, Dr William McGee, complained that the notorious Caddell's Entry houses harboured 'unfortunate children' whom the police regarded as 'public pests'. One brothel keeper, a Mrs Bickerstaff, was known to entice young girls away from their homes and introduce them to a life of prostitution and theft.[99]

Anderson's Row was the district which was most notorious for harbouring juvenile delinquents. Julius Rodenberg, who visited the street in the late 1850s, accompanied by a policeman, wrote:

The young fry I saw here are only partly born on the straw heaps of Anderson's Row; another and no small portion is stolen! The policeman showed me an old stout woman, with an unendurably roguish face, who had gained a name in this branch of industry. Her den is subjected to continued examinations, and is constantly under surveillance, and yet it has been impossible hitherto to catch this criminal in the act, although it is known that the majority of the youthful population quartered on her are stolen children of twelve or thirteen years of age. This woman keeps several young women, by whom the boys are corrupted in an unnatural way; they are instructed how to pilfer in the streets and the port, and seduce other boys by representations to Anderson['s] Row. In this way the criminal den is constantly filled afresh; and respectable parents who have lost their son on an errand, and whose traces they have tried in vain to find by advertisements, discover him again, years after, in the criminal, whom the magistrate sentences to lengthened imprisonment.[100]

The crimes committed by juveniles were mostly petty thefts, such as shoplifting or picking pockets. Some specialized in stealing clothes left on hedges to dry;[101] others were 'snappers', that is, children who stole from farmers' carts passing through the town.[102] As early as June 1821 it was pointed out that it was a 'common practice' to steal the brass and iron fittings in uninhabited houses: juveniles and indeed adults routinely plundered iron, copper, brass and lead

97. Ibid, 26 Nov. 1852.
98. Ibid, 12 Oct. 1855, 2, 27 Mar., 28 July 1857, 13 Apr., 30 Aug. 1858, 2 Aug. 1861, 21 June 1862, 6 Jan. 1865; *B.D.M.*, 18 July 1859.
99. *B.N.L.*, 11 Aug. 1855, 17 Dec. 1861.
100. Rodenberg, *Pilgrimage*, p.315.
101. For an example see *B.N.L.*, 3 June 1856.
102. Ibid, 3 Sept. 1857.

fittings ranging from door knockers to lead pipes and roofing metal from uninhabited, empty or partly-constructed houses. They found a ready outlet for their takings in the town's marine stores.[103] The owners of marine stores were not noted for making close enquiries about the origin of goods offered to them for sale; even if they did not openly collude with law-breakers and knowingly act as receivers of stolen property, they showed a remarkable lack of curiosity as to how children acquired various items of metal. They also readily purchased clocks, buttons, knives, flax, scissors, rope and cloth with a similar lack of curiosity as to their origin. The owners were frequently condemned as receivers of stolen goods.[104] There were some twenty-eight marine stores in Belfast in 1851, as well as 110 dealers in second-hand goods.[105] The latter, colloquially known as 'gather ups', were also implicated in receiving stolen goods,[106] especially from children. They were described in February 1848 as 'those prowling knaves, who sneak through the streets exchanging abominable "sweetmeats" for bits of iron, rags, bone and other refuse— thus teaching little children to pilfer at home, and become, even in their infancy, the accessories of crime'.[107]

The harsh penal system does not appear to have acted as a deterrent to Belfast's juvenile delinquents. It was not unknown for children aged from twelve to fourteen years to be sentenced to seven years' transportation for theft, especially if they were repeat offenders,[108] although most received prison terms with or without a whipping. By the 1840s transportation was imposed less often on both adult and juvenile offenders due to complaints from Australia that the colony was being used as a dumping ground for the United Kingdom's riff-raff; the remaining threat of a mere prison sentence held no terrors for Belfast's criminals, according to the assistant barrister at Belfast quarter sessions in 1850.[109] However, in the 1850s public opinion hardened against the idea of even a prison

103. For just some of the myriad examples see ibid, 1 June 1821, 4 May 1826, 1 Sept. 1851, 28 Mar., 9, 22 May, 1 June 1853, 25 June, 12 Oct. 1855, 19 Mar. 1856, 27 May, 26 June 1862; *N.W.*, 22 Feb. 1830, 10 Jan. 1837, 31 Oct., 5 Dec. 1840.

104. Town council committee on police affairs minutes, 21 Dec. 1847; *B.N.L.*, 7 Dec. 1853, 21 Nov. 1855, 23 Feb., 19 Sept. 1857, 14 Feb. 1859, 17 May 1862; *B.D.M.*, 9 Nov. 1859.

105. *B.N.L.*, 3 Jan. 1851.

106. *N.W.*, 12 Aug. 1824; *B.N.L.*, 25 Jan. 1848, 19 Sept. 1851, 10, 28 Jan. 1853, 1 Sept. 1857.

107. *B.N.L.*, 4 Feb. 1848.

108. Ibid, 13 Aug. 1816, 28 Jan. 1834; *N.W.*, 12 Aug. 1824.

109. *B.N.L.*, 3 July 1849, 2 July 1850.

sentence for juvenile offenders. One of the earliest critics of the practice of imprisoning juveniles was Reverend John Edgar, who complained in 1852 that a young child found guilty of theft 'is shut up in the common prison, branded with infamy, robbed of self-respect, perhaps whipped like a slave; and, at all events, exposed to the pollution of the vilest society, and the acquaintance and seduction of the most destructive agents of ill'.[110] In 1856 the *Belfast Newsletter* advocated the establishment of a reformatory school for young offenders, pointing out that 'We cannot go on tolerating the barbarism of flogging young criminals into harder and more dangerous depravity, or the folly of apprenticing them in jails to the trade of the burglar, the incendiary, or the assassin'. It also advocated the formation of a 'Shoeblack Brigade' for Belfast urchins in the hope that they would become enamoured of more honest ways of earning a living.[111] Early in the next year a Society for the Reformation of Juvenile Offenders was founded in Belfast, with the marquis of Donegall as president, the earl of Antrim and Viscount Massereene as vice presidents and a committee consisting of the mayor, Resident Magistrate Tracy and 'several other philanthropic gentlemen'. Its aim was to promote reformatory schools for young offenders, in which juveniles could receive 'religious instruction and moral training' and learn a trade, as an alternative to sending them to prison.[112] In August 1858 an act to establish reformatory schools in Ireland was passed. It allowed for sentencing juveniles under 16 years of age to at least two years in a reformatory school.[113] After this Catholic juveniles were sent to the reformatory in Monaghan or Glencree, Co. Wicklow, while Protestant youths were sent to the Malone Road reformatory. The much-vaunted 'Shoeblack Brigade' to provide employment for the 'City Arabs' was not organized until late 1861. Only twelve boys joined its ranks.[114]

OTHER CRIME

Of course, not all crimes in Belfast were committed by children: adults proved more than adept at criminal activity. A particularly

110. Revd John Edgar, 'The dangerous and perishing classes' in *Belfast Social Inquiry Society*, no. 5 (1852), 7.

111. *B.N.L.*, 12 Feb. 1856.

112. Ibid, 3 Feb. 1857.

113. Jane Barnes, *Irish industrial schools, 1868–1908: origins and development* (Dublin, 1989), pp.32–33.

114. *B.N.L.*, 17 Sept., 1 Nov., 21 Dec. 1861.

nasty offence which adults committed was that of child-stripping—enticing young children to a secluded place, stealing their clothes and pawning them.[115] Pickpockets were a more significant presence in Belfast's streets. In the 1820s pickpockets preyed on the crowds that gathered to hear ballad singers perform, and on the farmers who attended Smithfield market.[116] They also plied their trade amongst the crowds that gathered for the arrival of the Dublin coaches. The *Northern Whig* complained in September 1829 that:

Our town has become proverbial with all the strangers that visit it. To say nothing of various other abuses that daily meet the eye, a traveller cannot alight off one of the stage coaches without running the risk of having his pocket picked, or being robbed of his trunks, by the crowd of blackguards that immediately surround him, jostle him about, and seize upon his luggage.[117]

The markets were still favourite areas of operation for pickpockets at the end of the period;[118] they also operated in churches,[119] and the Maze races attracted the attention not only of native pickpockets but also the 'swell mob' of England.[120] Pickpockets from as far away as Monaghan and Armagh congregated on the quays and fleeced passengers while pretending to help them with their luggage.[121] The pickpockets were not awed by the efforts of the police force to suppress their activity; the *Belfast Newsletter* claimed in October 1861 that 'Occasionally a detective's pockets have been picked, just to remind him that his acquaintances have not all been removed from their country for their country's good'.[122] Pickpockets, thieves and burglars could operate because they had a ready outlet for their pickings in the numerous pawnbroker shops in the town. The number of these rose from just thirty in 1833 to forty-nine in 1837; it fell to just thirty-three by 1851, but by 1865 it had risen again to

115. For some examples see ibid, 2 Aug. 1822, 25 May, 27 Aug. 1829, 13 July 1848, 26 July, 1 Nov. 1850, 21 Feb., 22, 27 July, 7 Sept., 14 Dec. 1853, 16, 18 Jan., 11 Oct. 1856, 2 Feb. 1865; *N.W.*, 25 Sept. 1828, 30 Apr. 1829, 9, 16 May 1833, 10 July, 25 Oct. 1838, 19 Oct. 1839.
116. *B.N.L.*, 13 Apr. 1819, 14 May 1824, 28 Mar. 1826.
117. Ibid, 15 Nov. 1822; *N.W.*, 17 Sept. 1829.
118. Town council committee on police affairs minutes, 28 Oct. 1851; *B.N.L.*, 26 Apr. 1852, 5 June 1854, 4 May 1855, 29 Apr. 1861, 30 Jan. 1864.
119. *B.N.L.*, 21 Apr. 1852, 27 May 1858; *B.D.M.*, 25 June 1859.
120. *B.N.L.*, 21 July 1854, 23 July 1856, 27 July 1861; *B.D.M.*, 25 July 1859.
121. *B.N.L.*, 6 June 1851, 2 Aug. 1852.
122. Ibid, 15 Oct. 1861.

seventy-three.[123] The judicial authorities in 1826 considered that dishonest Belfast pawnbrokers were 'grievous nuisances to the community, and worse than thieves'.[124] While one cannot say with certainty that all Belfast pawnbrokers knowingly accepted stolen goods, there is no doubt that a minority fell into this category[125] while the lax attitude of others in accepting goods from their customers encouraged crooks to continue with their activity.[126] It probably did not pay pawnbrokers to enquire too closely of their customers where they had acquired their goods: in the course of an ordinary day, it was claimed in March 1838, a Belfast pawnbroker worked for fifteen hours and was 'awarded the filth, the risk of infection, and the abuse of the most troublesome set of customers on the face of the globe'.[127]

It is difficult to assess precisely the extent of crime in Belfast or to compare it with that of other cities such as Dublin, given the almost total absence of Belfast crime statistics for the period. We know that a total of 1,529 people were committed to the Belfast police office from 1816 to 1824, almost all of whom were convicted when tried; some 168 of the prisoners were transported, and four were hanged.[128] It is impossible to tell from the source what proportion of Belfast law-breakers was represented by the 1,529, as those accused who were proceeded against on summonses were not included. In a five-week period from August to October 1822 some 425 people were arrested for various offences, including 242 women (56.9% of the total) arrested for disorderly conduct at night.[129] If these figures were sustained throughout the year, they would suggest that the police made approximately 4,420 prisoners in 1822 alone.

Contemporaries felt that despite the presence of the police the crime problem increased over time. The most serious offences,

123. *Report from the select committee on pawnbroking in Ireland; together with the minutes of evidence, appendix and index,* H.C. 1837–38 (677), xvii, 173, pp.147–48, 158; *The Belfast almanac, for the year of our lord 1851* (Belfast, 1851), p.62; *The Belfast and province of Ulster directory for 1865–66. Vol. VII* (Belfast, 1865), pp.534–35.

124. *B.N.L.,* 11 Apr. 1826.

125. Belfast police committee minutes, 18 Oct. 1831; *N. W.,* 18 Apr. 1837; *B.N.L.,* 11 June 1855.

126. *Belfast Monthly Magazine* (Mar. 1814), pp.199–210; *Select committee on pawnbroking in Ireland,* p.79; *B.N.L.,* 13 Aug., 12, 15 Sept. 1855, 8 Sept. 1860.

127. Letter from 'J.H.' in *N. W.,* 31 Mar. 1839.

128. *B.N.L.,* 23 Nov. 1824.

129. Ibid, 27 Aug., 3, 17, 24 Sept., 8 Oct. 1822.

indictable crimes, consisted mainly of thefts. Assistant Barrister William Mayne told the Belfast quarter sessions in 1834 that

the description of offences was much the same as on former occasions; that they consisted mostly in [sic] offences against property—a species of crime always supposed to exist in such a large commercial town as Belfast, and which it was impossible, even by the most judicious arrangements and strictest vigilance of police authorities, to prevent.[130]

Drunk and disorderly cases, 'almost without an exception, of the very lowest dregs of society', were the most frequent non-indictable offences. Adulterated whiskey was popular with the lower classes. One brand was known as 'Corduroy', because of the 'rough feeling which it imparts to the palate', while that known as 'Kill the Beggar' requires no elaboration. Reverend John Edgar, a leading temperance advocate, stated that 'in houses where pickpockets, thieves, and such pests are kept and trained, it is customary for a portion of spirituous liquor to be given to them, to prepare them by false courage for going out to their work of plunder or blood'.[131] In 1837 'repeated and unchecked robberies and house-breakings' prompted the banks to employ night guards.[132]

The *Northern Whig* lamented in the following year that 'The streets are swarming with pickpockets and robbers, of every age and of both sexes, and it behoves persons coming from the country, or servants driving jaunting cars, to be on the alert, as no town in Great Britain or Ireland is worse off than Belfast, in regard to police protection'. An estimated 10,000 cases were tried at petty sessions in Belfast from October 1837 to October 1838.[133] Assistant Barrister John Gibson, when presiding at Belfast quarter sessions in July 1840, even asserted that the 'manifest inefficiency' of the police in preventing burglaries and thefts suggested that the night constables 'must actually be in league with the depredators'.[134] The *Belfast Newsletter* did not go quite so far as that in the following year. Instead it blamed the population explosion for the town's crime problem: 'When it is recollected that the scoundrelism of three or four counties is occasionally poured in upon us, it is no wonder that our [criminal]

130. *Northern Herald*, 19 Apr. 1834.

131. *N.W.*, 11 Apr. 1833; *Report from the select committee of inquiry into drunkenness, with the minutes of evidence, and appendix*, H.C. 1834 (601), viii, 1, pp.70, 72.

132. *N.W.*, 7 Nov. 1837.

133. Ibid, 27 Oct., 13 Nov. 1838.

134. Ibid, 9 July 1840.

calendar should sometimes assume an enlarged appearance.'[135] At first sight the statistics of the cases tried by the magistrates at Belfast petty sessions from 1840 to 1842 do not bear out the general picture of a rise in crime: the number of minor cases declined from 9,861 in 1840 to 7,925 in 1841 and 5,914 in 1842.[136] However, as most non-indictable offences consisted of drunkenness, and these years coincided with the height of Father Mathew's temperance campaign, it appears reasonable to assume that the fall in the number of non-indictable cases can be attributed to a (temporarily) greater degree of sobriety among the Catholic lower classes.

By the early 1850s the judicial authorities once again were expressing despair at the town's crime level, and their apparent inability to curb the activities of criminals.[137] By this decade the popularity of summer excursions to the seaside added to the problems of the police, as burglaries of holidaymakers' houses became more frequent. From the summer of 1852 the Belfast police kept a special list of families who went to the 'shore' so that the day and night constables could keep a particular watch over the vacant houses. It was hoped that this would foil the 'crib crackers', as the burglars were called.[138] As for minor offences, they still consisted mostly of drunkenness and disorderly behaviour[139] and some commentators felt that drunkenness was at the root of most other crimes.[140] Monday mornings in particular saw large numbers of drunk and disorderly cases, following the weekend revels.[141] Drunken 'Amazonian' quarrels, as fights between women were sometimes described, figured prominently. The cases involving women at loggerheads taxed magistrates, as 'it would puzzle a Minos to discover on which side the aggression commenced', while the foul language that accompanied the cases was 'one of the most painful inflictions to which the magistrate can be subjected in the exercise of his duty'.[142] When the petty sessions court sat on Wednesday, 20 December 1854 the attendance was astonished that there was not a single female prisoner for trial, 'a

135. *B.N.L.*, 15 Jan. 1841.

136. *N.W.*, 5 Jan. 1843.

137. *B.D.M.*, 5 July 1854.

138. *B.N.L.*, 3 May 1850, 1, 17, 24 Sept. 1851, 18, 20, 21 June, 11, 13 Aug. 1852, 28 July 1856, 27 July 1857, 30 Apr. 1860; Town council committee on police affairs minutes, 24 June 1856.

139. *B.N.L.*, 2 July 1852, 15 June, 28 Dec. 1853.

140. Ibid, 1 Dec. 1852, 1 June 1853; *B.D.M.*, 1 July 1859.

141. *B.N.L.*, 18 Aug. 1852, 7 Aug. 1855, 27 May 1862, 23 June 1863.

142. Ibid, 22 Sept. 1851, 12 Jan. 1852, 6 Apr., 4 May 1853, 24 Sept. 1861.

circumstance unprecedented in the police annals in the remembrance of the oldest living member of the service'.[143]

REPEAT OFFENDERS

It is probably stating the obvious to point out that most of those who contributed to Belfast's crime statistics came from the lower classes. While many members of the lower class never fell foul of the law, quite a considerable number appeared in court on an astonishing number of occasions. The first individual with an especially note-worthy record whom the author has noticed was George Warnock, a cripple who clocked up sixty-five convictions before he was finally transported for seven years in July 1837 for a 'grievous assault' on Day Constable John Leonard.[144] A few months earlier a young man of around twenty-three years of age, Owen Christie, was found guilty of vagrancy at the assizes and sentenced to seven years' transportation unless he 'betake himself to honest pursuits' within three months. Australia thus lost a prospective immigrant, and Belfast gained a fowl dealer—the trade which Owen took up to avoid trans-portation—of extraordinarily dissolute habits. No single individual chalked up as many convictions as Owen Christie during the period of the municipal police's existence. The convictions were mostly for public drunkenness, although occasionally assaults on women and policemen and petty theft accompanied the intoxication charges. By October 1850 he had eighty-six court appearances for drunken-ness on his record. The total appearances for all offences had increased to 179 by September 1853. Christie had been imprisoned 136 times for a total of over ninety months by January 1858. In November 1861 it was estimated that he had paid the astonishing amount of £100 in fines for his misdemeanours. Owen's final number of offences by September 1865 was 221, and this would have been even higher had he not given up drink for two years before 1865.[145] A contemporary with almost as notorious a reputation was the 'Gypsy King of the North', Matthew Mulholland, who had ninety-six fines for drunkenness imposed by November 1840 but had paid the penalty only once. His wife had sixteen court appear-ances for the same offence by that date. On his 126th court appearance for drunk and disorderly conduct, in January 1853,

---

143. Ibid, 22 Dec. 1854.
144. *N.W.*, 6 July 1837.
145. Details from ibid, 11 Mar. 1837; *B.N.L.*, 22 Oct. 1850, 12 Sept. 1853, 26 Jan. 1858, 29 Nov. 1861, 5 June, 18 Aug. 1865.

there was a 'conspiracy for his defence amongst the solicitors, who felt a sort of reverence, not to say honour or esteem, for the patri- archical champion of law-breaking and drunkenness'. Mulholland had 143 convictions from 1837 to 1857. His total number of con- victions for drunk and disorderly behaviour would probably have exceeded even Owen Christie's but for the fact that Owen often paid the fines inflicted while Matthew rarely did. His lengthy residences in jail slowed down his overall record of drunkenness.[146]

Other frequent attenders at Belfast Police Court in this period included Elizabeth Barry, Jane Feeny and Mary Johnston. When Elizabeth Barry was arrested for drunk and disorderly conduct in notorious Robert Street, where she was 'cursing the pope and otherwise exercising her powers of malediction' in September 1856, Chief Constable Lindsay informed the magistrates that he had ceased counting her 'drunken delinquencies', but that she had been more than 150 times in police custody. By April 1857 the police considered that the old woman's record closely approximated to that of Owen Christie. Two months later Resident Magistrate Tracy proclaimed her 'the worst woman in Ulster' on account of her drunkenness, disorderly behaviour and cursing the pope.[147] Sarah Jane Feeny had been prosecuted for drunkenness on more than 100 occasions by May 1854. If one were to believe her own account of her motivation there was a certain amount of selflessness in her drunken behaviour. Constable Moses Jamison, who found Feeny lying hopelessly drunk at Bishop Denvir's door, cursing 'pope and popery' in a loud voice in December 1855, stated to the magistrate that Sarah told him that 'she got drunk to give you something to do'. Sarah explained to the magistrate, 'I did not want your worship, like 'thella, to have no occupation'. On at least fifty occasions Feeny tried to excuse her inebriety by claiming that one of her friends was about to emigrate to Australia and she had had a farewell drink with her. She was clever enough to always insist on being brought to the police office in a car after her arrest. According to the bemused Chief Constable Lindsay in November 1857, she had 'cost the authorities so much in car hire as would take him to Killarney and back'. It is not clear how often Feeny was convicted, but it is known that she was imprisoned in Crumlin Road jail, which was opened in 1850, on 154 occasions by January 1860.[148] It was stated in June

146. Details from *N.W.*, 14 Nov. 1840; *B.N.L.*, 20 Aug. 1851, 30 Aug. 1852, 24 Jan. 1853, 15 Sept. 1856, 29 Sept. 1857.
147. *B.N.L.*, 23, 24 Sept. 1856, 25 Apr., 18 June 1857.
148. Ibid, 19 May 1854, 20 Dec. 1855, 8 Nov., 13 Dec. 1856, 24 Nov. 1857, 21 Jan. 1860.

ATROCIOUS & INHUMAN OUTRAGE.

WHEREAS on the Night of SUNDAY the 9th January instant, the Body of WILLIAM QUAIL, a Private in the 3d Company of Belfast Yeomanry, which had been that day INTERRED in the Burying Ground of Friar's-Bush, near this Town, was inhumanly RAISED out of the EARTH; and carried to the New Bridge near ORMEAU, where it was left exposed until the following day, the Coffin being considerably broken.

Now we whose names are hereunto subscribed, contemplating with just abhorrence the perpetration of a crime of so revolting a nature, and with a view to bring to condign punishment the authors of this atrocious outrage, do hereby promise to pay, in proportion to the Sums annexed to our Names,

ONE HUNDRED POUNDS

to any Person or Persons who shall, within Six Months from the date hereof, discover and prosecute to conviction any of the persons concerned in the perpetration of this savage action.—And also a REWARD of

THIRTY POUNDS

to any person who may, within said time, give such private information as may lead to such discovery, and their names kept secret if required.

726)   Belfast, January 14, 1814.

Name	£	s.	d.	Name	£	s.	d.
Donegall	50	0	0	Charles Standfield	3	8	3
Thomas Verner, Sovereign of Belfast	20	0	0	John Stewart	2	5	6
				Wm. Stewart	2	5	6
				James Taylor	2	5	6
Edward May	20	0	0	Wm. Taylor	2	5	6
Gilbert M'Ilveen	11	7	6	Robert Egan	2	5	6
Narcissus Batt	11	7	6	Wm. Patrick	2	5	6
Thomas Batt	11	7	6	John M'Kee	2	5	6
George Bristow	11	7	6	James Huddleston	2	5	6
H. A. S. Harvey	11	7	6	Saml. Huddleston	2	5	6
George Black	11	7	6	Samuel Tucker	2	5	6
C. M. Skinner	11	7	6	Anth. Thompson	2	5	6
F. Coulson	11	7	6	James Wilson	2	5	6
Robert Gordon	11	7	6	George Snell	1	2	9
Francis Taggart	5	13	9	John M'Mullen	1	2	9
Stephen Daniel	5	13	9	Richd. W. Thorpe	1	2	9
John & T. Cunningham	5	13	9	Hamilton Fulton	1	2	9
				James M'Dowell	1	2	9
James Law, sen	5	13	9	James Johnston	1	0	0
Archer Bayly	5	13	9	John Reilly, for 1st company Belfast Infty.	5	13	9
Sam. M'Naghten	5	13	9				
James Law, jun	5	13	9				
Samuel Law	5	13	9	Thos. Caldwell, for 2d ditto	5	13	9
J. Thompson	5	0	0				
A. Handcock	5	0	0	J. Coates and J. Brady, for 3d ditto	10	0	0
C. Salmon	5	0	0				
S. Cupples	5	0	0				
Phillip Johnston	5	0	0	Richd. Freeman, for 4th ditto	5	13	9
Edward Cupples	5	0	0				
William Guy	5	0	0	John Rice, for Belfast Loyals	10	0	0
John Atkinson	5	0	0				
Arthur Woods	5	0	0	Loyal Falls Infantry	5	13	9
Walter Ferral	5	0	0				
F. Huddleston	4	11	0				
A. Scott	3	10	0		£375	13	11

1. *Belfast Newsletter* advertisement detailing reward for information about the perpetrators of an outrage in Friar's Bush graveyard, 1814.

DREADFUL OUTRAGE AND REWARD.

WHEREAS, on WEDNESDAY morning the 28th February, instant, about FOUR o'Clock, an Armed Party attacked the Dwelling-House of Mr. FRANCIS JOHNSON, in Peters-hill, in the Town of Belfast, and after breaking the Windows, introduced some extremely combustible preparation, which exploded with such violence, as to destroy a great part of the said House and imminently endangered the lives of the whole family, (consisting of Thirteen Persons).

Now we, whose Names are hereunto annexed, viewing with indignation and horror this infamous and malicious attempt to involve in destruction not only the Property of this respectable Gentleman and the lives of himself and Family, but those of all the neighbourhood, and anxious to bring to Condign Punishment the Perpetrators of this atrocious and diabolical outrage, do hereby promise to pay, in proportion to the sums to our names annexed, a REWARD of

TWO THOUSAND POUNDS, Sterling,

to any Person or Persons, who shall, within Twelve Months from this date, discover on, and prosecute to conviction the Person or Persons, or any of them, concerned in this atrocious outrage ; and we also hereby engage to pay a REWARD of

FIVE HUNDRED POUNDS,

for such Private Information as may lead to the discovery and conviction of any Person or Persons who were concerned aiding or assisting therein, and the name of the Person or Persons who shall make such private communication will be kept secret.

Application will also be made to Government for obtaining his Majesty's most gracious Pardon for any Person or Persons implicated in the above outrage, who shall give such information as may lead to conviction.

941)   Belfast, 29th February, 1816.

---

2. *Belfast Newsletter* advertisement detailing reward for information about a bombing outrage, 1816.

NIGHTLY WATCH.

PURSUANT to a NOTICE from the SOVE-REIGN of BELFAST, agreeable to Act of Par-liament,

A MEETING of the POLICE COMMIT-TEE will be held at their COMMITTEE-ROOM, on THURSDAY 5th September next, at the hour of ELEVEN o'Clock, for the purpose of appointing a NIGHTLY WATCH, to consist of

25 MEN at NINE SHILLINGS per week.

4 CONSTABLES at HALF-A-GUINEA per week.

1 HEAD CONSTABLE at FIFTEEN SHILLINGS per week.

ALL those Persons who are duly qualified, and wish to fill any of the above situations, must appear personally, and bring with them certificates of ability and good conduct.

LAMP-LIGHTING.

And on SATURDAY, the 7th Sept. next, the COMMITTEE will proceed to ELECT SEVEN MEN, to LIGHT the LAMPS during the ensu-ing Season.—None need apply but active well-be-haved men.—(By Order,)

JAMES HYNDMAN, Clerk.

3. Advertisement for recruits to the Belfast police, August 1816.

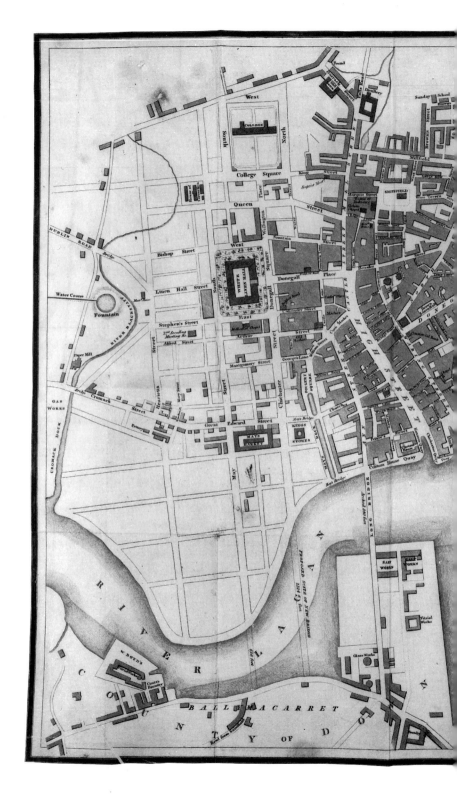

4. Map of Belfast in 1822.

A

NEW & CORRECT PLAN

OF THE

TOWN OF BELFAST,

Drawn & Engraved

EXPRESSLY FOR THE PRESENT WORK;

— 1822. —

Burying
Ground

Poor
House

NEW
BARRACK

Carrickfergus

Street

ARTILLERY
BARRACK

STREET

INFIRMARY

Green Mount

Bridge

MILL WATER

Carrickfergus   Road   York Bridge

FORT

STREET

STREET

Henrick

William
Street

Street

York Street

Donegall Street

COURT
HOUSE

Henry

Patrick   Street

Thomas   Street

Hercules Street

CORPORATION

STREET

Corporation
Ground

Street

STREET

Quay

Ritchies
Ship
Yard

Governors Dock No 1

Governors Dock No 2

Ritchie
& Sons
Ship
Yard

C
H
A
N
N
E
L

J. THOMSON ESQ?

Reclaimed Ground

Engraved by J.T

5. The Long Bridge, *c.*1822: 'haunt of beggars, thieves, and thieves' compeers'.

6. High Street, *c.* 1830.

7. Map of Belfast in *c.*1842.

AST

Brick Field

Brick Field

New Burying Ground

Cotton Factory

Old Grave Yard

NEW ANTRIM ROAD

School Ho.

NEW BARRACK

Artillery Barrack

Linen Factory

QUEEN STREET

Trafalgar Street

Presbyterian Church

YORK STREET

FREDERICK STREET

GREAT GEORGES STREET

CORDUKES PLACE

Little York Street

HENRY STREET

EARL STREET

Nelson Street

Nelson Street

Street

JAMES STREET

GT PATRICK STREET

CORPORATION STREET

Tomb Street

Gamble Street

HATCHICK DOCK

Donegall Quay

Custom Dock

Dunbar Dock

Paran Street

MAILS FROM BELFAST

To	Start from	o'Clock	cost
BANGOR	Ann St.	5 P.M.	2 Hours
DERRY	Corn Market	7 A.M.	15
DONAGHADEE			
SCOTLAND & NORTH OF ENGLAND	Do. Do.	30 8 A.M.	
DOWNPATRICK	Chichester St.	10 1 P.M.	5 22
DUBLIN	Castle Place	{ 5 A.M.	12
SOUTH & WEST OF IRELAND & ENGLAND		{ 6 P.M.	
ENNISKILLEN	Do. Do.	20 5 P.M.	14
LARNE	High St.	15 8 P.M.	5¼

STEAM PACKETS

Sail for LONDON FALMOUTH & PLYMOUTH *every week.* LIVERPOOL *3 times a week.*
DUBLIN *once a week* GLASGOW *every day except Sunday* STRANRAER *once a week.*

J. Kirkwood S?

Borough of Belfast.

LAWS AND BYE-LAWS

FOR BETTER REGULATING

Coaches, Carriages, Chariots, Landaus, Landaulets, Cabriolets, Sociables, Flys, Jaunting-Cars, Gigs, Cabs,

AND OTHER SUCH LIKE CARRIAGES,

PLYING FOR HIRE,

AND

THE OWNERS AND DRIVERS THEREOF.

BELFAST:
PRINTED BY JAMES WILSON,
13, HIGH-STREET.

1850.

INSTRUCTIONS

TO

THE BELFAST POLICE FORCE.

1856.

Belfast:
PRINTED AT "THE BELFAST DAILY MERCURY" OFFICE.

MDCCCLVI.

8. Title page of the Belfast police manual, 1856.

9. Title page of printed regulations for coach and other vehicle drivers in Belfast, 1850.

10. Buttons from Belfast police uniforms. Top: brass button, *c.* 1830, made by John Woodhouse, Dublin; Middle, right: officer quality gilt brass, *c.* 1845, made by John Woodhouse; Bottom: blackened brass button from night-duty uniform, *c.* 1845; Middle, left: brass button, *c.*1845, made by John Woodhouse.

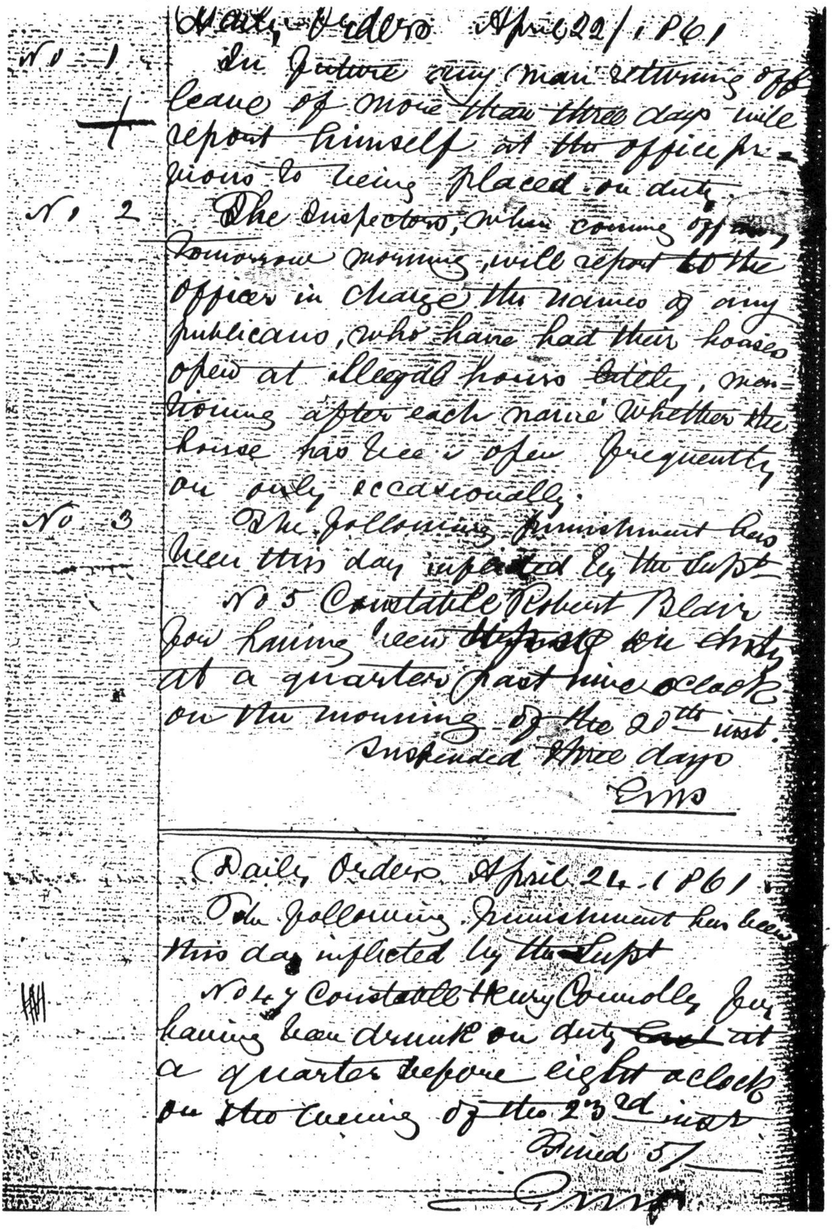

Daily Orders April 22/1861

No 1 In future any man returning off leave of more than three days will report himself at the office previous to being placed on duty

No 2 The Inspectors, when coming off duty tomorrow morning, will report to the officer in charge the names of any publicans, who have had their houses open at illegal hours lately, mentioning after each name whether the house has been open frequently or only occasionally.

No. 3 The following punishment has been this day inflicted by the Supt.

No 5 Constable Robert Blair for having been [illegible] on duty at a quarter past nine o'clock on the morning of the 20th inst.

Suspended three days

[illegible]

Daily Orders April 24 1861

The following punishment has been this day inflicted by the Supt

No 47 Constable Henry Connolly for having been drunk on duty last at a quarter before eight o'clock on the evening of the 23rd inst

Fined 5/-

[illegible]

11. Extract from the day book of the Belfast police, 22 April 1861. The extract is transcribed at pp. 146–47 below.

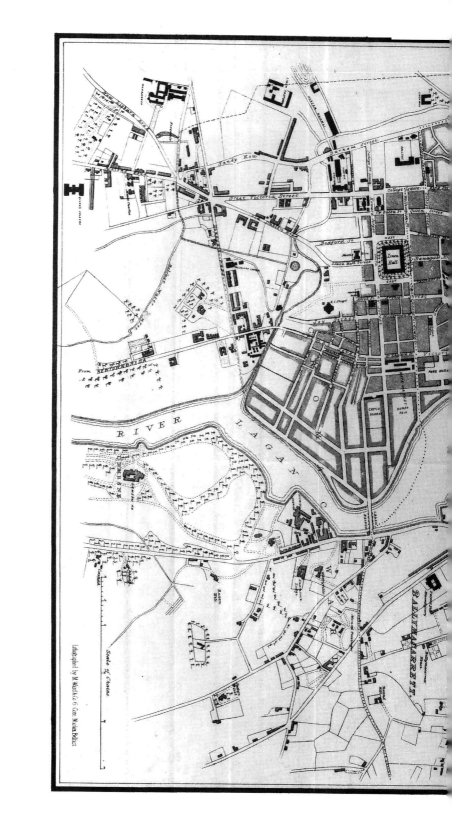

RIVER LAGAN

From NEWTOWNBREDA

BALLYMACARRETT.

Lithographed by W. Ward & Co. 6 Corn Market, Belfast.

Scale of Chains

12. Map of Belfast in *c.*1849.

13. Belfast in 1860, with The Queen's Bridge in the foreground.

AST.

ON STEEL BY MARCUS WARD & Co

14. Captain Eyre Massey Shaw, superintendent of the Belfast police from June 1860 to August 1861. Shaw, the last superintendent of the force, was the first superintendent of the London fire brigade. He is pictured here in the uniform of the latter force.

15. Scene from the 1864 riots: Protestants and Catholics in fire-
fight in front of St Malachy's Catholic church.

16. Scene from the 1864 riots: The Irish Constabulary open fire on a Protestant mob.

17. Scene from the 1864 riots: Protestant ship-carpenters firing on Catholic navvies.

18. Abbey Street, off Peter's Hill, in 1912.

1851 that one unfortunate woman, known to the police as 'Jenny on the Shelf', 'possesses suicidal propensities so fully developed, that the constables are in terror, every time she is locked up for drunkenness—which is at least two or three times a week—that she will be found suspended from the grating of the cell'.[149] Another unfortunate woman, Mary Johnston, had about 100 charges for drunkenness by January 1862; by January 1863 she had made 147 court appearances for drunkenness, disorderly conduct and using 'profane language'.[150]

Other frequent offenders whose records are known with some accuracy include Charles O'Neill, who made his 101st court appearance for being drunk and disorderly in September 1860; Ann Fitzsimons, whose 100th appearance on similar charges occurred in May 1862; Isabella Kane, who was charged for the 110th time in June 1863 for inebriation and disorderly behaviour, and William Gardiner, who was found guilty of drunkenness 'upwards of a hundred times' by June 1865.[151] There were many other people who appeared with monotonous regularity before the court but whose number of appearances are not recorded so precisely as those we have already seen. They included a prostitute named Betty Mackay, described in November 1862 as 'an emaciated, wasted looking woman' who was 'a habitual frequenter of the court during the last thirty-five years'; John McCallum, a blind man, who according to Constable McGibbon 'is a very troublesome fellow. I have been reading him lectures over and over again'; an old drunken woman named Mary Cassidy, stated in May 1864 to spend more than half of her time in prison, and a 'miserable-looking' beggarwoman named Fanny Drew, who according to Chief Constable McKittrick in December 1864 was 'one of the greatest nuisances in Belfast'.[152]

No discussion of Belfast's crime would be complete without noting John Massey, a 'haggard and squalid wretch', charged in June 1851 with assaulting Constables Hawkes, McGibbon and Taylor. The *Belfast Newsletter* described Massey as

the most arrant, artful and incorrigible begging impostor who has trodden the pavement of Belfast. He is in the habit of throwing himself down in the streets, and feigning excruciating cramps in the stomach. He is enabled to stimulate agony by a singular command over the muscles of

149. Ibid, 2 June 1851. For an account of another female prisoner who frequently attempted suicide in her cell see ibid, 8 Sept. 1857, 25 June 1861.

150. Ibid, 23 Jan. 1862, 3 Jan. 1863.

151. Ibid, 13 Sept. 1860, 26 May 1862, 17 June 1863, 9 June 1865.

152. Ibid, 27 Nov. 1862, 25 May, 24 Sept., 3 Nov., 15 Dec. 1864.

the diaphragm and abdomen, and excites so much commiseration from the soft-hearted and gullible that he is enabled to get drunk three or four times a day. The constables pounced upon him during one of his performances; but, although all stalwart fellows (Hawkes is the Goliath of the police force), they were heartily tired of their prisoner ere they reached the lock-up.[153]

Other noted offenders mentioned in 1851 were Anne Kinsley, 'an elderly woman, who is so often in jail for her jollifications that her hair is never allowed time to grow', and Thomas Bradley, a 'fierce-looking quay porter', described in July 1851 as 'a foe to the police' because of his repeated disorderly conduct. Bradley was 'one of the most ferocious of all the rough characters about our quays, and has been known, when wanted by the police, to take to water, and swim about for an hour with his clothes on' in an effort to evade arrest.[154] He would have recognised a kindred spirit in Mary O'Hare, whose name 'has long been in the habit of figuring in the police books, side by side with charges of rioting, drunkenness, thumping the night watch, &c, &c'.[155]

Thomas Morrow, who was arrested in December 1854 for being drunk and disorderly in North Street, where he was 'challenging to fight any "heretic" in that or any other locality', was a 'celebrated character in local police history'.[156] In the same year the municipal police described James Higgins of Millfield as 'a notorious drunkard, and one of the worst characters in Belfast,' while Arthur Duffy, a pickpocket residing in Hudson's Entry was known as 'The Boomerang' because of the number of times that he had been in and out of jail.[157] A drunkard named Peter Slavin was one of the most unruly of the drunk and disorderly prisoners taken by the police towards the end of our period. He usually caused the police 'much annoyance' when arrested, and was considered one of those characters who 'cannot by any means keep out of the dock'. He was only thirty-three years old in December 1864, by which month his court appearances were 'innumerable'.[158] In March 1856 Resident Magistrate Kelly described a prostitute named Margaret Kelly, who was repeatedly convicted 'for practising robbery and vice of all descriptions', as 'one of the

153. Ibid, 16 June 1851.
154. Ibid, 30 July, 27 Aug. 1851.
155. Ibid, 13 June 1853.
156. Ibid, 22 Dec. 1854.
157. *B.D.M.*, 11 Oct., 1 Nov. 1854.
158. *B.N.L.*, 15 Jan. 1856, 27 July 1858, 18 Nov. 1863, 12 Dec. 1864.

worst women in Belfast'. In the following month he called John Hagans, a Hudson's Entry householder, 'one of the most notorious blackguards in the province of Ulster,' who had committed every offence 'short of those crimes that bring a man to the gallows'. In August of the same year an old drunkard named Margaret Nunn was described as one of 'the regular occupants of the dock,' who usually had to be brought to the police office in a car.[159]

In May 1857 Mary O'Rorke, who was sentenced to a fine of 20*s.* and costs or fourteen days in prison for unruly conduct in York Street, was considered 'A notorious character ... one of that class of persons who spend more of their lifetime under the surveillance of the police and in prison enclosures than in the enjoyment of freedom and independence'. In the same month the *Belfast Newsletter* published brief details of the trial of a woman for breaking a window in Dock Street. She had made her debut in the dock only a year previously, but in the meantime had acquired such an unsavoury reputation that the newspaper heralded her court appearances under the headline of 'The Notorious Mrs McCance'. The headline 'Mrs McCance again!' was repeated frequently in the following years. By October 1863 Sarah Jane McCance had more than 100 convictions for drunkenness combined with disorderly conduct, theft, assaulting policemen or indecency in the street. In June 1865 the Belfast court authorities thought that they had seen the last of Mrs McCance when she announced at her trial for being drunk and disorderly that she had recently received £25 from her husband in America to pay for her emigration passage. She was let off on the charge as she promised to leave for Liverpool immediately. Within a week she was in court again, charged with attempting to stab the editor of the *Belfast Morning News* because of the unwelcome publicity which his newspaper directed at her actions.[160]

Other individuals who were closely acquainted with the police in the period were Sylvester Gartlan, 'a very troublesome old man' who was prosecuted more than fifty times by October 1857 for beating his wife; a brothel-keeper named William Rice who 'resides half his time in the county jail'; Mary Watts, arrested in October 1858 for disorderly conduct in May's Lane, who was described as 'a thief, and everything that is bad, and [she] has been a thief since she was a child'; and Celia Kelly, 'a most disorderly character', who made so many court appearances that the police stopped counting

159. Ibid, 20 Mar., 18 Apr., 26 Aug. 1856.
160. Details from ibid, 22 May, 18 June, 13 July, 26 Oct. 1857, 5 Sept. 1862, 17 Mar., 16 Oct. 1863, 12 Apr. 1864, 29 June, 8 July 1865.

them—she made at least four suicide attempts in police custody.[161] One should also include John Thistle, a middle-aged man stated in September 1860 to be prosecuted 'almost every Monday morning' for 'drunkenness, rioting, and disorderly conduct'; Agnes Martin, a 'stout, strapping six-footer' whose nickname of 'Lamp Post' aroused her ire and was the cause of the trouble which ensured her frequent appearance in the dock; and Jane Wright, described in March 1863 as 'an elderly Amazonian woman, who has been frequently punished for assaulting police constables'. Jane explained that she had ten children but her husband lived with another woman, and 'Always, when I get drink, I think of these things, and then I go clean mad'.[162]

161. Ibid, 31 Oct. 1857, 16 Oct. 1858, 16 Dec. 1861; *N.W.*, 6 Sept. 1858; *B.D.M.*, 3 Mar., 17 June, 21 Sept. 1859.
162. *B.N.L.*, 11 Sept. 1860, 27 Dec. 1862, 17 Mar. 1863.

CHAPTER SIX

Police response to Belfast's growth

INTRODUCTION

FROM 1816, POLICING arrangements in Belfast developed in response to a number of factors, the most important of which were the town's population growth and the subsequent increase in crime.[1] Another of the factors shaping Belfast's police system was the fact that the pace of the town's expansion, particularly from the 1840s onwards, outstripped the capacity of the municipal coffers to pay for a local police throughout all of Belfast, especially in some newly-built areas. What came into being was a hybrid police system, with the bulk of the burden of policing Belfast falling on the shoulders of the municipal force but with the Irish Constabulary taking responsibility for the remaining outlying districts of the rapidly-growing city. While the main focus of this work is on the municipal police, one also has to be aware that the Irish Constabulary played a significant role in policing Belfast. This chapter gives a brief sketch of the growth of the area of the Belfast police's 'beat', shows how the Irish Constabulary from 1824 onwards played an important role in reinforcing the local police, and indicates some of the innovations in policing methods which the local force introduced in response to the demands placed on it as a result of Belfast's growth.

THE GROWTH OF BELFAST

In 1813 there were an estimated 28,000 people living in Belfast 'within the lamps',[2] that is, in the area for which the police board was responsible. This area covered approximately 230 acres in 1822.[3] One cannot be more exact about the extent of the police

---

1. Increased sectarian tensions were another of the important factors behind innovations in Belfasts's policing. This topic is dealt with in chapter 8.
2. *Belfast Monthly Magazine*, vol. xi (Aug. 1813), p.145.
3. *B.N.L.*, 22 Mar. 1822.

board's jurisdiction because it was not precisely fixed; the 1800 Belfast police act merely stated that the night watch should operate in the town of Belfast 'and precincts thereof'. When Samuel Lewis visited Belfast in 1837 he reported that the town police's jurisdiction extended on the north to the Milewater, on the south to the Blackstaff and on the east to the Lagan, but that the western boundary was 'imperfectly defined', which made for plenty of disputes about taxation.[4] The police district was not identical with the area covered by the borough. The police board tended to try and extend its district in line with the built-up area of the town. Newly-constructed areas were lighted and 'watched', that is, patrolled by the municipal police, when they paid the police rates.[5] The extent of the borough, however, lagged behind that of the built-up area. When it was fixed in 1845 the borough's area was based on that planned by the Irish Municipal Corporations Act of 1840, which area in turn had been planned by government commissioners several years previously. As a result the borough area did not correspond to the built-up area. As the newly created town council could only operate legally within the borough area as defined by the 1845 act, its police were obliged to withdraw within the new boundaries (except for Ballymacarrett, which remained under the supervision of the Irish Constabulary), leaving much of the built-up area without a municipal police presence, as well as lacking basic amenities such as water, sewers and paved streets.[6]

By 1853 one quarter of the town on the Antrim side of the Lagan was outside the borough area.[7] The Belfast Borough Extension Act of 1853,[8] which passed on 20 August and came into effect on 1 December, considerably extended the size of the borough, and hence the area over which the municipal police had jurisdiction. Following the passage of this act the town council, in November 1853, proposed extending the lighted and watched district from York Road in the north, Agnes Street in the west, and to Botanic Gardens and the Ormeau Road as far as Glenfield Place in the south: this comprised virtually the entire built-up area on the Antrim side

4. Samuel Lewis, *A topographical dictionary of Ireland* (2 vols., London, 1837), i, 197.

5. The 'police rates' did not entitle rate payers to policing alone, but also to the range of services outlined in the 1800 Belfast police act for which the police board was responsible.

6. *N.W.*, 4 Nov. 1845; Town council minute book, 1 Jan. 1853 (Belfast City Hall).

7. *The Belfast and province of Ulster directory for 1865–66. Vol. III* (Belfast, 1865), p.21.

8. 16 & 17 Vict, c.114.

of the Lagan.[9] The extension resulted in a considerable loss of civic revenues, due to the expense incurred in providing sanitation, lighting and other amenities in the newly built-up areas,[10] and made the town council wary of further extending its area of responsibility. While building continued apace in the Belfast borough area the local force confined their activity to Belfast 'within the lamps', that part of the borough which was lighted and paved and which paid police rates in return. The town police could have patrolled the newly-constructed outskirts but found that they had more than enough with which to occupy their time in the lighted area of the borough. The parts of the town which did not pay police taxes and received no municipal amenities were policed by the Irish Constabulary, but the rapid expansion of Belfast in the 1850s meant that it was often difficult to determine where the two forces should operate.[11] Proposals to include the Ballymacarrett and Windsor districts of the borough within the lighted and watched area, as well as most of the Shankill and Crumlin Road areas, met with stubborn resistance from councillors who were opposed to the older districts of the town subsidizing the amenities of the outlying areas. As a result the Crumlin Road was not added to the lighted district until January 1865, some eight months before the municipal police were abolished, while Ballymacarrett was never policed by the town force.[12]

THE IRISH CONSTABULARY IN BELFAST

As indicated earlier in this chapter, the absence of the municipal police from certain outlying districts of Belfast did not mean that these areas had no police presence. In addition to the municipal police, a small force of County Constabulary (after the 1836 reforms it was named the Irish Constabulary) was stationed in the town for most of the period. The constabulary mainly policed the outskirts of the town, rather than Belfast 'within the lamps'. Antrim and Down were amongst the last Irish counties to receive detachments of the County Constabulary. The first ninety-six men for Antrim were appointed in December 1824, much to the dismay of the

9. Town council committee on police affairs minutes, 15 Nov. 1853; *B.N.L.*, 2 Dec. 1853.

10. *B.N.L.*, 3 Jan. 1855.

11. *1857 riots inquiry*, p.99; *B.N.L.*, 13 July, 23 Sept. 1858.

12. *B.N.L.*, 2 Feb. 1860, 17 Feb., 3 Nov. 1863, 2 Jan., 2 Dec. 1864, 3 Jan. 1865; Town council committee on police affairs minutes, 22 Dec. 1862, 26 Jan. 1863, 3 Nov. 1864.

Northern Whig which considered it insulting that relatively tranquil
Antrim and Down should be treated in the same manner as unruly
Munster counties.[13] Major D'Arcy, the provincial inspector of the
constabulary in Ulster, had his headquarters in McClean's buildings
in Belfast.[14] The small Belfast contingent was part of the Ballymena
constabulary district. At first its number was insignificant: there
were only nine constabulary (including two mounted men) stationed
in Belfast early in January 1833, which number was increased to
twelve later in the month following an appeal from Stephen May,
sovereign of Belfast, to Sub-inspector John Clarke in Ballymena.
In February 1833 the lord lieutenant agreed to station twenty-five
constabulary in Belfast,[15] but this strength was not kept up for
long. In August 1838 the Belfast magistrates complained that there
were only seventeen county constabulary in the town, including
those in Ballymacarrett. They requested the establishment of constabulary barracks in the suburbs outside of the area patrolled by
the night watch. They suggested the main roads as ideal locations,
especially as the outlying areas were the places mainly affected by
robberies in the winter. Barracks at the gasworks on the Ormeau
Road, at the Malone Road and Falls Road turnpikes, and on the
Crumlin Road and Antrim Road, it was felt, would curb winter
robberies and 'provide an effectual check to party disturbances',
especially if half of the men were stationed as a reserve in a central
barracks near Smithfield. The officer in charge of the Belfast constabulary, Sub-inspector Flinter, explained that the Belfast force
had been reduced to meet the requests of the Antrim grand jury for
the reinforcement of the barracks at Portglenone and the establishment of a barracks at Whiteabbey. He added that 'it has been
my opinion, ever since I came to this county, that the force in Belfast
was not half strong enough for the duty they have to perform', and
that 'the men are worn off their legs, marching prisoners to
Carrickfergus which duty would be quite sufficient without any
other for the men ... stationed here'.[16]

This duty was not only tiring but highly unpleasant, as can be
gathered from the following vivid description of prisoners being

13. *N.W.*, 23 Dec. 1824, 13 Jan., 15, 29 Sept. 1825.

14. *B.N.L.*, 27 Sept. 1825; Gaffikin, *Belfast 50 years ago*, p.30.

15. Stephen May to Earl O'Neill, 28 Jan. 1833; Under Secretary Sir William
    Gossett to Sub-inspector John Clarke, 23 Feb. 1833; May to Clarke, 19 Feb.
    1833, and Clarke to [?], 26 Apr. 1833 (NA, C.S.O.R.P. 1833/597).

16. Belfast magistrates to Under Secretary Thomas Drummond, 15 Aug. 1838;
    Sub-inspector E.S. Flinter to Inspector General Duncan McGregor, 20 Aug.
    1838 (NA, C.S.O.R.P. 1838/1650).

escorted from Carrickfergus jail for trial at the quarter sessions in Belfast:

long before the prisoners arrive, the street by which the procession enters is thronged by a rabble composed of the friends and associates of the prisoners—of those whom the police have not yet been able to get into their hands. Thus, the inhabitants and their families are exposed to the oaths and obscenity of these degraded wretches. But, when the procession itself arrives, the scene is absolutely revolting to every well-regulated mind. A long double file of men and boys, separated by a rope, to which they are attached, forms one portion of the procession, while the females are elevated aloft, on open carts; the entire is guarded by soldiers and police. The dialogues which take place, over the heads of the guard, are truly edifying. The hurry, bustle, and confusion, the oaths and shouts of the men, the obscenity shouted forth by the women, must, in short, to a stranger, afford a good idea of the high pitch of civilization to which we have attained in this part of the country.[17]

Despite complaints of an under-strength constabulary the Dublin Castle authorities were slow to augment the force in Belfast, probably due to the presence of the municipal watch. In September 1843 the Belfast police board claimed that the constabulary strength averaged from nineteen to twenty-four men, while Belfast's share of county cess entitled the town to an average of at least thirty-one to thirty-two men.[18] The dramatic increases in Belfast's population and area were not matched by similar increases in constabulary strength: by 1855 there were only thirty-two Irish Constabulary men stationed in Belfast, including barracks on the Malone and Falls Roads, North Queen Street, Bradbury Place and Durham Street.[19] In April 1856 a new barracks housing a constable and six sub-constables was erected on the Crumlin Road, following representations from the magistrates and local residents.[20] After the extensive riots in July and September 1857 the permanent constabulary force assigned to Belfast, including Ballymacarrett, was fifty-one men and officers in eight barracks. In addition to the barracks mentioned above there was a barracks at Cromac Street, while the Durham Street party were moved to a new premises at Albert Crescent to allow for a more rapid response to rioting between Sandy Row and Pound district mobs. The Antrim county inspector

17. Letter from 'Anti-Nuisance' in *N.W.*, 29 Oct. 1839.
18. Belfast police commissioners' minutes, 20 Sept. 1843.
19. *B.N.L.*, 25 Apr. 1848, 12 July 1850, 10, 17 May 1852, 13, 26 Sept. 1855.
20. Ibid, 19 Apr. 1856.

also moved his headquarters from Ballymena to Belfast.[21] Following the 1864 riots the permanent constabulary force was increased to seventy-one men and officers.[22] By 1865 the constabulary and the 160 men of the municipal force were responsible for policing a town of approximately 130,000 inhabitants.[23]

'BULKY' RESPONSES TO BELFASTS'S GROWTH: PLAIN-CLOTHES AND DETECTIVE POLICEMEN

The task of dealing with the types of crime described in the previous chapter mainly fell on the shoulders of the Belfast municipal police. In this task the force relied primarily on the preventive beat or patrol, the standard anti-crime procedure adopted by nineteenth-century Irish and British police forces. The main *raison d'être* of the night force was the prevention of burglaries;[24] while this was also a function of the day police, a large part of their activity also involved enforcing the various town bye-laws. The period saw no change in the basic 'philosophy' on the part of the Belfast police—this continued to be the 'prevention and detection of crime'. There were, however, a number of changes introduced to the way in which the municipal force went about its crime-fighting role. The establishment of a day police (despite the police board's having no statutory authority to do this) can be viewed as one important instance of the Belfast force's adapting to Belfast's changing circumstances.[25] To increase the force's efficiency in preventing and detecting offences, in July 1838 the police authorities began a policy of retaining watchmen on their respective beats on a permanent basis[26] (before this the men served on different beats each night). This was obviously designed to improve the men's knowledge of the residents on their beat. Thereafter watchmen always served on the same beat, with each beat consisting of several streets. The street in which a policeman resided was never included in his beat. Men were removed to another beat only if civilians complained of their inefficiency or incivility, or if they neglected their duty.[27]

21. *1857 riots inquiry*, p.49; *Ulsterman*, 20 July, 4 Sept. 1857.

22. *B.N.L.*, 14 Mar. 1865.

23. *1864 Belfast borough inquiry*, p.357.

24. Ibid, pp.83, 91, 258.

25. See above, pp.24–26.

26. Belfast police commissioners' minutes, 26 July 1838.

27. *N.W.*, 4 Sept. 1838; Belfast police commissioners' minutes, 29 July 1840; Town council committee on police affairs minutes, 6 Jan. 1847; *B.N.L.*, 14 Sept. 1857.

Another feature of police procedure which was developed over time was the use of plain clothes on duty. The force was authorised to wear plain clothes on duty for the first time in January 1833. The day constables were allowed to perform plain-clothes duty until 11 a.m., while the night men could wear them in the evenings 'after dark' until 10 p.m., after which time they had to revert to the 'town livery'.[28] In December 1836 day constables were allowed wear plain clothes to catch people who broke the police acts by driving carts upon the footpaths, not sweeping their pavements on time, or by 'furious driving'.[29] Plain-clothes work gradually became a regular feature of police duty. The *Northern Whig* in December 1839 records a good example of how plain-clothesmen were employed by the Belfast police authorities. Following a spate of robberies from farmers' carts leaving Belfast while their drivers were drunk, six policemen—three of the Irish Constabulary and three of the municipal police—dressed in 'coloured clothes' (the police description of plain clothes) to try and catch the people responsible for the robberies. Two of the police, feigning drunkenness, drove carts from George's Lane along Carrick Hill to Millfield; two others pretended to be asleep in the carts, while two policemen followed the carts at a distance. Four thieves eventually took the bait. One of the 'sleeping' policemen, Day Constable John Campbell, had his handkerchief and trousers stolen in the operation, but the four culprits were caught in the chase after the robbery.[30] In another instance of police use of plain clothes, some thirty members of the municipal force were sent on plain-clothes duty to a bazaar and fete on Queen's Island in September 1851 to catch pickpockets.[31] In 1857 seventeen policemen were especially supplied with plain clothes by the town council. They performed a wide variety of duties, ranging from reporting on 'nuisances', catching shoplifters and arresting vagrants to preventing boys from letting off fireworks for fear that they might spark off riots and watching for pickpockets 'and other bad characters' in the markets. They and their uniformed counterparts from the early 1850s were also ordered to arrest known thieves found at large in the streets 'under circumstances sufficient to warrant the presumption that they are about to commit felonies'.[32]

28. Belfast police committee minutes, 15 Jan. 1833.
29. Ibid, 27 Dec. 1836.
30. *N.W.*, 24 Dec. 1839.
31. *B.N.L.*, 8 Sept. 1851.
32. Ibid, 6 June 1851, 18 Dec. 1858, 2 Dec. 1861, 17 Dec. 1864; Town council committee on police affairs minutes, 29 May 1855, 24 Mar. 1857; *B.D.M.*, 17 Oct., 13 Dec. 1859.

Full-time detectives were not employed until the mid-1840s. The introduction of detectives should be seen as another important innovatory approach by the Belfast force to tackling Belfast's increasing crime. The first mention of detective police in the police minutes relates to an incident in May 1845, which means that the Belfast police were at the most only half a year behind the D.M.P. in using detectives. In June 1846 Detective John Kane was rewarded with about £46 for apprehending John Anderson after he absconded from his employers with a 'considerable' amount of money.[33] Two full-time detectives were appointed in 1852, and from the middle of the 1850s onwards there were three full-time detectives in the municipal force.[34] Their numbers were occasionally augmented by detectives from the Dublin and Glasgow police, as for instance when policing the Royal Agricultural Show in August 1861.[35] The detectives' pay was considerably higher than that of all other members of the force, with the exception of the superintendent and the chief constables: from May 1853 their wages were increased from £1 a week to £1 5s. a week (£65 a year).[36] The detectives' main role was to trace offenders rather than to prevent crime, which latter task was the main duty of the uniformed police patrols. A particularly important activity of detectives was tracing stolen property, which involved frequent visits to pawnbroker shops, marine stores and second-hand goods shops, as these were used as outlets by burglars, thieves and prostitutes. They also routinely searched premises in Hudson's Entry and other infamous localities. The public viewed the detectives' role as a useful if unsavoury one, given the type of character with whom they often had to deal. One critic in 1856 alleged that detectives had 'intemperate habits, which they were obliged to learn when associating with thieves from whom they received information'.[37] Their alleged fondness for drink does not appear to have affected their ability as detectives, however. Towards the end of the period it was felt that Belfast, despite its small detective department, had a comparatively high rate of recovery of stolen property and detections in burglaries.[38] The use of the telegraph in the last years of the period also proved

33.   Town council committee on police affairs minutes, 24 June 1846.
34.   Ibid, 5 Oct. 1852, 24 Nov. 1859; *The Belfast and province of Ulster directory for 1856. Vol. III* (Belfast, 1856), p. 407; *B.N.L.*, 14 May 1858.
35.   Town council committee on police affairs minutes, 18 July 1861.
36.   Ibid, 24 May 1853.
37.   *B.N.L.*, 2 Apr. 1856.
38.   Ibid, 14 May 1858, 5 Jan. 1861.

invaluable to the detectives in catching suspects from other parts of Ireland or from Britain arriving in Belfast by rail or ship, or fleeing the town to enter other parts of the kingdom.[39]

Summing up, then, we can see that the municipal police responded gradually to the exigencies posed by Belfast's rapid population expansion and resultant growth in crime by adopting a number of specialised approaches to fighting crime. Introducing plain-clothes and detective police was clearly a response to the growing crime problem. It would, however, be a mistake to view these innovations as signs that the Belfast police gradually adopted a 'modern' approach to policing that was absent in the early days of the force. The plain-clothes and detective police were simply innovatory additions to a uniformed, patrolling force which already had the 'prevention and detection of crime' as its goal. The period 1816–1865 saw some changes in method, but none in the basic 'philosophy' of the Belfast force.

39. *B.D.M.*, 30 June 1859; *B.N.L.*, 14 May 1860, 5 Jan., 26 Mar., 27 Apr. 1861, 16 Sept. 1862.

CHAPTER SEVEN

The police and the public

INTRODUCTION

THE RELATIONSHIP BETWEEN the Belfast police and the Belfast public was shaped by many factors, including the force's efficiency in tackling crime, its role in preventing riots and disorder in the streets, its intervention in numerous aspects of Belfast's social life and, of course, the increasing sectarian tensions in the town down to 1865.[1] We have already seen that in the 1820s there were many complaints about the inefficiency of the new force. Indeed in January 1821 the *Belfast Newsletter* advised that Belfast's shopkeepers should form their own association for the prosecution of shoplifters, as the 'depredators' were operating almost with impunity.[2] A hostile observer some four years later commented that 'Our own constables might do some good, in going about the town, putting the commissioners' orders in execution, but they prefer lounging about the police office eating cockles'.[3] Complaints about the inefficiency of the force continued over the following decades but by the late 1850s the propertied classes, to judge from newspaper comments, were reasonably satisfied by the force's handling of crime. Undoubtedly the work of the detectives was partly responsible for this favourable view. The magistracy, town council and the Irish Constabulary serving in Belfast similarly felt that the municipal police were effective when it came to tackling ordinary crime.[4]

However, the people who judged the police on their crime prevention and detection abilities alone represented only one section of Belfast's population. It is probably accurate to say that it was the propertied classes who worried most about burglars, shoplifters and pickpockets and police activities against them. The opinions of many other inhabitants towards the force were often formed as a result of being on the receiving end of unwanted police attention.

---

1. The topic of the Belfast police and sectarianism is discussed in chapter 8.
2. *B.N.L.*, 19 Jan. 1821.
3. Letter from 'B.B.T.' in *N.W.*, 16 June 1825.
4. *1857 riots inquiry*, p.29; *1864 Belfast borough inquiry*, pp.64, 83, 136, 259, 275.

For example, the numerous people who were brought before the magistrates and fined for not having their footpaths swept within the specified hours[5] are unlikely to have had a high regard for attention shown to that particular duty by prosecuting policemen. This chapter gives a detailed examination of how various groups responded to the municipal force's policing of their activities. It has already been shown above that 'the general enforcement of good order' was one of the main duties of the Belfast police.[6] This, of course, did not merely mean the prevention and detection of crimes against property, but also involved imposing decorous behaviour on Belfast's lower class. This was a familiar duty to police forces in the rest of Ireland and in Britain.[7]

CARMEN

One group who did not wholeheartedly appreciate the force's regulatory activity were Belfast's carmen and assorted cart drivers. These were most likely to receive unfavourable attention from the police when they drove carelessly or on the incorrect side of the road or, most commonly, when they were guilty of 'furious driving'. As early as September 1816 the *Belfast Commercial Chronicle*, exasperated by carmen's ignoring the rules of the road, published a rhyme for their enlightenment:

The rule of the road is a paradox quite,
While riding or driving along,
If you keep to the left, you are sure to go right,
If you go to the right, you go wrong.[8]

5. Belfast police commissioners' minutes, 4 Dec. 1822, 20 Feb. 1839, 20 Jan. 1841; *B.N.L.*, 23 Jan. 1824, 15 Jan. 1828, 15 Dec. 1852, 21 Jan. 1861; Belfast police committee minutes, 8 Dec. 1829, 1 Jan. 1833, 12 Jan. 1836; *1856 police instructions*, p.24.

6. See above, p.24.

7. R.D. Storch, 'The plague of the blue locusts: police reform and popular resistance in northern England, 1840–57' in *International Review of Social History*, xx, part I (1975), 61–90 and idem, 'The policeman as domestic missionary: urban discipline and popular culture in northern England, 1850–1880' in *Journal of Social History*, ix (1976), 481–509.

8. *Belfast Commercial Chronicle*, 2 Sept. 1816. As late as October 1863 the police authorities printed 5,000 handbills warning carmen and carters about driving in the middle or on the right hand side of the road: Town council committee on police affairs minutes, 15 Oct. 1863.

Furious driving, especially by drunken carmen, was a recurring problem in Belfast's streets throughout the period.[9] Even if carmen drove on the correct side of the road at a leisurely pace they were still subject to police scrutiny as the force checked that they were duly licensed, that names and numbers were on their vehicles, that they were sober, honest and clean, and that they plied for hire at the authorised locations. The Irish Constabulary stationed in Belfast were given similar powers of supervision under the terms of the 1845 Belfast Improvement Act.[10] Carmen often showed their distaste at police interference by using insulting or threatening language towards policemen or by assaulting them.[11] Bernard Hughes, a member of the town council's police committee in 1857, claimed that there was 'a bad feeling' between carmen and policemen who enforced the council's car regulations and brought them before the committee to be fined. According to Hughes, 'they would not wish a greater delight than to get those police committee men into their cars, and they would drive them three times as far as they wanted [to go], and would be willing to break a spring, if they by so doing could break their necks'.[12] In 1860 many carmen felt that they were subject to 'scorn, abuse and tyranny' from the police and that they were fined 'on the most trivial pretences'. They adopted the strategy of clubbing together to pay the fines imposed on colleagues hauled before the courts for infractions of the town council's regulations.[13]

PUBLICANS AND DRINKERS

The town's drinkers and publicans were another group who regarded the municipal force with a jaundiced eye, for obvious reasons.[14]

9. *Irishman*, 2 July 1821; Belfast police commissioners' minutes, 4 Dec. 1822, 28 Oct. 1835, 1 Dec. 1841; *N.W.*, 26 Oct. 1829; *B.N.L.*, 25 Apr. 1848, 21 June 1852, 9 May 1853, 29 July 1856, 11 Oct. 1861.

10. Belfast police commissioners' minutes, 13 Jan. 1819, 29 Mar. 1826; *N.W.*, 26 Apr. 1830; *B.N.L.*, 4 Feb., 5 Sept. 1848; *Borough of Belfast. Laws and bye-laws for better regulating coaches, carriages, chariots, landaus, landaulets, cabriolets, sociables, flys, jaunting-cars, gigs, cabs, and other such like carriages, plying for hire, and the owners and drivers thereof* (Belfast, 1850), pp.12, 34; Act for the improvement of the borough of Belfast (8 & 9 Vict, c.142).

11. For some examples see *B.N.L.*, 25 May 1853, 18 May, 30 July 1857, 7 Aug. 1863; *Ulsterman*, 6 July 1857; Town council committee on police affairs minutes, 28 Oct. 1858, 9 June 1859.

12. *1857 riots inquiry*, p.240.

13. *B.N.L.*, 17 Mar., 15 Aug. 1860.

14. The D.M.P. also found themselves to be the object of scorn from Dublin's

Drunks' resentment stemmed partly from the fact that most of them could not afford the fines imposed on them by the magistrates and thus they ended up in jail, usually for from two weeks to a month, in default.[15] Many publicans resented what they considered an over-officious enforcement of the licensing acts by the Belfast police. The publicans were warned as early as November 1816 that the laws regulating drinking hours would be strictly enforced, and that drinkers would be cleared from public houses and 'dram shops' when they were found on the premises after authorized hours.[16] The police board was particularly concerned with unruly public houses, which promoted 'drunkenness and debauchery'; their owners were threatened with loss of their licence if they did not conduct their businesses in a more seemly manner. From September 1836 special patrols were sent to check on the public houses on Saturday nights, in an effort to curb illegal early-hours drinking on Sunday mornings.[17] While the municipal force carried out the surveillance of public houses, from 1836 it was the constabulary sub-inspector who had the task of opposing or approving the renewal of publicans' licences, based on the advice of the Belfast police.[18] There was a total of 554 public houses in the borough district in 1847, and in the entire built-up area there were an estimated 800 establishments.[19] By 1853 the total had risen to 889, but in April of that year the municipal authorities launched what turned out to be a three-year campaign to reduce the number of public houses in the town. The impetus behind this move came from the vociferous temperance lobby. At a vestry meeting at St Anne's church Arthur Hill Thornton, one of the churchwardens, pointed out the need for twenty overseers of public houses. These had been authorized by acts of parliament,[20] and some had been appointed in the 1830s, but they had had a short-lived existence.[21] Thornton appealed for the re-introduction of overseers as Belfast was 'competing with Glasgow in the race of

drinkers. See Brian Griffin, '"Such varmint": the Dublin police and the public, 1838–1913' in *Irish Studies Review*, xiii (1995–96), 21–25.

15. *B.N.L.*, 16 Sept., 13 Dec. 1860.
16. Ibid, 8 Nov. 1816.
17. Belfast police commissioners' minutes, 22 Mar. 1820; Belfast police committee minutes, 1 Apr. 1820, 18 Oct. 1831, 6 Sept. 1836.
18. *N.W.*, 27 Nov. 1838; *B.N.L.*, 19 Oct. 1853, 13 Sept. 1855, 2 Oct. 1856, 25 Sept. 1857, 15 Sept. 1863.
19. *Belfast People's Magazine* (Nov. 1847), p.266.
20. 3 & 4 Will IV, c.68 and 6 & 7 Will IV, c.68.
21. *N.W.*, 17 Nov. 1838.

demoralization'. He painted a lurid picture of Belfast's numerous public houses:

Numbers of them are never closed, day or night, during the whole year, particularly from Saturday night till Monday morning. The very worst and most degraded characters of the human race—men, women, and children —are allowed to remain together night and day. As it may well be imagined, all sorts of obscenity, wickedness, and lewdness, and other crimes that nature must shudder at the bare idea of, are practised. Not satisfied with this, they are in the habit of sallying forth in the streets, where they will continue to brawl both day and night, particularly from Saturday till Monday.[22]

In April 1853 a number of magistrate-appointed overseers, led by Thornton, began to visit the public houses on Saturday nights and Sunday mornings and evenings to check that the owners were obeying the legal opening hours. The municipal police were ordered to escort and protect the overseers on their rounds.[23]

By November 1854 the campaign to reduce the number of public houses had resulted in a noticeable decrease to 726 premises, approximately one to every nineteen houses. There was a considerable concentration of licensed premises in North Queen Street, Barrack Street and Smithfield. Reverend William Johnston, a leading temperance advocate, claimed that 'in those localities where the greatest number of these shops prevailed … the largest amount of misery and vice was to be found'.[24] The heightened offensive against irregularly-conducted public houses had a number of results. Firstly, in the short term it gave rise to a number of 'low and illegal retail shops' which supplied thirsty drinkers both before and after the legal hours kept by the closely-watched public houses.[25] Secondly, it prompted many harassed publicans to hire look-outs to warn of the approach of policemen, who were now regarded as 'the enemy'.[26] Most importantly, the police role in protecting the hated overseers inevitably meant that the force came in for its share of the public's odium. The overseers were extremely unpopular—even one resident magistrate considered that they were informers—and but for their police protectors they would have got short shrift from enraged

22. *Ulsterman*, 30 Mar. 1853.
23. Town council committee on police affairs minutes, 19 Apr., 3, 31 May 1853; *B.N.L.*, 25 Apr., 4 May 1853.
24. *B.N.L.*, 1 Nov. 1854.
25. Ibid, 18 May 1853.
26. Ibid, 24 Oct., 23 Dec. 1853; Whiteside, 'Captain Shaw', p.18.

Belfast publicans and drinkers. The overseer scheme was eventually scrapped in 1855 because of the bad feelings which it engendered amongst the lower classes, although the police continued their screening of licensed premises.[27] The redundant overseers were not overly impressed with the results. Arthur Hill Thornton claimed in June 1856 that an eleven-hour walk through the town uncovered as many as 288 publicans selling outside of legal hours. Whatever the accuracy of this claim—one solicitor suggested that Thornton made up the figure in an effort to have the overseers restored—the police crackdown on 'bad places' meant that by June 1857 there were only around 650 licensed premises in the town. The total would have been even smaller but for the fact that Belfast publicans hired as many as three solicitors to defend them in court, and their 'badgering' frequently frustrated constables' prosecutions.[28] Towards the end of the period the municipal police were relieved of the duty of visiting public houses to check for after-hours drinkers when, following legal advice from the law officers in Dublin Castle in 1860, it was decided that the 1845 Belfast Improvement Act gave this power to the Irish Constabulary alone. The Belfast force could enter only in very limited circumstances after legal hours.[29]

POPULAR PASTIMES: CHILDREN'S GAMES AND ADULT CELEBRATIONS

The police supervision of the drink trade was only one aspect of their wide-ranging intervention in the social life of Belfast. Both the police board and the town council were concerned to impose order on the town's streets. This order extended not merely to paving footpaths, lighting and naming streets and collecting refuse, but to regulating the conduct of the town's inhabitants and suppressing the more unruly aspects of their behaviour. Unseemly pastimes were especially frowned upon, and police efforts at imposing social control earned them the opprobrium of Belfast's lower classes. Even relatively innocuous activity such as boys playing with hoops on the street was deemed an 'annoyance' worthy of police attention.[30] Children were also frequently arrested for playing cards, pitch and toss (sometimes for money, sometimes for buttons),

27. *B.N.L.*, 8 June, 9 Sept., 9, 28 Dec. 1853, 1 Sept. 1854, 14 Feb., 2, 9 Mar., 1, 13 June, 3 Aug. 1855.
28. Ibid, 18 June, 2 Oct. 1856, 30 June 1857.
29. Ibid, 17 Aug., 28 Sept. 1860, 30 Mar. 1861.
30. Belfast police commissioners' minutes, 26 May 1821.

football, shinty or hurling in the streets, or for throwing snowballs and making slides in winter.[31] The popular sport of bullets or road bowls was another activity which the Belfast police were expected to suppress, especially on the outskirts of the town.[32] In the early 1820s the authorities were particularly determined to suppress Sunday drinking and to arrest hurlers, footballers and wrestlers on that day as 'the profanation of the Sabbath has become habitual in this town and its vicinity'.[33] The police also tried to stop people who indulged in such excessively exuberant behaviour as firing pistols in the air on St Patrick's Day, July 12th and especially on Christmas Day.[34] In the 1850s and 1860s the practice of burning tar barrels to celebrate weddings seems to have been a popular activity in Belfast, and it too came in for a share of police suppression.[35]

POPULAR PASTIMES: BLOOD SPORTS

Reverend A. McIntyre wrote in his diary in October 1854 that 'if a low singing-room, theatre, or any exhibition of buffoonery is to take place, a constable takes his stand at the door, as a matter of course'.[36] The diary extract gives us a good idea of the routine surveillance of popular pastimes undertaken by the municipal police. From an early date the force took action against a pastime which was very popular in Belfast, that of blood sports involving cruelty to animals. Thomas McTear, born in Belfast in 1800, recalled that in the early years of the nineteenth century cock fights were 'very frequent, and were attended by gentlemen of the town, as well as by poorer people: and no one had any idea that either bull-baiting or cock-fighting was anything else than a most proper and gentlemanly amusement'. The Point Fields, between York Street and the Lagan, was a popular rendezvous for cock fights, dog fights, bull-baiting and prize fights. Baiting badgers with terriers was another popular

31. For some examples see *B.N.L.*, 15 Oct. 1816, 10 Apr. 1821, 13 July, 7 Sept. 1853, 4 May, 12 June 1856, 3 Feb., 23 Apr., 2 June 1857, 21 Dec. 1860, 12 Dec., 28 Oct. 1861, 24 Dec. 1862, 14, 20, 21 Feb., 25 May, 2, 12, 15 June 1865; *N.W.*, 7 Feb. 1837, 10 Mar. 1858; *B.D.M.*, 16 Mar. 1859.

32. *B.N.L.*, 3 Sept. 1816, 1 July 1825, 16 June 1851, 7 Aug. 1857, 18 May 1858.

33. Ibid, 20 Apr. 1821.

34. Ibid, 21 Mar. 1820, 25 Mar. 1834, 26 Dec. 1851, 13 July, 28 Dec. 1853, 27 Dec. 1854, 8, 14 Jan., 27 Dec. 1855, 28, 29 Dec. 1857, 27 Dec. 1861, 27 Dec. 1862; *N.W.*, 15 July 1824.

35. *B.N.L.*, 24 Aug. 1853, 21 Mar. 1858, 11 Jan. 1865, 15 Feb. 1865.

36. Diary of Revd A. McIntyre, 15 Oct. 1854 (PRONI, D.1558/2/3).

Belfast pastime.[37] The first recorded action against blood sports was the suppression in June 1825 of a Berry Street cock pit.[38] Blood sports, however, retained a popular following. Cock and dog fights were reported to be especially popular around Easter in the fields near Belfast.[39] In September 1841 the Belfast branch of the Society for the Prevention of Cruelty to Animals (S.P.C.A.) requested the police commissioners to authorize Day Constable James Watt to devote his time to implementing the anti-cruelty policies of the organization. The appointment was sanctioned. Watt continued to wear the uniform of the Belfast police and to be subject to the same regulations as the other constables, but the S.P.C.A. paid his wages. In 1857 there were two constables wearing Belfast police uniform and concentrating on stamping out cruelty to animals, which led to a noticeable rise in convictions.[40]

Despite the vigilance of the police force in general and of the S.P.C.A.–paid men in particular cock and dog fights remained a popular if secretive form of lower class amusement. Once the authorities set their faces against blood sports the wealthier sections of Belfast society seem to have lost their taste for them. In September 1847 the *Belfast People's Magazine* claimed that cockfighting was 'almost exclusively confined to the very dregs of society'.[41] Badger baiting does not appear to have held its appeal among the lower classes, although it did not vanish entirely. As late as March 1863 an ex-member of the municipal police and a partner hired a badger for dog fights for 2d. per fight. The police found it impossible to convict the pair as their erstwhile colleague saw through whatever disguise they wore when they went to his partner's house.[42] The exertions of the police did, however, force blood-sports enthusiasts to indulge in their pastimes in secrecy, and even to leave Belfast for the purpose of enjoying their sport. For example, on 17 April 1856 thirty car loads of enthusiasts left the town to hold a dog fight in Carrickfergus. In 1861 the S.P.C.A.'s honorary secretary stated that

37. *B.N.L.*, 20 Sept. 1822; Thomas McTear, 'Personal recollections of the beginning of the century' in *Ulster Journal of Archaeology*, v (Feb. 1899), 70; Gaffikin, *Belfast 50 years ago*, pp.7, 25.

38. Monaghan, 'Belfast 1801–1825', p.489.

39. *N.W.*, 30 Mar. 1839; *B.N.L.*, 18 Apr. 1840, 27 Apr. 1849.

40. Belfast police commissioners' minutes, 22 Sept. 1841; *1857 riots inquiry*, p.41; *B.N.L.*, 5 Dec. 1857, 5 Aug. 1861; *N.W.*, 12 Feb. 1858.

41. *N.W.*, 3, 10 Jan. 1843; *Belfast People's Magazine* (Sept. 1847), p.198; *B.N.L.*, 4 June 1852, 10 Aug. 1853, 11 Apr. 1855, 15 Oct. 1856, 4 Feb. 1857, 8 Mar. 1860, 30 July 1863.

42. *B.N.L.*, 25 Mar. 1863.

cock and dog fights were held 'in some obscure and carefully-concealed locality, and even this [is] not so hidden but that a sudden termination is generally put to the proceedings by the appearance of the police'.[43] The enthusiasts are unlikely to have held a high opinion of a force which placed such difficulties in the way of their amusement. Nor would they have been endeared by the tone of moral indignation used by the S.P.C.A. to describe their activities. As with the English S.P.C.A., Belfast's anti-cruelty society consisted to a large extent of evangelical clergymen and other individuals who viewed the lower classes with both contempt and fear. The campaign against their unruly pastimes had the ultimate aim of transforming their manners. Blood sports were viewed not merely as exercises in cruelty but also as activities which could potentially lead their practitioners into more dangerous acts against the social order.[44] Belfast S.P.C.A. activists often condemned blood sports in language which voiced their fears of more serious mischief: Reverend D. Hamilton in April 1848 considered dog and cock fighting as 'two especial engines of Satan'.[45] Eight years later Sir Robert Bateson addressed the annual meeting of the Belfast society in the following terms:

the youngest children indulged in cruelty to animals, and progressed until they expiated the greatest crime on the gallows. How often did they read in the papers of the most barbarous and savage cruelties? Every week it was reported that a husband had half murdered his wife, if he did not kill her outright. A mother had murdered her child not long ago on account of what she might receive from the burial club. Drunkenness prevailed to a great extent in this town and neighbourhood, and well might it be said to have its origin, to a great extent, in the vicious practices of cruelty in youth.[46]

The 1859 annual meeting was told by its chairman, John Clarke, JP, that cock and dog fighting were 'an evil not only to the animals engaged, but also one that was productive of the greatest moral mischief to those who encouraged and promoted such sports— productive of cruelty, dissipation, drunkenness, and rioting of every description'.[47] The S.P.C.A.'s rhetoric undoubtedly struck a

43. Ibid, 30 Apr. 1856, 13 Feb. 1861.
44. For more on this topic see Harriet Ritvo, *The animal estate: the English and other creatures in the Victorian age* (London, 1990), pp.130–35.
45. *B.N.L.*, 14 Apr. 1848.
46. Ibid, 15 Feb. 1856.
47. *B.D.M.*, 1 Mar. 1859.

receptive chord with the municipal authorities, concerned as they already were with the disruptive behaviour of the town's lower orders.

Organized blood sports were only one example of the cruelty practised on animals by the Belfast public in this period. Most of the people who were brought before the courts by the police for cruelty were carmen and carters who drove animals with welts or ulcers on their backs, or who overloaded their animals. They were also condemned by the S.P.C.A., but it is unlikely that public opinion shared their view that such treatment was unacceptable. There was a considerable tolerance level for abuse of work animals, and the Belfast police are unlikely to have increased their popularity with the lower class by arresting carmen who overworked their horses. When the *Northern Whig* in October 1829 referred to 'the daily acts of brutality exercised towards horses in every one of our streets'[48] it merely underlined the fact that a certain amount of mistreatment of animals was accepted as inevitable. The *Belfast Newsletter* recognised this in its article on cruelty to animals in March 1853, when it stated that 'Few, in these busy days, will devote their time and go the trouble of deposing on oath to what [cruelty] they must often witness in the streets'.[49] Commenting on a case in October 1860, in which a group of boys from the York Street area suspended a cat from a clothes line for an hour and stoned it to death, 'the cries of the writhing creature all the time being piteous in the extreme', the *Newsletter* asserted that such incidents were 'scarcely to be wondered at when the incessant and unnecessary use of the lash to beasts of burden in the streets—the miserable ass as well as the overworked cart horse—is remarked by every stranger as disgraceful to Belfast'.[50]

Apart from the regular mistreatment of or cruelty towards work animals there were other quite horrific instances of cruelty reported in the press. For example, in June 1851 and February 1853 there were sickening cases of dogs being killed by people dashing their brains out against a wall.[51] In May 1858 and December 1859 two men were convicted of driving a horse and a bullock, each with a broken leg, through the town.[52] In February 1858 a Belfast man killed two rats with his teeth for a 5*s*. wager. The rats' tails were fastened to a table with nails, and the gambler had to kill the rats

---

48. *N.W.*, 20 Oct. 1829.
49. *B.N.L.*, 14 Mar. 1853.
50. Ibid, 6 Oct. 1860.
51. Ibid, 16 June 1851, 14 Feb. 1853.
52. Ibid, 18 May 1858; *B.D.M.*, 3 Dec. 1858.

in less time than it took a dog to kill three rats which were turned loose on the floor. The dog won the race. The sportsman's face was bitten 'severely' by one of the hapless rats on the table.[53] Hugh Mathews was fined £1 for cruelty to a dying horse in a field near the Falls Road in October 1862. Mathews severely kicked the animal in the head to speed up its death, explaining that he was 'in a hurry for the skin'.[54] Constable Heaney spotted a woman named Bella Kane suspend a dog over a pond in Millfield by a rope tied round its neck, while William John Stewart pelted it with stones. When the dog was nearly dead they lowered it into the pond and drowned it.[55]

The previous examples were just some of the many instances of cruelty recorded in the Belfast newspapers. There is little evidence that the public felt revulsion at the suffering inflicted on animals, so one cannot say with certainty that the municipal police's crackdown on cruelty won them significant popularity with the public. There are only two occasions known to the author in which bystanders showed their abhorrence at the cruelty cases. The first occurred in July 1853 when a man was sentenced to a fine of 10s. or fourteen days in jail for 'dragging a bag full of ducks through Calendar [sic] Street, in such a manner as to excite the indignation of the passers by'. The second instance occurred some years later, in June 1862. In that month a scripture reader named John Wiley killed a boy's dog on the Shankill Road by running the prongs of a pitchfork through its eyes and disembowelling it with a knife. When Resident Magistrate William Samuel Tracy sentenced Wiley to a fine of £5 or three months in prison, as well as £1 10s. compensation to the boy or an additional one month's imprisonment, his judgment 'was received with evident approbation by a crowded court of both sexes, who had listened with horror to the details of such barbarity'.[56]

POPULAR SPORTS: PRIZE FIGHTS

Given the S.P.C.A.'s desire to reform the behaviour of Belfast's lower classes, it is not very surprising that it also included prize fighting on its list of cruel and degrading activities.[57] Although prize

53. *N.W.*, 20 Feb. 1858.
54. *B.N.L.*, 11 Oct. 1862.
55. Ibid, 27 Aug. 1863.
56. Ibid, 20 July 1853, 21 June 1862.
57. Ibid, 18 May 1860.

fighting was only a minor spectator activity in Belfast when compared to cock or dog fighting, it was still subject to similar pressure from the police. In February 1851 a prize fight for a purse of £100 between Hugh McVeigh, a drunken labourer, and Peter Doran had to be held at Carrickfergus Common to evade the attentions of the police. The fight stirred up considerable interest in Belfast, to judge from the numerous broadsheet-hawkers who sold ballads commemorating the bout, which Doran won in thirteen rounds.[58] In May 1859 McVeigh was involved in another prize fight with Peter McCann, a foundry worker. The contest, disguised as a foot race, was held at Appletree, near Ballymena, again to foil police efforts at suppression. Some 200 Belfast spectators went by special train to witness the bout, which lasted for sixty-seven rounds. McCann won the fight, knocking down McVeigh, who was blinded for the last twelve rounds from blows to his eyes, no less than sixty times. The pair were afterwards guests of honour at a ball held in the Nelson Rooms, an indication of the interest that the fight aroused among the Belfast public.[59] The police suppression of prize fights was simply an extension of its activity in stamping out 'riots' or disorderly congregations and petty brawls on Belfast's streets.[60]

PUBLIC RESENTMENT OF THE POLICE

One result of the police force's intervention in lower class activity such as drinking and various other leisure pursuits was a hostility based on the belief that the force was unduly active in working-class areas. This was expressed well by a resident of Corporation Street in August 1854, when he claimed that 'truly the constables of our town often make a bad use of their power, not as regards persons of influence, to whom they are always the most sneaking and fawning of creatures, but to the lower classes they generally act in the most malevolent manner'.[61] Plebeian hostility towards the police often took the form of assaults on constables. Most of the examples for which we have details come from the 1850s and 1860s, but we can infer that police assaults were also a serious problem earlier from the fact that in February 1839 the police

58. Ibid, 26 Feb. 1851.
59. *B.D.M.*, 1, 13, 17 June 1858.
60. Belfast police committee minutes, 11 Oct. 1831, 5, 12 Mar. 1833, 22 Apr. 1834, 23 June 1835; Belfast police commissioners' minutes, 11 May, 5 Dec. 1838.
61. *B.D.M.*, 30 Aug. 1854.

committee ordered uniforms made in England which were 'extra milled expressly for police purposes'. The committee were unable to procure material in the Belfast market 'sufficiently strong to resist the wear and tear, and violent attacks to which the men are exposed'.[62] Superintendent Shaw claimed in August 1861 that the Belfast force had been subjected to serious assaults 'from time immemorial'.[63] In August 1833 the police committee pointed out that areas which were dimly or inadequately lit by street lamps were insecure for watchmen. North Street was one of the districts where it was unsafe for the police to venture at night in the early period— one watchman in January 1833 refused to pursue a man who had robbed a woman of her shawl and some money into North Street for fear that he would 'get his brains knocked out'.[64]

It is possible to give a comprehensive account of the physical dangers faced by the Belfast police only for the 1850s and 1860s, given the nature of the newspaper evidence. An examination of the assaults on policemen in the ten years from 1855 to 1864 shows that, as was the case with the R.I.C. and D.M.P., by far the single most common source of physical attack on policemen was the drunk and disorderly prisoner.[65] In each year most assaults occurred either before or shortly after taking drunks into custody.[66] The next most common recorded reason for assaults on the police, that of their intervention in family disputes, accounted for about only one tenth of the total caused by drunk prisoners. One should not ascribe sectarian motives for these assaults. There is absolutely no evidence to suggest that a Protestant drunk was in any way more inclined to go quietly to the police office than a Catholic drunk. When two municipal constables intervened in a fight between two brothers on the Old Lodge Road in August 1853, the solicitor of one of the unruly men complained that his client had been arrested because he had 'too much of the good old Presbyterian iron in his nature to obey the arbitrary command of a night policeman. He did not run to his own door like a whipped dog at the orders of this mighty official'.[67] The fact that plebeian hostility towards the police

---

62. Transmiss from police committee in Belfast police commissioners' minutes, 13 Feb. 1839.

63. *B.N.L.*, 20 Aug. 1861.

64. *N.W.*, 24 Jan. 1833; Belfast police committee minutes, 13 Aug. 1833.

65. Griffin, 'Irish police,' pp.187–89.

66. For statements on the particular fondness of Belfast drunks for assaulting policemen see *B.N.L.*, 6 June 1851, 30 Mar. 1853, 21 Apr. 1854.

67. *B.N.L.*, 19 Aug. 1853.

Table 2. *Assaults on Belfast Policemen, 1855–1864*

Year	No.	*Committed by drunk/ disorderly prisoners*	*Committed after intervention in family disputes*
1855	89	50 (56.2%)	6 (6.7%)
1856	123	76 (61.8%)	15 (12.2%)
1857	115	71 (61.7%)	6 (5.2%)
1858	211	124 (58.8%)	16 (7.6%)
1859	164	101 (61.6%)	10 (6.1%)
1860	190	131 (68.9%)	12 (6.3%)
1861	145	110 (75.9%)	6 (4.1%)
1862	143	98 (68.5%)	7 (4.9%)
1863	148	100 (67.6%)	7 (4.7%)
1864	234	181 (77.4%)	13 (5.6%)
Total	1,562	1,042 (66.7%)	98 (6.3%)

Source: Belfast Newsletter, 1855–1858, 1860–1864; *Belfast Daily Mercury*, 1859. (The assaults upon the police during the communal riots of July and September 1857 and August 1864 are not included).

crossed the sectarian divide can be gauged by the statement of a solicitor in December 1856 that it was 'a particular taste of the lower orders of Belfast to beat the constables'.[68] Resident Magistrate J.C. O'Donnell declared in December 1864 that the municipal policemen were 'the common target of all the ill-conducted people in the town'.[69]

Some individuals were noted for their frequent attacks on policemen. These included a 'violent rough' named John Hill, 'whose hobby in his cups is to maul a constable, if he can foregather with an isolated one in a secluded region'; John Timney, described as 'the natural enemy of the blue frocks', who was 'prone to indulge in the expensive luxury of beating a constable now and again'—he had thirteen convictions for assaulting policemen by January 1858; Michael Quinn of George's Court, who 'kicked and beat' four constables 'severely' in Rosemary Street in April 1861, also had numerous police assault convictions on his record; and John Nolan, described in May 1863 as 'frequently before the court for assaulting

68. Ibid, 27 Dec. 1856.
69. Ibid, 17 Dec. 1864.

constables and women of bad character'.[70] Not all assaults on policemen were of a severely physical character, however. For example, when Constable Coburn tried in November 1854 to persuade drunken John Walker to allow his wife and two children to re-enter their Vere Street home, Walker 'precipitated a chamber vessel, full of offensive matter, on the head of the constable'. The assault committed on Constable Fennessy in July 1856 consisted of Ann Matthewson, whom he arrested for disorderly conduct in Ann Street, throwing milk over him in the police office. When Constables Scott and Anderson were assaulted by drunk and disorderly prisoner James Keogh in May 1864, Constable Scott stated that Keogh 'did not strike him, but covered his face and hat with very disagreeable spittles', and agreed with Resident Magistrate Edward Orme that he would have preferred to be struck on the head than be spat upon.[71] The police authorities assigned their tallest men to the more turbulent localities, but stature alone was not sufficient to prevent violent assault. For example, the *Belfast Newsletter* stated in August 1851 that Constable Norwood, 'the giant of the local day force', was routinely put on 'quarrelsome' beats, and 'meets with an undue share of hard knocks'. Even 6' 4" tall Constable Hawkes, whose beat included Hudson's Entry, admitted in June 1851 to having a 'very tough job' in conveying two drunk and disorderly women to the police office from North Street.[72]

Historians have examined the massive riots in Belfast in 1857 and 1864,[73] but no attention has been given to those more frequent mass attacks on policemen which were neither political nor sectarian in their origin. These crowd attacks were typical symptoms of lower-class hostility towards arrests made in working-class areas. It is not suggested here that working-class districts served as 'no go' areas for the police, as obviously it would have been impossible for unarmed policemen to operate a beat system in such circumstances, but rather that the ever-present distrust towards policemen frequently manifested itself in large-scale attacks upon constables when they made arrests which were unpopular. The mere appearance of policemen in lower-class areas was not enough to spark off attacks. Sometimes the police handled drunk prisoners with

70. Ibid, 30 June 1852, 18 June 1856, 18 Jan. 1858, 27 Apr. 1861, 14 May 1863.
71. Ibid, 17 Nov. 1854, 31 July 1856, 23 May 1864.
72. Ibid, 26 June, 27 Aug. 1851, 11 June 1852.
73. Boyd, *Holy war*, passim; Jonathan Bardon, *A history of Ulster* (Belfast, 1992), pp.349–52; W.A. Maguire, *Belfast* (Keele, 1993), pp.51–52, 89–90; A.C. Hepburn, *A past apart: studies in the history of Catholic Belfast* (Belfast, 1996), pp.35–36.

excessive violence, which led to angry protests or assaults from bystanders. The police were expressly ordered to treat drunk prisoners carefully, and not to strike them unnecessarily or to use provocative language towards them, whatever their class. When constables had to use force to restrain prisoners they were warned never to strike them on the head.[74] Incidents from July and November 1852 are good examples of the type of opposition which the police often met with in working-class areas. When Constable Hawkes arrested a drunk and disorderly person in Winetavern Street on a Sunday morning in July he was instantly struck and kicked by his prisoner. The altercation attracted a crowd of around 100 people, and Hawkes and Constables Storey and McGibbon were 'pelted front and rear' with stones until they emerged from North Street. In November Constable McCrea was assaulted by David Lewis after he arrested him in North Street for drunk driving and for whipping his horse in the face. The struggling pair attracted a crowd of hundreds of people 'shouting against the constable'. According to Constable Hawkes, if police reinforcements had not arrived on the scene to rescue McCrea from the mob the beleaguered constable 'would never have stood another day on duty'.[75] These incidents do not mean that the local residents were utterly opposed to the police operating in their area, or that all arrests met with popular resistance. For instance, the North Street inhabitants cheered the four night constables who arrested spirit-level maker John Cappo for severely assaulting his wife in July 1856. The *Belfast Newsletter* stated that 'Mobs generally sympathise too strongly with the party in custody, but on this occasion they encouraged the force in the most enthusiastic manner. Had the prisoner been allowed to escape they would have likely laid violent hands upon him'.[76]

There were several instances of mass attacks on constables in the 1850s and 1860s after they had taken prisoners, which might account for the advice given to constables to be sparing in the use of their rattles as the noise often led to crowds collecting.[77] In April 1853 Constable David Duff arrested two youths in Catholic Hercules Street who were playing pitch and toss, one of whom assaulted the policeman while the other attempted a rescue. The fracas sparked

74. Belfast police commissioners' minutes, 3 Nov. 1841; Town council committee on police affairs minutes, 24 Apr. 1849; *B.N.L.*, 15 Jan. 1855, 11 May 1858, 16 Sept. 1862; *1856 police instructions*, pp.11, 33.

75. *B.N.L.*, 7 July, 19 Nov. 1852.

76. Ibid, 28 July 1856.

77. *1856 police instructions*, p.10.

off 'a furious attack of stones and brick-bats' on three policemen who came to Duff's aid.[78] A mob of over 200 people opposed the police who arrested a man for assault in Protestant Durham Street in June 1853.[79] On 9 July in the same year Constable Bingham arrested Hugh Coburn for disorderly conduct in a Union Street public house. Coburn resisted arrest which, as frequently happened, attracted 'a considerable crowd'. The prisoner, 'observing that amongst them he had awakened a sort of sympathy, immediately knocked down the constable and began to kick and abuse him most unmercifully'. Constables Lyons, Taylor and Hawkes rushed to the scene where they found 'several hundred people' assembled. They secured, and were assaulted in turn by, the prisoner, and also 'stones and brick-bats came upon them from the mob abundantly'.[80] When Constable Armstrong arrested a drunk man in September 1853 after repeatedly warning him about his disorderly behaviour it proved to be 'the signal for the general rising of the Smithfield Republic', as the *Belfast Newsletter* commented. A crowd of from 200 to 300 people assailed Armstrong and several other constables and a party of soldiers who went to his aid with stones, sticks and bricks.[81] Around 150 people attacked Constables Kennedy and Kelly who arrested a drunk and disorderly man in Donegall Street in August 1854. The court was amused by an eye-witness's account of how one of the badly assaulted constables was 'kicked in all imaginable parts of the body'.[82] In May 1855 an estimated 1,000 people opposed the attempts of two municipal constables and four soldiers to take into custody a man arrested for assaulting policemen in Smithfield.[83]

A crowd of from 200 to 300 people in the Lagan Street area stoned four constables who interfered in a family dispute there in March 1856. In another incident, when three constables arrested a disorderly soldier in McGlade's public house in Smithfield in March 1857, his appeals for a rescue led to a mob attack by about 500 to 600 people, obliging the police to take refuge in a Berry Street shop. On Christmas night in the same year numerous constables were assailed by a mob of about 200 people when attempting

78. *B.N.L.*, 18 Apr. 1853.
79. Ibid, 29 June 1853.
80. Ibid, 13 July 1853.
81. Ibid, 21 Sept. 1853.
82. *B.D.M.*, 22 Aug. 1854.
83. *B.N.L.*, 7 May 1855.

to secure a drunk and disorderly prisoner in Hill Street.[84] Two municipal constables who arrested a drunk and disorderly man at Pinkerton's Row in August of the following year were chased by an angry mob of about 300 people. They took refuge in a public house until they were rescued by constabulary from the North Queen Street barracks. Many members of the local force and of the constabulary were injured in clashes with a large crowd in Hill Street on 9 August 1861. The disturbances were sparked off by the local police arresting a number of people 'who seemed rather inclined to carry on the vary dangerous amusement of firing off squibs'. A stone-throwing mob estimated at 300 to 400 people obliged Constables Richey and Kelly to take shelter in a Little Patrick Street house after they arrested a drunk and disorderly man in August 1862. A mob of approximately 1,000 people stoned Constable Waller after he arrested a drunk and disorderly person in Henry Street on 19 June 1864.[85] There were numerous other instances of non-political crowd attacks on policemen in this period in which no estimate of crowd strength is given.[86] Justice of the Peace W.T.B. Lyons declared gloomily of the crime calendar in October 1858 that 'there was nothing but beating constables, which was not the case in any other town in Europe but Belfast'. His lament was echoed in June 1864 by Resident Magistrate Orme, who stated that 'constables were beaten night after night, and day after day' in Belfast.[87]

84. Ibid, 29 Mar. 1856, 10 Mar., 26 Dec. 1857.
85. Ibid, 18 Aug. 1858, 10, 12, 16, 17 Aug. 1861, 19 Aug. 1862, 21 June 1864.
86. Ibid, 4 May 1853, 18 Jan., 1, 25 Feb., 5 Apr., 16 Aug. 1858, 12 Apr. 1865; *N.W.*, 2 Oct. 1858; *B.D.M.*, 18 Mar. 1859.
87. *B.N.L.*, 2 Oct. 1858, 1 July 1864.

CHAPTER EIGHT

The Belfast police and the sectarian problem

ANOTHER REASON FOR the unpopularity of the police with the lower class, or at least with the Catholic portion of the lower class, was the alleged sectarian nature of the municipal force. Andrew Boyd in his study of the 1857 and 1864 sectarian riots argues that the Belfast police were disliked by Catholics because they were a biased force. He suggests a number of reasons why Catholics held this belief: the almost totally Protestant representation in all ranks, many of whom were allegedly Orangemen who participated in 12th of July processions outside Belfast; observations by 'the more liberal Protestants' of the town that the municipal police were partisan; allegations that the town police failed to arrest assailants attacking Catholics or encouraged the mobs in their bloody work.[1] Anyone familiar with the present Troubles in the North knows how rumours circulate about violent incidents and become accepted as fact. It is the aim of this chapter to try and sort out rumour from fact about the municipal force, and to assess the validity of the allegations that it was a sectarian force.

---

1. Boyd, *Holy war*, pp.13–15, 30, 54–55, 68. Boyd's book remains the best modern published account of the 1857 and 1864 riots. Readers are referred to that work for a more detailed account of these disturbances. Briefly, Boyd shows that the numerous clashes of July and September 1857 arose as a result of the inflamed Catholic and Protestant response to firebrand street preaching by Reverend Thomas Drew, grand chaplain of the Grand Orange Lodge of Ireland, and by 'Roaring' Hugh Hanna. Hanna, in particular, was greatly to blame as he insisted on giving an anti-Catholic speech despite appeals from the authorities to desist. The initial spark of the even more extensive rioting of August 1864, in which at least eight people and probably more were killed, was an attack on the Catholic Pound district by a Sandy Row mob on 10 August. The attack on the Pound was the most serious of a number of incidents since 8 August, the day on which the foundation stone of the O'Connell memorial was laid in Dublin. The ceremony in Dublin greatly irritated lower-class Belfast Protestants. The Pound attack led to widespread and bloody Protestant-Catholic clashes and battles with the police and military down to 22 August. During the 1864 riots, in addition to the municipal police force, over 1,300 troops and 1,000 members of the Irish Constabulary were deployed in the attempt to preserve order on Belfast's streets.

Probably the most useful starting-point when discussing the force's role in the 1850s and 1860s is to remind oneself that it was never intended by the police authorities that the local police should suppress communal disorder of the magnitude which occurred in July and September 1857 and August 1864. Until 1844 the night constables were armed with pikes while the day men carried truncheons only. In July 1844 the pikes were cut up and the thrifty town council supplied the night men with 'sticks' from them.[2] There is some confusion over whether these were what we would call truncheons or whether they were a type of walking stick. Down to 1861 they are usually described as oak sticks or walking sticks; one contemporary described the weapons as being similar to 'a serviceable grazier's walking stick'. It seems that the day men carried truncheons, while the night men carried these 'sticks'.[3] In 1862, following representations from the Belfast magistracy that truncheons were more useful in riots, the entire force was supplied with truncheons or batons.[4] Clearly a force thus armed was almost powerless in the face of the 1857 and 1864 rioters, many of whom were armed with firearms. It would have been foolhardy indeed for the twenty unarmed municipal policemen to attempt to arrest those armed Protestants who opened fire on the Pound Loaning on 18 July 1857, the only incident in those riots cited by Andrew Boyd where the local police did not attempt to tackle Protestants engaged in violence when they could have made an attempt to arrest them.[5] In December 1845 the mayor of Belfast and Resident Magistrate Walter Molony suggested that the force be armed with cutlasses, but this proposal was not acted upon by the town council. Similar suggestions in August 1848 and October 1864 were not followed through.[6] In August 1857 a local magistrate, Captain Thomas Verner, proposed to the town council that the Belfast police should be armed with muskets and bayonets but his suggestion was shelved, which was probably fortunate for the peace of the town as the Catholic *Ulsterman* newspaper warned that if the plan went ahead 'the humble Catholic population will, with natural distrust, arm themselves too'.[7]

---

2. Town council committee on police affairs minutes, 10 July 1844.
3. Ibid, 10 Jan. 1861; *B.N.L.*, 16 Aug. 1861; F.F. Moore, *The truth about Ulster* (London, 1914), p.20.
4. Town council committee on police affairs minutes, 13 Nov. 1862; *B.N.L.*, 15 Dec. 1862.
5. Boyd, *Holy war*, p.30.
6. Town council committee on police affairs minutes, 3 Dec. 1845, 15 Aug. 1848, 24 Oct. 1864.
7. *Ulsterman*, 3, 7 Aug. 1857.

There were two main reasons why the town authorities did not arm their police with weapons more formidable than pikes or truncheons. Firstly, in the early years there was no reason for supplying the Belfast force with firearms: murderous communal sectarian conflict was not a serious problem in Belfast before the 1830s. But more importantly the presence of an armed constabulary force from 1825 made it less necessary to arm the municipal force. The local police concentrated almost entirely on routine police duties, and were not expected to tackle violence more serious than Saturday night drunken brawls. When more serious violence erupted the civic authorities relied mainly on the armed constabulary or the military to suppress it, while the municipal police played a secondary, supporting role. The *Northern Whig* commented on the constabulary's primary function as the suppression of disorder in December 1825, in an account of the force's charging a Donegall Street mob after a fancy dress ball held at the Exchange. It felt that there were so few opportunities for the constabulary to prove its worth that the force was 'likely enough to create disturbances, which they do not find in existence, for the purpose of proving to those who have placed them in office, that there is work for them to perform: and that they are therefore not entirely useless in the situation which they occupy'.[8] One of the few occasions in which the force had to prove its utility in riot control occurred in February 1829 when the constabulary and the municipal police suppressed clashes between Protestants and Catholics in Smithfield following the funeral of an Orangeman.[9] On 20 January 1833 a Catholic funeral procession going to and returning from Friar's Bush graveyard was attacked by a Protestant mob near Sandy Row. A combined force of cavalry and constabulary dispersed the rioters.[10]

It is instructive to note that at this period the Catholic community did not look on the municipal police as a sectarian force. It was the County Constabulary which they felt was unduly favourable towards Protestants. There were probably good grounds for this belief, as before the reform of the constabulary in 1836 the Ulster constabulary was not only predominantly Protestant but many of its members were Orangemen.[11] In contrast, the Belfast police board

8. *N.W.*, 23 Dec. 1825.

9. Ibid, 19 Feb. 1829.

10. Sovereign Stephen May to Earl O'Neill, 28 Jan. 1833 (NA, C.S.O.R.P. 1833/597).

11. S.E. Baker, 'Orange and green: Belfast, 1832–1912' in H.J. Dyos and Michael Wolff (ed.), *The Victorian city: images and realities* (2 vols., London, 1973), ii, 805.

was determined to remove any taint of sectarianism from its force. In December 1828, during the investigation of a case of police cruelty towards a child, for which a constable was dismissed, the police committee discovered that the policeman had neglected his duty and attended pro-Orange Brunswick Club meetings instead. The committee determined that in future recruits had to pledge that they were not members of, and would not belong to, any political club or society while they were in the police force. In May 1831 the police were told that any policeman who quarrelled over 'party matters' would be dismissed, and in April 1835 a regulation was introduced that any policemen guilty of using 'party expressions' would also be removed from the force.[12] During the post-election riot on 22 December 1832 between the Catholic Hercules Street residents and an 'Orange body' armed with bludgeons, the arrival of the *constabulary* on the scene led to shouts of 'Here is the Protestant police' from the Tory supporters. In the mêlée the constabulary, estimated at from fifty to 100 men, opened fire on the Catholics, killing four, including two boys, and wounding several. Not surprisingly Belfast Catholics looked upon the 'Peelers' as an unsteady, partisan force. The *Northern Whig* declared that 'less bloodshed always takes place, when the regular army is engaged in quelling disturbances, than when the semi-military constables are let loose on men to whom they are, frequently, politically opposed ... They rather excite a mercurial mob to acts of violence, than tend to repress its intemperance'.[13]

The *Northern Whig*, however, also claimed that the municipal police were a sectarian force. It distrusted the police committee which, after the formation of the Tory Belfast Society, became almost totally dominated by Tory activists. In November 1837 the newspaper alleged that everybody appointed by the committee had to display 'ardour in the Tory cause'.[14] However, there is no solid evidence that the municipal police were biased against the Catholic population at this period. In fact, in July of the following year the same newspaper reported that during the 12th of July riot in Donegall Street, when the Catholic chapel and the house of Bishop Denvir were attacked, the Orange mob 'made a number of the night watch fly before them, for their lives'.[15] It is unlikely that the unarmed police would have placed their lives in danger if they were

12. Belfast police committee minutes, 23 Dec. 1828, 31 May 1831, 21 Apr. 1835; *N.W.*, 1 Jan. 1829.
13. *N.W.*, 24, 27 Dec. 1832, 10 Jan. 1833; *B.N.L.*, 28 Dec. 1832.
14. *N.W.*, 4 Nov. 1837.
15. Ibid, 14 July 1838.

as bigoted as the newspaper alleged that they were. On 19 January 1841, following a public dinner for Daniel O'Connell in the new Music Hall in Upper Arthur Street, Protestant mobs rioted in several parts of Belfast; the allegedly-biased municipal police and the reformed Irish Constabulary clashed with them.[16] Both forces also combined on 12, 14 and 15 July 1843 to suppress fights between Protestant and Catholic mobs in Peter's Hill. These were the worst disturbances in the town since July 1835, when the constabulary and military were sent to pull down arches in the rival Barrack Street and Sandy Row areas and the military killed a Protestant man and wounded two women with gunfire.[17]

How should one assess the frequently differing perceptions of the partiality of the two police forces involved against Belfast rioters? Perhaps the fairest statement to make is that in the bitterness and animosity engendered by the sectarian cockpit which Belfast was developing into from the 1830s onwards both police forces were regarded with suspicion by the disputing parties in periods of tension. The O'Connellite *Vindicator* stated of the Irish Constabulary stationed in Belfast in September 1843 that 'the majority of the present body of "green police" are little better than Orange partisans', and that all of the Belfast constables, and most of the sub-constables, were Protestants. This, however, was not enough to endear them to the Protestant lower class, who 'hate their own dear friends in the green frieze almost as religiously as they love to gulp the Boyne water or guzzle ox beef when an election brings them a God-send'.[18] In the 1850s public perceptions of the character of the two police forces had changed somewhat. There is no evidence to suggest that the denominationally-mixed Irish Constabulary were viewed as biased against either of the conflicting parties in Belfast. The case was rather different for the municipal police, however. It was frequently alleged by Catholics that the local force was sectarian, and its unpopularity with the Catholic lower classes during the 'marching season' is beyond dispute. The nicknames used to describe the force reflected the change. The force when under the police board's authority were nicknamed 'Charleys'.[19] Assaulting a watchman was known as 'slating a Charley'.[20] In the 1850s the nickname of 'Bulkies'

---

16. Ibid, 12 Jan. 1841.

17. *B.N.L.*, 14, 17 July 1835, 14, 18, 21 July 1843; John Barrow, *A tour round Ireland, through the sea-coast counties, in the autumn of 1835* (London, 1836), pp.34–35.

18. *Vindicator*, 20, 24 Sept. 1843.

19. '*Northern Athens*', p.45; *1864 Belfast borough inquiry*, p.175.

20. *N.W.*, 28 Nov. 1840.

was used more commonly than that of 'Charleys' to describe the force. The origins of the term are obscure. One suggestion is that the nickname derived from the bulky appearance of the men when they wore capes.[21] While this might explain the origin of the term, there is no doubt that the word 'Bulky' was intended as a term of abuse. In March 1855 Constable Jamison, in prosecuting a person who called him a 'Bulky', sheepishly admitted that he could not explain what the term meant. The defending solicitor caused laughter in court when he ironically suggested that it could be a term of 'endearment or adulation'.[22] Resident Magistrate James Law McCance of Newry stated in 1864 that it was a 'violent' expression, used in a similar sense to 'blackguards'.[23] Whatever its exact pejorative intent may have been, it was a widespread term of abuse towards the end of the period.[24] The nickname of 'Hornies' was also used pejoratively. Its precise meaning is also unclear, but it was not a term of abuse confined solely to Belfast. It was also used to describe members of the D.M.P. at this period.[25]

Undoubtedly one of the reasons for Catholic hostility towards the town police was its almost exclusively Protestant membership in the 1850s and 1860s. The surviving records do not enable us to state what proportion of the force was Protestant or Catholic before the 1850s, but it is possible that many of the early police were Catholics. The evidence for this is circumstantial and of a later date. One suggestive piece of evidence is the fact that the police commissioners, who were mainly Whigs in politics and thus somewhat responsive to the sensitivities of the Catholic population of Belfast, opposed the transfer of power to the Tory-dominated town council on the grounds that it could not be trusted to deal impartially with those who differed from the Tories in politics.[26] It was claimed later that because the police board had been balanced between Tories and Whigs its police appointments were free from political or sectarian bias.[27] However the recruitment records do not enable us to determine accurately the religious composition of the police membership before the late 1850s.

21. See above, p.5, n.19.
22. *N.W.*, 27 Mar. 1855.
23. *1864 Belfast borough inquiry*, p.145.
24. *B.N.L.*, 26 June 1851, 31 Dec. 1862, 28 Apr., 28 July 1864, 22 Mar. 1865; Boyd, *Holy war*, p.14.
25. *Freeman's Journal*, 22 Dec. 1843, 19 Mar. 1858, 22 Jan. 1866; *B.N.L.*, 14 Feb. 1859, 31 Aug. 1864.
26. Belfast police commissioners' minutes, 28 Apr. 1843.
27. *1864 Belfast borough inquiry*, pp.157, 224.

The earliest year for which there are reasonably precise statistics of the religious denominations of the police is 1857. In that year it was estimated that all but six or seven of the force were Protestants.[28] In 1864 only five of the 160 officers and men were Catholics, and all of the officers were Protestants.[29] Apart from their religious composition, an examination of their origins shows that they came from a similar background to the men of the D.M.P. Just as most Dublin policemen came from the counties nearest Dublin, most of the Belfast force came from the counties nearest Belfast. In 1864 some eleven members of the force were natives of Belfast, nine of whom came from the Antrim side of the Lagan; another eighty-five came from counties Antrim and Down. Fifteen men came from Tyrone, three were natives of Armagh, two came from Monaghan, and there was one person from each of Dublin, Fermanagh, Derry and King's County. The King's County native was a Catholic named Thomas Murphy who had served in the Irish Constabulary before joining the Belfast police.[30]

The social background of the Belfast men was very similar to that of the D.M.P., most of whom were small farmers' sons or agricultural labourers before they joined the Dublin force. In February 1856 a member of Belfast Town Council's police committee stated that applicants to join their force were working as gardeners or porters before their recruitment.[31] In September 1857 it was stated that many of the police were 'the sons of farmers—broken-down farmers who have become reduced in circumstances'.[32] The regulations in the 1850s stated that a recruit should be no older than twenty-eight years of age, although in certain circumstances slightly older men would be accepted (the town council had stricter requirements for qualification than the police board had, as the police board imposed an age-limit of forty years for recruits in the 1830s but sometimes appointed older men). He also had to be at least 5'9" tall, healthy, be able to read and write and be 'generally intelligent'. He was expected to be able to read a legibly-written address on a letter or parcel. He also had to produce testimonials of character from 'persons of undoubted respectability', one from his employer and two from householders, describing his behaviour

28. *1857 riots inquiry*, p.4.
29. *1864 Belfast borough inquiry*, pp.359–61.
30. Ibid.
31. *B.N.L.*, 11 Feb. 1856.
32. Ibid, 25 Sept. 1857.

for at least the five preceding years.[33] The general impression is that of young Protestant men, from poor rural backgrounds, with a modest level of education: Alderman Lindsay described the police in November 1864 as 'drafted mainly from the farming classes— men who have been brought up, perhaps, scantily enough as regards this world's comforts, but who have got good constitutions, and have got a certain amount of education without which they are unfit to perform the duties of a constable'.[34] An examination of the occupations pursued by the 160 men in the Belfast force in 1864 before their recruitment reveals clearly their plebeian origins: 116 were labourers, seventeen weavers, six farmers and six soldiers; there were two gardeners, shoemakers, porters and bleachers, and one letter carrier, car driver, nailer, gamekeeper and member of the Irish Constabulary. Two stated that they had no occupation before they joined the force.[35]

The surviving evidence enables us to look closely at the pre-police experience of only a few members of the force. One constable, a Catholic named Hugh Heaney, was a native of Larne. A labourer, he had worked in Fermanagh, Cavan and Tyrone before going to Belfast to join the police.[36] Constable William Moffatt was a native of Edenvaddy townland in Tyrone. The police returns describe him as a labourer, although he described himself as a farmer. He had spent around twelve years in Belfast before he joined the force when aged thirty-seven, in June 1856. He ran a grocery shop in Sandy Row before joining the force and for about a year afterwards, as well as keeping a number of cows whose milk he sold in his shop. In his own words, he would not have joined the police 'if I was not broken down by trust': that is, if he had not extended credit to his customers.[37] Another constable, Richard Coulter, a native of Dublin, had been in the army before joining the police force. Letters of recommendation from officers in his regiment secured his appointment.[38] William Scott, a labourer from Derriaghy, first joined the force in August 1856. He was dismissed in October 1858 for drunkenness and for threatening to assault civilians. He then joined

33. Belfast police committee minutes, 30 Jan. 1834; Belfast police commissioners' minutes, 26 July 1838; *B.N.L.*, 5 Sept. 1848; *1856 police instructions*, pp.33–34, 36–37; *1857 riots inquiry*, p.41; *1864 Belfast borough inquiry*, p.199.
34. *B.N.L.*, 18 Nov. 1864.
35. *1864 Belfast borough inquiry*, pp.359–61.
36. *1857 riots inquiry*, p.81.
37. *1864 Belfast borough inquiry*, pp.310–12.
38. Ibid, p.313.

a militia regiment; after its disbandment his officer, whom he served as a messman, procured employment for him with the Co. Antrim sheriff as a footman. During the Antrim assizes he met the police superintendent, Captain Shaw, who invited him to re-join the force.[39]

While the social and geographical origins of the police are of interest to the social historian, there is no doubt that the most important biographical feature as far as the lower classes in the 1850s were concerned was the men's religion. As the previous chapter suggests, the police would have been unpopular even had Belfast been free from sectarian animosities; Councillor Samuel Brown's observation in 1864 that the people of Sandy Row regarded the municipal force with 'suspicion' and that both the Catholic and Protestant lower classes had disliked the police even before the intensification of sectarian strife, bears this out.[40] But by the late 1840s Belfast's lower classes were highly polarised along religious lines,[41] and their attitudes towards the local police diverged during times of heightened sectarian tension. During the riots of 1857, which had their origin in the rash behaviour of certain street preachers, the municipal force continued to patrol Protestant districts but could not venture into Catholic areas without military or Irish Constabulary escorts. Catholic policemen were quietly warned by residents of the Pound that they should stay away from the area as it would be an unhealthy district for 'Bulkies' who were foolhardy enough to enter it.[42]

Why were there such differing attitudes on the part of the lower classes towards the police during the disturbances? A principal factor was the preponderance of Protestants in the police ranks. Lower-class Catholics did not distinguish between a man's being Protestant and his being an Orangeman; in their eyes the two were indistinguishable, and naturally in times of increased sectarian tension Catholic mobs assumed that the police were on the same side as their Protestant opponents.[43] It is instructive to note that in the mid- to late 1850s a similar belief existed among Dublin Protestants that the D.M.P. was a sectarian force, the 'proof'

39. Town council committee on police affairs minutes, 26 Aug. 1856, 7 Oct. 1858; *1864 Belfast borough inquiry*, pp.316–17.
40. *1864 Belfast borough inquiry*, pp.200–01.
41. Ian Budge and Cornelius O'Leary, *Belfast: approach to crisis: a study of Belfast politics 1613–1970* (London, 1973), p.77.
42. *1857 riots inquiry*, p.52.
43. *Ulsterman*, 20, 22 July 1857; *1864 Belfast borough inquiry*, pp.169, 182, 256, 306.

consisting mainly of the fact that a majority of the force were Catholics. Lurid rumours of anti-Protestant actions by the D.M.P. circulated and were believed by the more credulous of Dublin's Protestant population, and almost led to the D.M.P.'s abolition in 1858 and its replacement by the Irish Constabulary.[44] In a mirror image of Dublin Protestants' hostile perception of the D.M.P. in the 1850s, much of the basis for Belfast Catholics' opinion that the Belfast municipal force was anti-Catholic grew from the initial fact of the force's being predominantly Protestant; rumours and exaggerated or inaccurate reports of police anti-Catholic attitudes and actions helped cement this belief.

Discriminatory recruitment practices by the town council's police committee were blamed for the low Catholic representation in police ranks. It is difficult to believe committee members' claims that they were unaware of an applicant's religion when interviewing him for employment in the police. One did not have to be a professional genealogist or mind-reader to know that men named Elias Branagh, Isaac and Samuel Finlay, Absalom and Amaziah Hewitt, Moses Jamison, Isaiah Linn, Samuel McChestney, Zebulon Savage and Abel George—to choose some names of 1864 policemen—were Protestants.[45] Even if an applicant's name did not make his religion obvious his letters of recommendation, most of which were written by clergymen, should have made it apparent. The repeated assertions by committee members that they never asked a prospective recruit his religion (claims that were supported by Catholic policemen)[46] should be treated as disingenuous attempts by embarrassed councillors to deny having knowingly discriminated against Catholic applicants. The only recorded instance in which an applicant's religion was openly discussed puts the police committee in an unfavourable light. In April 1856 William Pope was appointed a supernumerary constable. Pope, a member of the Irish Constabulary, had originally been a Catholic but had converted to Presbyterianism. This proved an unpopular move with his Catholic comrades. When stationed in Newtownbreda he 'could not get any peace from the Roman Catholic sergeant over him'; he transferred to Newcastle, but 'they treated him worse there, and called him a "Souper"'. His application to join the Belfast force was a source of

44. Brian Griffin, 'Religion and opportunity in the Irish police forces, 1836–1914' in R.V. Comerford, Mary Cullen, J.R. Hill and Colm Lennon (ed.), *Religion, conflict and coexistence in Ireland: essays presented to Monsignor Patrick J. Corish* (Dublin, 1990), pp.226–31.

45. *1864 Belfast borough inquiry*, pp.359–61.

46. *B.N.L.*, 17, 19, 25 Sept. 1857; *1864 Belfast borough inquiry*, p.199.

amusement to the selection committee because of his name, but he was accepted into the force because he was 'a good Presbyterian' and had 'left the Papists'. His career was unusually brief; he resigned after just one day, considering that the duty was 'too severe'. Alderman Hamilton stated that he subsequently 'returned to his own mother church', and that he was a 'horrible wretch'.[47]

The method of police recruitment employed by the town council in the 1850s and 1860s was similar to that used by its police board predecessor. Whenever vacancies occurred, an advertisement to that effect was placed on the wall of the police office.[48] This had the effect that only people who frequented the police office were aware that positions were vacant, and in practice this meant that friends and relatives of serving policemen were more likely to be selected. If the selection committee should have a bias against appointing Catholics or towards appointing Protestants, as that of the 1850s and 1860s certainly had, this system of closed advertising had the effect of further limiting the number of Catholic policemen.[49] One of the results of the recruiting method was that members of the same family frequently joined the force, as is best exemplified by the fact that in 1864 Chief Constable Thomas Green, Inspectors Francis Green and Samuel Green, and Acting Constable Joseph Green, all from Magheragall, were brothers.[50] The close-knit character of the force can also be gauged from the fact that sixty of its 160 members in 1864 came from the villages of Glenavy, Magheragall, Derriaghy and Drumbo alone.[51] It was understandable that there was 'a notion among the Roman Catholics something like "No Catholic need apply"' regarding police vacancies.[52] The explanations offered by members of the police committee to the 1864 parliamentary commission into the Belfast riots that year, for the small number of Catholic policemen, were not very convincing. One, Mayor John

---

47. Town council committee on police affairs, 22, 29 Apr. 1856; *B.N.L.*, 2 Oct. 1857; *1857 riots inquiry*, p.240; *1864 Belfast borough inquiry*, pp.59, 208.

48. Belfast police committee minutes, 19 May 1835, 25 Apr., 5 Sept. 1837; Belfast police commissioners' minutes, 15 Aug. 1838; Town council committee on police affairs minutes, 15 May 1844, 26 Mar., 5 Nov. 1845, 29 Apr. 1846.

49. *Report of the commissioners of inquiry, 1864, respecting the magisterial and police arrangements and establishments of the borough of Belfast*, H.C. 1864 [3466], xxviii, 1, p.6 (hereafter *Report of the commissioners of inquiry, 1864*); *1864 Belfast borough inquiry*, p.305.

50. *1864 Belfast borough inquiry*, pp.164–65, 359–60.

51. Ibid, pp.359–61.

52. Ibid, p.200.

Lyttle, claimed that the explanation was simple: Catholic applicants simply refused to present themselves.[53] Another pointed to the alleged larger stature of Ulster Protestants: 'We appointed the biggest men—men most likely able to knock other men down. Belfast is inhabited by two races of people—the colonial or Scotch race, and the other the native or Celtic race; and the Scotchmen are the biggest, and that is the way they [the police] are Protestants.'[54] David Taylor, an Antrim magistrate who was chairman of the town council's police committee for three or four years in the 1850s, admitted that if a Protestant and a Catholic candidate equal in all respects offered themselves for a police vacancy the Protestant was more likely to receive the appointment.[55]

There is no doubt that the almost exclusively Protestant town council practised discrimination against Catholics in its police appointments in the 1850s and 1860s. But is that enough evidence to condemn the men of the police force as partisan or sectarian, accusations which were levelled at the time and which have been repeated more recently?[56] There is sufficient evidence to suggest that this view of the force is a caricature of the reality, and that the police were understandably if incorrectly lumbered with the image of being a sectarian force partly because of the recruiting policies of their paymasters. The most successful and prominent promoter of the idea that the Belfast police were biased against Catholics was a solicitor named John Rea, the most vociferous Belfast Liberal during the town council's control of Belfast's policing. Rea's grandfather had fought at Saintfield in 1798, and Rea was a Presbyterian Young Irelander who had been jailed in Kilmainham in 1848. His many enemies delighted in rousing his temper by calling him a 'Kilmainham spy', suggesting that he was released without charge as a result of turning informer. Since his release Rea conducted a passionate crusade against the Tory-dominated town council; it was he who brought the famous Chancery case against the council in the 1850s charging several leading councillors with various corrupt or shady transactions. His animosity was given a more personal edge in 1854 when his father was dismissed as clerk of the Belfast markets. On numerous occasions court cases and town council meetings ended in pandemonium as Rea gleefully levelled accusations of slander, conspiracy, corruption, perjury, cowardice and 'other

53. Ibid, p.182.
54. Ibid, p.82.
55. Ibid, p.139.
56. Boyd, *Holy war*, passim.

crimes of the vilest description' against councillors, policemen and magistrates alike. In July 1864 he was even dragged from the House of Lords when he advocated one of his many passionately-held causes with too much ardour. He was enormously popular with lower-class Catholics or, as the *Belfast Newsletter* put it in August 1863, he was a hero to 'the wretched scum of the back purlieus'. Before his attendance at council meetings proceedings were conducted in a relatively orderly fashion, but Rea's frequently outrageous performances were so popular with his supporters or so infuriated his opponents that railings had to be installed to hold back the mob.[57] In December 1862 a typical Rea performance included opposing a vote of thanks to the outgoing mayor of Belfast, earning himself the description of 'town pest … more offensive and loathsome than any turbid stream that oozes between banks of slime' after he caused the town council meeting to end in uproar. A few days later he repeated the performance in a row over the appointment of a clerk of the markets, a position which Rea felt that his father should hold. The *Belfast Newsletter* reporter wrote of the confusion which followed: '"Felon", "liar", "blackguard", "low ruffian", "forger", were repeatedly heard. Libels were uttered with unparalleled profusion. Threats of personal violence were made, and would have been fulfilled but for the interposition of peacemakers' and the intervention of Chief Constable Green, who eventually managed to clear the chamber!'[58]

Rea skilfully attacked the town council throughout the 1850s by condemning its police appointments as sectarian. In court cases he repeatedly asked policemen if they were members of Orange lodges; despite the fact that he never proved membership in a single instance, Rea skilfully planted the suggestion in Catholic minds that the majority of policemen were Orangemen. In July 1854 he alleged that three-quarters of the police were Orangemen, and that membership in that organisation was 'the only qualification' required of a recruit.[59] A good instance of how Rea operated occurred in September 1851. During the trial of four Catholics who were part of a mob estimated at 500 to 600 people that attacked Day Constables Murray, Constable and Lynass on 6 September after they arrested a drunk and disorderly man in Hill Street, Rea tried

57. Details from *B.N.L.*, 15 Nov. 1850, 4 Oct. 1854, 2 Oct. 1856, 24, 30 Sept. 1857, 3, 9 Feb., 2 Apr., 7 Aug., 2 Sept., 2 Dec. 1863, 18 Feb., 7 July, 2 Aug. 1864; *1857 riots inquiry*, p.146; *A.G. (ex.rel. Rea) v. Belfast Corporation* (1855) 4 Irish Chancery Reports 119.

58. *B.N.L.*, 8, 10 Dec. 1862.

59. *B.D.M.*, 18 July 1854.

to give a 'party' colouring to proceedings by producing in evidence a piece of paper in which Constable Samuel Lynass of Stanfield Street was addressed as 'Sir Knight and Brother'. Rea's aim was to prove that the police prosecution was brought solely on sectarian grounds, as Lynass's being an Orangeman meant that he was motivated by hatred towards Catholics in making the charges. In fact it was pointed out some years later that the salutation on the paper was a freemason title, but in the meantime Rea was convinced that he had found clear proof of Orange membership on the part of one of the municipal police.[60] Rea also alleged that the town council required the police to live in houses of a rateable value sufficient to qualify them for the franchise (since September 1849 the police were required to reside in the borough, in houses which were not in 'unhealthy locations') and that their votes swung every election in the Tory interest. A survey in 1857 showed how uninformed or at least exaggerated Rea's claims were. In fact only twelve police qualified for the parliamentary and eight for the municipal franchise, scarcely enough to have the effect claimed by Rea even if all of the police votes went to Tory candidates.[61]

Another of Rea's allegations, that Belfast police participated in Orange processions outside of Belfast, was similarly lacking in foundation. It arose from a selective interpretation of an incident in which two municipal policemen who were going to a funeral at Tullyrusk on 13 July 1857 found the road blocked by an Orange march. An investigation found that the policemen were not involved in the parade, although many Catholics believed otherwise. This incident seems to be the basis for Andrew Boyd's claim that 'Several [of the Belfast police] were Orangemen who walked, despite the law, in Twelfth of July processions outside Belfast'.[62] Rea was on

60. *B.N.L.*, 15 Sept. 1851; *N.W.*, 13 Sept. 1851; *1857 riots inquiry*, p. 152. It is true that freemason policemen were unlikely to have been regarded much more favourably by Belfast Catholics than Orange policemen, given the hostility shown by the Irish Catholic church (especially under the leadership of Cardinal Paul Cullen) towards the masonic order. It is also likely that masonic and Orange membership overlapped to a large extent. Nevertheless, masonic membership, unlike Orange membership, *was* open to Catholics. Significantly, the Irish Constabulary and D.M.P. were forbidden to join any secret society, with the sole exception of the freemasons, and some Catholic policemen did join the order. What is significant for the discussion here is not, however, the denominational make-up of the freemasons but the accuracy of Rea's allegations of police membership of the Orange order. In Lynass's case, Rea failed to substantiate his allegation.

61. Town council committee on police affairs minutes, 25 Sept. 1849; *B.N.L.*, 19, 25 Sept. 1857.

62. *Ulsterman*, 15 July 1857; Town council committee on police affairs minutes, 6

surer ground when he stated that the superintendent of the police force in the 1850s, Adam Hill, was an Orangeman of long standing. Hill had joined the organisation as far back as 1797 and had fought in the Yeomanry against the United Irishmen in 1798. He was a member of the town council's police committee in 1844, and was appointed sub-treasurer to the town council in July 1849. In 1852 he was appointed superintendent of the town police. While the fact of a person of Hill's background being in charge of the police might at first glance appear to substantiate Rea's charge of partiality, one should bear in mind that the aged Hill's superintendentship was little more than a sinecure. Most of his time was taken up with matters other than looking after the police. He was also a water commissioner, an auditor of the County Down Railway Company, an agent for a marine insurance company and notary public to the Northern and Provincial Banks. He did not even appear at the head of the local police during the 1857 disturbances. Hill, who retired in 1860 on a pension of £100 per annum, was dismissed as little more than a clerk by a police committee member in 1864.[63]

Even Rea's oft-repeated assertions that the Protestant policemen were mainly Orangemen cannot be substantiated. Some, indeed, had been members of the society *before* they joined the police. Those who admitted to past membership included Inspector McIlroy in July 1854, who insisted that 'he feels as much for a Roman Catholic as an Orangeman; and he did not sympathize with Orangemen if they be in the wrong'. In 1857 those who owned up to being ex-members included Constable Robert Blair who gave up his association with Dundrod no. 553 Lodge a year and a half before he joined the police; Constable John McClelland, who gave up his membership of Brookhill no. 187 Lodge some five years before he became a policeman; Constable Hugh McMullan, who ceased

Oct. 1857; *1857 riots inquiry*, pp.244–47; Boyd, *Holy war*, p.14. As late as 1886 Dr Alexander Dempsey, JP, a member of the Catholic Committee, formed by wealthy and prominent Belfast Catholics to present evidence to the 1886 parliamentary commission into the extensive Belfast riots of that year, claimed that the municipal police 'were every one of them Orangemen, and it was quite customary for them to take part in Orange processions'. He stated that he would prefer 'a police republic under a dictator' rather than return to the days when the town council controlled the police: *Report from the select committee on Municipal Regulation (Constabulary &c) Belfast Bill; together with the proceedings of the committee, minutes of evidence, and appendix* (London, 1887), p.108.

63. Details of Hill's biography from *N.W.*, 4 June 1844; *B.N.L.*, 1, 2 Oct. 1857, 3 Nov. 1862; Town council committee on police affairs minutes, 21 June 1860; *1864 Belfast borough inquiry*, p.81; Boyd, *Holy war*, pp.14–15.

being an Orangeman some six months before joining the force, and Constables James Miller and George Wright who similarly gave up their association with the order before they joined the police.[64] The author failed to discover a single instance in which John Rea proved Orange membership on the part of serving policemen, although for years the solicitor cross-examined policemen in court as if they were members—for example, by addressing them as 'Brother'. Undoubtedly police confessions of past membership in the Orange Order fuelled Catholic suspicions of the force, but Rea's repeated and inaccurate accusations against the police were also blamed for the Catholic community's distrust.[65] The town council's refusal to bring in a rule explicitly forbidding Orange membership was a useful aid to Rea's campaign of vilification. The reason why no regulation on the subject was introduced was straightforward: councillors who voted for such a measure were likely to be unseated by Protestant electors at the next municipal election. Assurances from Chief Constable Green that there were no policemen known to be in Orange lodges, and that any policeman proven to be a member of the Orange Order would be discharged,[66] are unlikely to have impressed Belfast Catholics. The claims of Catholic policemen that they had never experienced discrimination in the force, and that Catholic and Protestant members worked harmoniously together similarly failed to correct the belief that the municipal force was biased against Catholics; so did the statements of Irish Constabulary members with many years' service in Belfast that they had never seen the town council's force behave in a partisan manner.[67]

It is open to question whether John Rea really believed that the Belfast police were partisan, or whether he merely used this allegation as a convenient stick with which to beat the Tory-dominated town council. It is certainly odd to find the fiery solicitor urging in February 1856 that the municipal force should be paid as much as the Irish Constabulary, a measure which was rejected by the town council.[68] In August 1856 he praised the force's efficiency and urged an increase in pay due to the high cost of living in Belfast, and 'the severe duty which the men had to perform'.[69] A satirical verse entitled 'I am the Popular Man' poked fun, in part, at Rea's efforts on behalf of the local police:

64. *B.N.L.*, 24 July 1854, 26 Sept., 29 Oct. 1857.
65. *1864 Belfast borough inquiry*, pp.109–10, 157, 166, 211, 218, 220, 250.
66. Ibid, pp.190–91, 214, 218.
67. *B.N.L.*, 17, 19, 25, 26 Sept. 1857; *1864 Belfast borough inquiry*, pp.297–98.
68. *B.N.L.*, 11 Feb. 1856.
69. Ibid, 25 Sept. 1857.

The police, those much under-paid fellows,
Whom I loudly abused long ago,
I proposed to make friends of for ever,
For five shillings a fortnight or so.[70]

But most of Rea's comments about the force were uncomplimentary
and designed to give the impression that it was hostile to Catholics.
A typical instance occurred during the parliamentary investigation
into the sectarian riots of 1857. When questioning a policeman
named Lavery as to how he had joined the force, Rea and his
colleague Mr O'Rorke felt that they had found proof of sectarian
influence in the police. O'Rorke's query about Lavery's sponsor for
entry into the force received the reply, 'The Rev Mr Hanna'. A
newspaper extract describes the scene: 'Mr Rea (bouncing up)—
Oh—now we have it. Mr O'Rorke—Ay, this is it.' Clearly the two
interrogators felt that Lavery was referring to the controversial
Bible-thumper 'Roaring' Hugh Hanna. Their reactions prompted
the following reply from Lavery: 'Wait, gentlemen, you're in too
much haste—it was the Rev Mr Hanna, priest at Bryansford, who
recommended me—(laughter)—together with other gentlemen.'
Neither Rea nor O'Rorke knew that Lavery was a Catholic.[71]

The extract exemplifies the atmosphere of suspicion with which
the municipal force was held at the time by many people in Belfast.
The town council's discriminatory recruitment practices, which
resulted in a force drawn overwhelmingly from one side of the community, were bound to raise doubts about the force's impartiality.
In the hysterical atmosphere engendered by the sectarian riots of
1857 frequently fantastic allegations and rumours about the municipal force's siding with Orange rioters became accepted as fact by
many lower-class Catholics. The Catholic newspaper, the *Ulsterman*,
was affected by this readiness to believe the worst of the municipal
police. In April 1857 it praised the supposedly-biased day and night
police for their exertions in preventing a Protestant mob from
attacking St Malachy's church in the Markets area; however, in July
1857 James McLoughlin, the newspaper's proprietor, seriously
asserted that 'it was rather a common occurrence for policemen to
beat Catholics, when they can get the opportunity', and that each
July the town council paid their force a bonus 'for creating the July
riots from year to year'. He claimed that 'regularly every year, as
regularly as July comes round, the corporation police of Belfast
have an inducement offered them to secretly instigate riot, and to

70. Ibid, 11 Nov. 1856.
71. Ibid, 26 Sept. 1857.

urge on their fellow Orange brethren to outrage and bloodshed'.[72] This was a rather wild interpretation of the fact that since July 1842 the police authorities periodically awarded extra pay to the force for the additional duty they performed over the July 12th period.[73]

It is not the author's intention to claim that the allegations of sectarian behaviour on the part of some of the Belfast police were entirely without foundation. It would have been astonishing had a force recruited from the lower orders of the Ulster countryside been totally free from the taint of bigotry. One instance involved Night Constable James Connolly, who was dismissed from the force in October 1853 for absenting himself without leave and participating in a 'party' riot, for which he received a sentence of four months in prison at Newry quarter sessions.[74] George Leggatt or Ligget, a Catholic night constable, was dismissed for using party expressions and for drunkenness. Chief Constable Green wanted to retain him in the force but he was unable to keep him sober. On Ligget's final drunkenness violation, on 12 July 1863 on the Shankill Road, he was shouting that 'he was the best Catholic in the force; and he used very strong language ... Cursing Orangemen and Orangeism and everything appertaining to it'. He also assaulted a civilian in his home in the same incident.[75] In September 1858 four municipal policemen—William Scott, John Macaulay, Joseph Kinneard and Thomas Cairns, the last two of whom were ex-members of the Orange Order—were heard to make an Orange toast in O'Neill's public house in Smithfield, and when they were passing through Hudson's Entry the most inebriated of the four, Constable Scott, unwisely shouted out that he could 'beat ever a Papish' in the street. This led to a fracas with the local people, with one woman in particular threatening to 'knock the Orange sowls' out of the policemen with a 7lb weight. Scott, the principal instigator of the trouble, was dismissed from the force.[76]

The belief that the police had an animus against Catholics recurred during the 1864 riots. Undoubtedly claims that local policemen failed to prevent Sandy Row mobs from attacking Catholic women or, worse, that they actively encouraged them[77]

---

72. *Ulsterman*, 6 Apr. 1857; *B.N.L.*, 4, 22 Sept. 1857.

73. Belfast police commissioners' minutes, 20 July 1842; Town council committee on police affairs minutes, 24 July 1849; *B.N.L.*, 30 July 1858, 3 Aug. 1863.

74. Town council committee on police affairs minutes, 25 Oct. 1853.

75. Ibid, 23 July 1863; *1864 Belfast borough inquiry*, pp.216–17.

76. *B.N.L.*, 1 Oct. 1858; Town council committee on police affairs minutes, 7 Oct. 1858.

77. Boyd, *Holy war*, pp.54–55.

fuelled Catholic hatred of the force. It is argued in this chapter that the allegations of sectarianism against the force were understandable, but exaggerated. Writing more than a century after the events of that troubled year, it seems unfair to brand the entire force as sectarian because of the disgraceful behaviour or alleged behaviour of a few of its members. To gain a fuller view of the municipal force one should bear in mind its actions throughout the entire period of the riots. An examination of the newspaper reports and of the parliamentary investigation makes it clear that the unarmed local force acted in tandem with the hundreds of military and Irish Constabulary reinforcements rushed to the town to combat the mobs of both communities. To single out the few occasions when members of the municipal force allegedly expressed approval of the actions of Protestant rioters as typical of the sentiments of the force is to distort the true picture.

CHAPTER NINE

The Bulkies depart: enter the Peelers

THE END OF THE BULKIES

HOWEVER UNJUST OR EXAGGERATED the charges of sectarian behaviour may have been against most members of the municipal police, they undoubtedly were central in spelling the end for a force whose members were drawn disproportionately from one section of the community. The 1864 parliamentary commissioners considered that the unarmed municipal police were incapable of suppressing armed, communal rioting of the type experienced in July and September 1857 and in August 1864. They recommended abolition of the municipal force and its replacement by an expanded contingent of the Irish Constabulary. This would have the advantage not only of being armed and thus better equipped for opposing widespread public disorder, but if any constabulary men 'fell under the suspicion of becoming impregnated injuriously with local feelings' they could be transferred to other parts of the country.[1] For years the Belfast magistrates had recognised that the local force was inadequate for the task of riot control. In September 1857 the town council refused the magistrates' request that a further three or four lock-ups be provided in Belfast, where prisoners could be lodged 'in times of popular excitement'. The estimated cost of £220 was deemed excessive by the police committee.[2] The most attractive feature of Chief Secretary Lord Naas's plan in the following year to replace the local force with a sub-inspector, two head constables and 100 men of the Irish Constabulary was the savings which this would mean to the town council. However the plan was not endorsed because the constabulary did not perform duty throughout the night, which activity was considered the most important part of the municipal force's work.[3] The *Belfast Newsletter* proved hostile to the proposal because the Irish Constabulary was a largely Catholic

1. *Report of the commissioners of inquiry, 1864*, p.20.
2. *B.N.L.*, 2 Sept. 1857.
3. Ibid, 13 July 1858; *1864 Belfast borough inquiry*, pp.186, 253, 273.

force. It pointed to a fracas between local policemen and constabulary men on the Ormeau Road in April 1858 as an example
of the dangers awaiting Belfast's tranquillity should the Irish
Constabulary become entirely responsible for policing the town.
The April incident started when Night Constable James Hanlon,
on duty at the junction of Cromac Street and the Ormeau Road on
the night of the 10th, encountered Sub-constable Owen Conlan
of the Bradbury Place barracks and Sub-constable Patrick
McCafferty, stationed at Cromac Street. Both 'Peelers' were drunk
but Hanlon took no notice of them. Sub-constable McCafferty,
who had a grudge against the 'Bulkies' because one of them had
arrested him for fighting when in plain clothes in Legg's Lane,
'made a noise with his mouth in a disrespectful manner' when
passing Hanlon but Hanlon still ignored the two sub-constables.
Shortly afterwards Hanlon was attacked from behind by the two
constabulary men, and was kicked and stabbed several times, once
near the heart. He managed to spring his rattle, bringing several
other local night constables (at least two of whom had also been
drinking earlier) on the scene. McCafferty, who received a broken
arm in the fight, was arrested on the Ormeau Road. Conlan fled
through the fields but was captured later. The *Newsletter* claimed
that the incident 'conveys a lesson against placing implicit depen-
dence upon any civil force largely composed of Romanists, however
well disciplined or splendid in appearance'.[4]

The municipal authorities tried in vain to inject 'military'
features into their force in an effort to improve its utility in riot
situations. Captain Eyre Massey Shaw, who had served for five
years in the North Cork Rifles militia before his election as police
superintendent in May 1860, trained his men in 'battalion drill' to
accustom the police to acting in unison.[5] But the fact that most of
the men were married[6] and that there was no central barracks
highlights the fact that the force could not have been seriously
expected to quell large-scale public disorder. In this it contrasted
with the mainly bachelor D.M.P. and Irish Constabulary forces,
whose unmarried men lived in barracks. This meant that they could
be conveniently assembled and quickly despatched to the scene of
serious riots. It is significant that in October 1864 Chief Constables
Green and McKittrick recommended that the municipal police be
increased by 100 men, all of whom were to be unmarried and
residing in barracks to be constructed at the police office in Police

4. *B.N.L.*, 12, 13 Apr. 1858. Legg's Lane was a small street running between
   High Street and Rosemary Street.

5. *B.N.L.*, 10 May, 28 Sept. 1860; *1864 Belfast borough inquiry*, p.248.

6. *B.N.L.*, 30 Mar. 1861.

Square, at the old military barracks in Barrack Street, at the junction of North Street and Old Lodge Road, and in York Street. Each barracks was to be large enough to accommodate fifty prisoners. The officers hoped that if these changes were made 'we would be enabled in the event of disturbance to bring in a very short time a force of one hundred well armed men to bear upon the scene and crush in the bud what might otherwise become a formidable riot'.[7]

By that date the proposed changes were too late to allay pressure from Dublin Castle for the abolition of the municipal police. One police committee member admitted in November 1864 that the town council felt that their force was 'doomed'.[8] When the chief secretary, Sir Robert Peel, introduced his bill for the abolition of the Belfast force and its replacement by the Irish Constabulary in May 1865 the town council sent a deputation consisting of Sir Hugh Cairns, Conservative MP for Belfast, the mayor of Belfast, John Lyttle, and several members of the police committee in the hope of securing some concessions, especially regarding compensation for the police. They were left in no doubt that the Consolidated Fund would not pay the pensions or other allowances awarded by the council to the disbanded force; neither was the entire cost of the proposed 400 constabulary force for Belfast to be borne by the Treasury. The deputation was told that there was not the slightest hope of defeating the bill in the House of Commons.[9] The *Belfast Newsletter* maintained a forlorn opposition to the proposed reform of the policing of Belfast. It repeated the claim that the constabulary would be unsuitable for duty in the town because it did not perform night duty, and pointed to the example of Cork where 'private merchants' hired night watchmen because the constabulary did not patrol the streets at night on a round-the-clock basis. (Sir Robert Peel's bill actually proposed that the constabulary in Belfast should perform duty throughout the night, receiving an extra 6*d.* per night for this.) The newspaper also rather foolishly suggested that Peel's plan was due to 'a predilection for the force which is associated with his father's name'.[10] Almost two weeks after the bill passed the committee stage a petition against the abolition of the municipal police was begun in Belfast,[11] which was obviously bound to fail given its late start. The *Newsletter* stated that the

7. Town council committee on police affairs minutes, 24 Oct. 1864.
8. *1864 Belfast borough inquiry*, p.82.
9. Town council committee on police affairs minutes, 11 May 1865.
10. *B.N.L.*, 4, 18 May, 2 June 1865.
11. Ibid, 10 June 1865.

successful passage of the bill was 'viewed by the Roman Catholic factionists here as an unqualified triumph', while 'among Protestants it is regarded as an attempt to humiliate them'.[12] The disbandment of the 'Bulkies' was certainly a bitter pill for many of the Protestants of Belfast to swallow; even as late as 30 August, the second last day of the force's existence, the *Newsletter* complained that in order to 'satisfy the political malice of a faction' the local police were about to be 'cast off like a worn-out glove'.

The last night's duty performed by the force was on 31 August 1865. An observer stated that 'very few of them, in consequence of the wear and tear to which they have been subjected, will be able to engage in an occupation requiring much exertion'. This was probably an exaggeration, as a survey of the force late in May had disclosed that only fifteen policemen were older than forty years of age. In June 105 of the men aged below forty underwent a medical examination to determine whether they met the physical require-ments for entry into the Irish Constabulary, and seventy-three passed. (Only six men were subsequently accepted into the Irish Constabulary, however.) The reporter who wrote of the poor health of the police on their last day of duty was probably trying to arouse sympathy for them, especially among prospective employers. A street preacher named Mateer, who for several years previously had held open-air services in Police Square, gave a sermon to the police based on the quotation 'Trust in the Lord, and do good: so shalt thou dwell in the land, and verily shalt be fed'.[13] The words were obviously chosen to hearten the men who were losing their jobs, but they did not prompt the town council to recompense their employees over-generously. Just over a month later a delegation of clergymen attended a police committee meeting to support the petition of the discharged constables for pensions from the town council. Reverend Charles Seavers pointed out that the men, 'by being enlisted in the force, had been raised above the level in society to which they originally belonged, and now after service of twenty years and upwards it would be hard to ask them to resume their old positions, and go out spade in hand, to earn their livings'. The committee were not convinced by the delegation's arguments, however, and felt that the ratepayers should not be burdened with the cost of policemen's pensions. Instead they stuck to their earlier decision to grant gratuities to all of the force except Chief Constable Green, who was pensioned at £100 a year, and Chief Constable

12. Ibid, 17 June 1865.
13. Ibid, 1, 29 June, 1 Sept. 1865; Irish Constabulary general register, 1865, pp.156–57 (PRO (Kew), HO 184/16).

McKittrick, who received a pension of £80. Policemen with from seventeen to twenty years' service were given a gratuity of a year's pay, those with from twenty to twenty-three years' service received fifteen months' pay, while those with longer service were awarded eighteen months' pay. The other ex-policemen received gratuities of from two weeks' to ten months' pay.[14]

THE CONSTABULARY TAKE OVER

Some 450 of the denominationally-mixed Irish Constabulary replaced the borough force on 1 September 1865. The constabulary replacements were perceived by many Belfast Protestants as being a 'popish' force. 'Papist', 'papish looking b[ugge]r', 'fenian', 'bloody lot of fenians', 'popish rascal', 'popish pig-drivers', 'a parcel of ribbonmen', 'papist pup', 'papish brats', 'a popish set': these were just some of the abusive epithets hurled at the constabulary in Belfast by Protestant prisoners.[15] William Short's expressed desire in June 1866 to 'peel the nose off the papish Peelers' was undoubtedly shared by many of his co-religionists.[16] Not only was the new force disliked by Protestants because it was felt to contain an undue proportion of Catholics, but these were believed by some to be Catholics from outside Ulster, and were therefore even more repugnant to lower-class Protestants. In March 1866 Archibald Marks, following his arrest for being drunk, disorderly and assaulting a woman, 'cursed the police for Dublin papists'; in October 1866 Andrew Crawford of Ballymacarrett shouted out that the constabulary were 'papishes from Tipperary, and that they had come down to Belfast to trample over the Protestants'.[17] This antipathy towards a supposedly 'papist' force lasted a long time: during the Lady's Day disturbances in Belfast in 1880 a Dublin newspaper commented on the 'old enmity' between the Protestant rioters and the R.I.C.[18]

The hostility towards the new force was at first shared by many well-to-do Protestants, as one can gather from the complaint of the

---

14. Town council committee on police affairs minutes, 6, 7 Sept. 1865; *B.N.L.*, 3 Oct. 1865.
15. *B.N.L.*, 9, 28 Sept. 1865, 18, 28 Jan., 20, 28 Feb., 5 Mar., 14 Apr., 1, 4, 5, 9, 18 May, 20 June, 3, 10, 11 July, 2, 15, 29 Aug., 4, 18, 25 Sept., 8, 20, 24, 27, 31 Oct. , 27 Nov. 1866, 5 Jan. 1867.
16. Ibid, 12 June 1866.
17. Ibid, 13 Mar., 17 Oct. 1866.
18. *Freeman's Journal*, 19 Aug. 1880. The Irish Constabulary was re-named the Royal Irish Constabulary in 1867.

Belfast Newsletter, the Conservative organ, about the 'green badge of disgrace' that had been imposed upon the city.[19] The newspaper grumbled in September 1865 that 'Nothing could be more unconstitutional or improper than to have an armed police patrolling our streets', and alleged that the 450 constabulary men were 'by no means inclined to be civil', that they treated the public 'as though they were inferior animals', and that the men on night duty, instead of performing patrols, 'congregated in fours and sixes at the [street] corners, generally supporting the wall of some house'.[20] However, by the mid-1870s the newspaper had changed its tune, probably because by then the R.I.C. had proved itself both an efficient crime-fighting force and one that was more capable of suppressing serious disorder than the municipal force had been. In April 1876 the *Newsletter* stated that 'respectable persons have the fullest confidence in the Royal Irish Constabulary, armed or unarmed; but it is otherwise with the roughs, who are so often in their hands'.[21]

The constabulary received a mixed reception at first from lower-class Catholics. Old animosities died hard, and the insults of 'b[lood]y Orange pup', 'set of Orange Peelers', 'Presbyterian g[e]t', and 'Orange pig-drovers and Orange b[ugge]rs' suggest that many Catholics were no more enamoured of the new force patrolling Belfast's streets than they had been of the municipal police.[22] One Catholic woman arrested at Peter's Hill on 15 November 1866 declared that she 'would sooner have the skin of a policeman than [of] all the Orangemen in Belfast'.[23] However, Catholic constabulary men were, at first, welcomed by some lower-class Catholics as marginally more acceptable than Protestant police, as one can gather from the shout of a Cromac Street woman in July 1866 of 'To H[el]l with the police, especially the Protestant ones'.[24] A man who was arrested in October 1866 in Great Patrick Street for drunkenness at first stated that he was 'glad to see the good Roman Catholic police on duty on the street, and not the d[amne]d Protestants who were on before they came to Belfast'. However, following his arrest, he 'cursed the police for d[amne]d rascals'! In December of the same year a Catholic woman shouted out 'God bless the pope and the Tipperary Peelers, and to H[el]l with King William'; her good

19. Quoted in Budge and O'Leary, *Belfast: approach to crisis*, p.83.
20. *B.N.L.*, 2, 26 Sept. 1865, 11 May 1866.
21. Ibid, 29 Apr. 1876.
22. Ibid, 5, 26 June, 18, 19 July, 29 Aug., 27 Nov. 1866, 4 Jan. 1867.
23. Ibid, 17 Nov. 1866.
24. Ibid, 28 July 1866.

opinion of the 'Tipperary Peelers' probably changed following her arrest for using party expressions.[25]

The guarded welcome given to the Irish Constabulary by some lower-class Catholics changed as it became apparent that their duties were to be as obtrusive as those of the 'Bulkies' had been. As had been the case before September 1865, the month in which the constabulary assumed responsibility for policing all of Belfast, police intervention in the most popular working-class leisure activity—drinking—was deeply resented. In April 1866 James Toole was arrested by a constabulary man in the Catholic Pound Street area for 'wrangling with some women' when drunk. The women cried out for the men in the neighbourhood to rescue the prisoner, and 'a large crowd collected immediately' and 'pelted' the policeman with stones. He retained custody of his prisoner only by drawing his sword bayonet to keep the crowd at bay. According to Head Constable Jacques, 'whenever the police arrested any disorderly persons in the neighbourhood of Pound Street, the people assembled in large numbers, and attempted to rescue them'.[26] Some ten years later, in January 1876, Sub-inspector Blake claimed that another Catholic area, Cromac Street, was 'a place in which the police found it almost impossible to do duty. Whenever any person was arrested a regular crowd assembled, and the police were always assaulted, and sometimes severely'.[27] Crowd attempts to rescue prisoners were frequent in the city, and indicate how unpopular the constabulary were with the 'lower orders'.[28] John H. Otway, QC, commenting on Belfast's sectarian camps, at the Recorder's Court, in February 1880, stated astutely that 'there was nothing that united them more than this common hatred of the police'.[29]

It was the Belfast riots of June 1886, which left thirty-two people dead, most of them Protestant civilians who were shot by the constabulary, which ensured that Belfast Protestants were likely to have a greater aversion than Belfast Catholics to the R.I.C. During the riots, which started in the period of extreme tension accompanying the debate on the first Home Rule bill in the House of Commons, the constabulary were withdrawn from the Shankill

25. Ibid, 17 Oct., 28 Dec. 1866.
26. Ibid, 5 Apr. 1866.
27. Ibid, 4 Jan. 1876.
28. For some examples of crowd rescues or attempted rescues see ibid, 4, 24 Apr., 7, 29 Aug., 9, 19, 30 Oct., 23 Nov., 20 Dec. 1866, 3 Jan. 1867, 20 Jan., 18, 19 May 1876, 13 Jan., 2, 16 Mar., 6, 9 Apr. 1880.
29. Ibid, 18 Feb. 1880.

Road. Before they resumed patrolling in that area posters were put up demanding that a phrenologist test each man's skull, to ensure that he was not of 'murderous propensities'.[30] As a result of the disturbances the R.I.C. in Belfast were specially trained in the use of the truncheon in five-man groups, who were to be well-drilled and thus 'not likely to be seized with panic' when confronted by hostile mobs. Constables were warned to use 'sound discretion' before making arrests in 'dangerous localities', as an unwise arrest could spark off a riot or 'necessitate the use of firearms'. They were told that 'it is better that an offender should not be arrested, than that he should be rescued from custody after arrest',[31] the latter outcome being of frequent occurrence in Belfast.

These measures did little for the R.I.C.'s image in Protestant areas. During the period of the second Home Rule bill, in 1893, it was the military which policed the shipyard area and kept the Falls and Shankill mobs apart, and the Unionist mayor and Belfast magistrates showed scant sympathy for the R.I.C.'s troubles in times of exceptional tension. It should be borne in mind, however, that not all Protestant hostility towards the constabulary was a result of the force's actions in the 1886 riots. Although the bitter memory of the events of that year were an important factor, much animosity was also due to a natural dislike of the police in lower-class city areas. Even after partition and the establishment of the mainly Protestant Royal Ulster Constabulary, relations between the Protestant working class and the Belfast police remained strained. Sam McAughtry, recalling his youth in the 1920s in the Protestant working-class area of Tiger's Bay, states that the people of the district were 'distanced from the police', and that 'policemen came into the area with some trepidation and they came in twos and frequently one of them had trouble making it to the other side'.[32] McAughtry's statement, although it refers to the early twentieth century, could also be said to sum up the uneasy relationship between the 'Bulkies', the 'Peelers' and many working-class citizens of Belfast down to 1865.

30. *Belfast riots commission, 1886. Report of the Belfast riots commissioners. Minutes of evidence, and appendix,* H.C. 1887 (c.4925), xviii, 1, p.228.

31. Ibid, p.59; *Belfast police manual. Compiled for the use of the Royal Irish Constabulary serving in the town of Belfast* (Belfast, 1888), pp.13, 29.

32. Baker, 'Orange and green', p.218; Sam McAughtry, 'Being Protestant in Northern Ireland' in James McLoone (ed.), *Being Protestant in Ireland* (Belfast and Dublin, 1985), pp.35–36.

APPENDIX ONE

Extracts from *Instructions to the Belfast Police Force, 1856*

Source: Instructions to the Belfast police force (Belfast, 1856)

p.9

THE POLICE CONSTABLE

HE MUST STUDY TO recommend himself to notice by a diligent discharge of his duties and strict obedience to the commands of his superiors, recollecting that he who has been accustomed to submit to discipline will be considered best qualified to command.

He is at all times to appear neat in his person, correctly dressed in the established uniform, and respectful in his demeanour towards his officers, and individuals of every class.

He must cheerfully and punctually obey all orders and instructions of the Sergeants, Inspectors, Chief Constables and Superintendent. If they appear to him either unlawful or improper, he may complain, through his Superintendent, to the Police Committee, who will pay due attention to him; but any refusal to perform the commands of his superiors, or negligence in doing so, will be severely punished.

When for duty, he will take care to be at the appointed place a quarter of an hour before the time of being marched off; and, after inspection, and having received such orders as may be necessary, he will be marched to his beat, previously receiving from his Sergeant or Inspector a card, with the names of the streets, and so forth, forming his beat. A particular portion of the section will be committed to his care, and he will be held responsible for the security of life and property within his beat, preservation of peace, and general good order, during the time that he is on duty.

When proceeding through the streets together, either on or off duty, constables are not to walk three abreast; where the footway is very broad, two, but never more, may walk together abreast.

A constable should clearly understand what powers are given to him by law for the efficient execution of his duties. For this purpose he is directed to read repeatedly the 'Abstract of General Orders' and the instructions given to him in the 'Outline of the General Duties of a Constable'.

He should make himself perfectly acquainted with all parts of his beat; with the streets, thoroughfares, courts, and houses. He should possess such knowledge of the inhabitants of each house as would enable him to recognise their persons.

He is to see every part of his beat in the given time, walking at the rate of $2^1/2$ English miles per hour. This he will be expected to do regularly, so that any person requiring the aid of a constable, by remaining in the same spot for that length of time, may meet one.

p.11

He is to afford every possible information to strangers, or others making inquiries; and he is, on such occasions, to deport himself with the utmost civility and attention.

He is authorised to interfere when a crowd of persons is standing on the footways together, and must do all in his power to prevent the obstruction of the free passage of the thoroughfares.

He is, upon these and all other occasions, required to execute his duty with good temper, civility, and discretion. Any instance of unnecessary violence, by pushing persons off the footways, or striking a party in charge, will be severely punished. A constable is not to use his staff because the person in custody is violent in behaviour or language; but he may do so when his life is in danger, or to prevent the escape of felons. Whenever it is used, blows must not be given on the head or face, but only on the arms, back, or shoulders.

The constable must not use towards parties in custody, or otherwise, language calculated to provoke or offend them; such conduct often creates resistance in the party, and a hostile feeling amongst the persons present.

. . .

While on duty, he must not enter into conversation with any one – not even with other constables – except on matters relating to his duty. He is not to walk his beat in a slovenly manner, nor loiter about with his hands in his pockets.

He must remember that there is no qualification more indispensable to a police officer than a perfect command of temper, never suffering himself to be moved by threats or irritating language. If he does his duty in a quiet but determined manner, such conduct will tend to induce bystanders to render him assistance, should he require it.

When constables are walking along the streets, they should not shoulder past passengers, but give way in a mild manner. The more civil and respectful they are, the more likely they will be supported by the public in the proper execution of their duty.

Extracts from Belfast Borough Police Day Book, 1860–1863

Source: Daily order book of Belfast borough police, 1 July 1860–19 Dec. 1863 (Royal Ulster Constabulary Museum)

Daily Orders   April 15 1861

No 1   No 18 Constable Robert Stewart having been permitted to resign without the usual month's notice, is struck off the strength of the Force from this date.

No 2   In consequence of the resignation of the above named constable the following changes of numbers will be made from this date
        No 4 Constable John Hazlett will in future be numbered 18
        No 95 Constable David Carothers will in future be numbered 4

No 3   William Scott, having been appointed on the 14th inst by the Committee & finally approved by the Surgeon, is taken on the strength of the Force, from this date inclusive.

No 4   The following punishments have been this [day] inflicted by the Supt
        No 28 Constable Deveny for having been under the influence of drink on Saturday evening
                                            severely Reprimanded
        No 4 Constable Robert Steed for having been drunk on his beat in Donegall Place at ten minutes past three o'clock on Sunday afternoon   Fined 7/6
        No 58 Constable Robert Irwin for having been drunk in Divis St. at twenty minutes before three o'clock this morning (Not on duty)   Fined 2/6

Daily Orders   April 18 1861

No 1   No 100 Constable Patrick Magee having been permitted to resign without the usual month's notice is struck off the strength of the Force from this date.

No 2   Constables are reminded that it is their duty to remove orange peels off the footways. Some accidents have occurred during the past week through want of attention to this duty.

No 3   Attention is called to the following paragraph, which is taken from the 11th page of the Instruction book. A Constable, when on duty, must not enter into conversation with any one – not even with other Constables – except on matters relative to his duty. He is not to walk on his beat in a slovenly manner, or to loiter about with his hands in his pockets. In addition to this the Superintendent warns the Constables, that they must not sit down, or lounge against walls when on duty. The Inspectors are held answerable for the proper carrying out of this order.

No 4   It is notified for the general information of all ranks, that the Superintendent is ordered to prepare for the Committee at their next meeting some suggestions for their guidance, as to whether a rule should be made to the effect, that every man, who gets drunk, should be deprived of his good service pay.

Daily Orders   April 19 1861

No 1   Until further orders No 33 Constable William Wallace will take charge of No 47 Beat & No 23 Constable William Dodds of No 14 Beat by day.

No 2   Whenever a child is found straying the Constable of the Beat will take charge of it, & will remain with it near where it is found for a space of about five minutes, after which, in the event of it not being claimed, he will proceed with it to the Police Office, & deliver it over to the Officer on duty, who will make an entry of the matter in the occurrence book. An entry will also be made of returning the child to its friends.

Daily Orders   April 22 1861

No 1   In future any man returning off leave of more than three days will report himself at the office previous to being placed on duty.

No 2   The Inspectors, when coming off duty tomorrow morning, will report to the officer in charge the names of any publicans, who have had their houses open at illegal hours lately, mentioning after each name whether the house has been open frequently or only occasionally.

No 3   The following punishment has been this day inflicted by the Supt.

No 5 Constable Robert Blair for having been tipsy on duty at a quarter past nine o'clock on the morning of the 20th inst.   suspended three days

Daily Orders   April 24 1861

The following punishment has been this day inflicted by the Supt.

No 47 Constable Henry Connolly for having been drunk on duty at a quarter before eight o'clock on the evening of the 23rd inst.   Fined 5/-

Daily Orders   April 25 1861

No 1   The following punishment has been this day inflicted by the Superintendent

No 72 Constable Robert Hayes for having been in a house of ill fame in Little Edward St at a quarter past twelve o'clock last night, being at the time on the sick list

Suspended one week

No 2   The Police Committee has been this day pleased to permit Robert Stewart to withdraw his resignation and to pay the fine of 10/- awarded by the Supt. on the 2nd inst. This Constable is therefore retaken on the strength of the Force, & posted to the same scale of pay as before.

Daily Orders   April 26 1861

No 1   In future Constables will report any instances they may observe on their beats, in which parties change their residences, to the officer on duty. This order does not refer to persons going out of town for a short time, but to those who change permanently, & is issued for the purpose of assisting the collectors of police rates to ascertain the residences of parties who leave their residences without paying their taxes.

No 2   In making an arrest for any indictable offence, such as larceny, felony, murder, misdemeanour, & others of this class, it is the imperative duty of a Constable to warn the prisoner, at the earliest possible moment, that he is not bound to answer questions; or in any other way to criminate himself, & that anything he may choose to say after such warning, will be used in evidence against him, & Constables are commanded to be extremely cautious in abstaining from interrogating prisoners in their custody.

So jealous is the law in guarding against anything like entrapping a prisoner into an admission of guilt, that it has frequently in the highest courts been held that answers given to a Constable in reply to questions put by him, although he had given the prisoner a previous caution, were notwithstanding inadmissible in evidence.

No 3   No 31 Constable William Ross is suspended until further orders for having been implicated on last night in entrapping a woman into an admission of having committed theft, & for having afterwards arrested her on the charge.

Bibliography

I. PRIMARY SOURCES

A. Manuscripts
B. Parliamentary Papers
C. Newspapers
D. Contemporary Publications, and Reminiscences by Contemporaries

II. SECONDARY SOURCES

E. Later Books and Articles
F. Unpublished Dissertations

I. PRIMARY SOURCES

A. Manuscripts

Belfast City Hall

Belfast police committee minutes, Jan. 1800–Jan. 1844
Belfast police commissioners' minutes, Jan. 1800–Jan. 1844
Town council committee on police affairs minutes, Feb. 1844–Sept. 1865
Town council minute book, 1853

Public Record Office of Northern Ireland

D.46. Reports of the Belfast voluntary night watch, May–Nov. 1812, Feb.–May 1816
D.1558/2/3. Reverend A. McIntyre's diary of visits to the poor of Belfast, Aug. 1853–Aug. 1856
D.3361/3. Notes of talk given by 'an octogenarian' to the Belfast Naturalists Field Club, 1868 or 1869.

Royal Ulster Constabulary Museum

Daily order book of Belfast borough police, 1 July 1860–19 Dec. 1863.

National Archives

Chief Secretary's Office Registered Papers

National Library of Ireland

Ms 7600. Larcom Papers
Ms 19486. Joseph Patrick Carroll, 'Notes for a history of police in Ireland'

Public Record Office, Kew

HO 184/16: Irish Constabulary general register, 1865

B. Parliamentary Papers

Report from the select committee of inquiry into drunkenness, with the minutes of evidence, and appendix H.C. 1834 (601) viii 1

First report of the commissioners appointed to inquire into the municipal corporations in Ireland. Appendix, parts I and II: reports from the north-eastern circuit H.C. 1835 [27] [28] xxviii 199

Report from the select committee on pawnbroking in Ireland: together with the minutes of evidence, appendix and index H.C. 1837–38 (677) xvii 173

Minutes of evidence taken before the select committee of the House of Lords appointed to enquire into the state of Ireland since the year 1835, in respect of crime and outrage, which have rendered life and property insecure in that part of the empire, and to report to the House H.L. 1839 486–I 486–II xi 1.423

Report of the commissioners of inquiry into the origin and character of the riots in Belfast in July and September 1857; together with minutes of evidence and appendix H.C. 1857–58 [2309] xxvi 1

Report of the commissioners of inquiry, 1864, respecting the magisterial and police arrangements and establishments of the borough of Belfast H.C. 1865 [3466] xxviii 1

Minutes of evidence and appendix to the report of the commissioners of inquiry, 1864, respecting the borough of Belfast H.C. 1865 [3466–I] xxviii 27

Report of the commissioners of inquiry, 1869, into the riots and distur-bances in the city of Londonderry. With minutes of evidence and appendix H.C. 1870 (c.5) xxxii 411

Belfast riots commission, 1886. Report of the Belfast riots commissioners. Minutes of evidence, and appendix H.C. 1887 (c.4925) xviii 1

Report from the select committee on Municipal Regulation (constabulary &c) Belfast Bill; together with the proceedings of the committee, minutes of evidence, and appendix (London, 1887)

C. Newspapers *(published in Belfast, unless otherwise indicated)*

Belfast Commercial Chronicle
Belfast Daily Mercury
Belfast Monthly Magazine
Belfast Newsletter
Belfast People's Magazine
Comet
Freeman's Journal (Dublin)
Irishman
Northern Herald
Northern Whig
Ulsterman
Vindicator

D. Contemporary Publications and Recollections by Con-temporaries

Barrow, John. *A tour round Ireland, through the sea-coast counties, in the autumn of 1835* (London, 1836)

Batt, Reverend Narcissus G. 'Belfast sixty years ago: recollections of a septuagenarian' in *Ulster Journal of Archaeology*, vol. ii, no.2 (Jan. 1896), pp.92–95

Belfast and its environs, with a tour to the Giant's Causeway (Dublin, 1842)

Belfast police manual. Compiled for the use of the Royal Irish Constabulary serving in the town of Belfast (Belfast, 1888)

Borough of Belfast. Laws and bye-laws for better regulating coaches, carriages, chariots, landaus, landaulets, cabriolets, sociables, flys, jaunting-cars, gigs, cabs, and other such like carriages, plying for hire, and the owners and drivers thereof (Belfast, 1850)

Copy of the contract between the commissioners & committee of police, of the town of Belfast; and John & George Barlow, of the city of London (Belfast, 1834)

Doyle, J.B. *Tours in Ulster: a hand-book to the antiquities and scenery of the north of Ireland* (Dublin, 1854)

Edgar, Reverend John. 'The dangerous and perishing classes' in *Belfast Social Inquiry Society*, no. 5 (1852), pp.3–24

Gaffikin, Thomas. *Belfast fifty years ago* (Belfast, 1894)

Hall, S.C. and A.M. *Ireland: its scenery, character &c* (2 vols., London, 1841–43)

Instructions to the Belfast police force, 1856 (Belfast, 1856)

Le Fanu, W.R. *Seventy years of Irish life, being anecdotes and reminiscences* (London, 1893)

Lewis, Samuel. *A topographical dictionary of Ireland* (2 vols., London, 1837)

McTear, Thomas. 'Personal recollections of the beginning of the century' in *Ulster Journal of Archaeology*, vol. v, no. 2 (Feb. 1899), pp.67–80

Moore, F. Frankfort. *The truth about Ulster* (London, 1914)

O'Hanlon, Revd. William Murphy. *Walks among the poor of Belfast* (Memston, 1971 reprint of the 1853 original)

Rodenberg, Julius. *A pilgrimage through Ireland, or the island of the saints* (London, 1860)

Slater's national commercial directory of Ireland (Manchester and London, 1846)

Smith, J. Husband. *Belfast and its environs, with a tour to the Giant's Causeway* (Dublin, 1853)

The Belfast almanac, for the year of Our Lord 1851 (Belfast, 1851)

The Belfast and province of Ulster directory for 1865–66. Vol. VII (Belfast, 1865)

The 'Northern Athens'; or, life in the Emerald Isle (Belfast, 1826)

II. SECONDARY SOURCES

E. Later Books and Articles

Bardon, Jonathan. *Belfast: an illustrated history* (Belfast, 1984)

—— *A history of Ulster* (Belfast, 1992)

Baker, Sybil E. 'Orange and green: Belfast, 1832–1912' in H.J. Dyos and Michael Wolff (ed.), *The Victorian city: images and realities* (2 vols., London, 1973,), ii, pp.789–814

Barnes, Jane. *Irish industrial schools, 1868–1908: origins and development* (Dublin, 1989)

Benn, George. *A history of the town of Belfast from 1799 till 1810 together with some incidental notices on local topics and biographies of many well-known families* (London, 1880)

Blythe, Earnan P. 'The D.M.P.' in *Dublin Historical Record*, vol. 20, nos. 3–4 (June–Sept. 1965), pp.116–26

Boyd, Andrew. *Holy war in Belfast* (2nd ed., Tralee, 1972)

Boyle, Kevin. 'Police in Ireland before the union: I' in *Irish Jurist*, new series, vol. 7 (1972), pp.115–37

—— 'Police in Ireland before the union: II' in *Irish Jurist*, new series, vol. 8 (1973), pp.90–116

—— 'Police in Ireland before the union: III' in *Irish Jurist*, new series, vol. 8 (1973), pp.323–48

Brett, C.E.B. 'The Georgian town: Belfast about 1800' in J.C. Beckett and R.E. Glasscock (ed.), *Belfast: origin and growth of an industrial city* (London, 1967), pp.67–77

Broeker, Galen. *Rural disorder and police reform in Ireland, 1812–36* (London, 1970)

Cochrane, Nigel I. 'Public reaction to the introduction of a new police force: Dublin 1838–45' in *Eire-Ireland*, vol. xxii, no. 1 (spring 1987), pp.72–85

Connolly, S.J. *Religion, law and power: the making of Protestant Ireland 1660–1760* (Oxford, 1992)

Cox, Ronald. *Oh, Captain Shaw: the life story of the first and most famous chief of the London fire brigade* (London, 1984)

Critchley, T.A. *A history of police in England and Wales 900–1966* (London, 1967)

Crossman, Virginia. *Politics, law and order in nineteenth-century Ireland* (Dublin, 1996)

Fulham, Gregory J. 'James Shaw-Kennedy and the reformation of the Irish Constabulary, 1836–38' in *Eire-Ireland*, vol. xvi, no. 2 (summer 1981), pp.93–106

Greer, D.S. *Compensation for criminal injury* (Belfast, 1990)

Griffin, Brian. 'Religion and opportunity in the Irish police forces, 1836–1914' in R.V. Comerford, Mary Cullen, J.R. Hill and Colm Lennon (ed.), *Religion, conflict and coexistence in Ireland: essays presented to Monsignor Patrick J. Corish* (Dublin, 1990), pp.219–34

—— '"Such varmint": The Dublin police and the public, 1838–1913' in *Irish Studies Review*, no. 13 (winter 1995–96), pp.21–25.

—— 'The Irish police: love, sex and marriage in the nineteenth and early twentieth centuries' in Margaret Kelleher and James Murphy (ed.), *Gender perspectives in nineteenth-century Ireland: public and private spheres* (Dublin, 1997), pp.168–78

Hart, Jenifer. 'Reform of the borough police, 1835–56' in *English Historical Review*, vol. 70 (1955), pp.411–27

Henry, Brian. *Dublin hanged: crime, law enforcement and punishment in late eighteenth-century Dublin* (Dublin, 1994)

Hepburn, A.C. *A past apart: studies in the history of Catholic Belfast 1850–1950* (Belfast,1996)

Lampson, G. Locker. *A consideration of the state of Ireland in the nineteenth century* (London, 1907)

McAughtry, Sam. 'Being Protestant in Northern Ireland' in James McLoone (ed.), *Being Protestant in Ireland* (Belfast and Dublin, 1985), pp.34–47

McDowell, R.B. *Ireland in the age of imperialism and revolution 1760–1801* (Oxford, 1979)

—— *The Irish administration, 1801–1914* (London and Toronto, 1964)

Maguire, W.A. *Belfast* (Keele, 1993)

O'Brien, Joseph V. *'Dear, dirty Dublin': a city in distress, 1899–1916* (Berkeley, 1982)

Ó Ceallaigh, Tadhg. 'Peel and police reform in Ireland, 1814–18' in *Studia Hibernica*, no. 6 (1966), pp.25–48

O'Keeffe, Peter, and Simington, Tom. *Irish stone bridges: history and heritage* (Dublin, 1991)

O'Leary, Cornelius. 'Belfast urban government in the age of reform' in David Harkness and Mary O'Dowd (ed.), *The town in Ireland* (Belfast, 1981), pp.87–202

—— and Budge, Ian. *Belfast: approach to crisis: a study of Belfast politics 1613–1970* (London, 1973)

Osborough, W.N. *Law and the emergence of modern Dublin: a litigation topography for a capital city* (Dublin, 1996)

Palmer, Stanley H. *Police and protest in England and Ireland 1780–1850* (Cambridge, 1988)

Pearson, Michael. *The Age of Consent: Victorian prostitution and its enemies* (Newton Abbot, 1972)

Ritvo, Harriet. *The animal estate: the English and other creatures in the Victorian age* (London, 1990)

Stead, Philip John. 'The new police' in David H. Bayley (ed.), *Police and society* (London, 1977), pp.73–84

Storch, Robert D. 'The plague of the blue locusts: police reform and popular resistance in northern England, 1840–57' in *International Review of Social History*, vol. 20, part I (1975), pp.61–90

—— 'The policeman as domestic missionary: urban discipline and popular culture in northern England, 1850–1880' in *Journal of Social History*, vol. ix, no. 4 (1976), pp.481–509

—— 'Police control of street prostitution in Victorian London: a study in the contexts of police action' in David H. Bayley (ed.), *Police and society* (London, 1977), pp.49–72

Tobias, J.J. *Crime and police in England 1700–1900* (Dublin, 1979)

Whiteside, J.A. 'Policing Belfast under Captain Shaw' in *Ulsterview* (Feb. 1966), pp.17–20

F. Unpublished Dissertations

Cochrane, Nigel I. 'The policing of Dublin, 1830–46: a study in administration' (unpublished M.A. thesis, University College Dublin, 1984)

Griffin, Brian. 'The Irish police, 1836–1914: a social history' (unpublished Ph.D. thesis, Loyola University of Chicago, 1991)

Monaghan, John Joseph. 'A social and economic history of Belfast 1801–1825' (unpublished Ph.D. thesis, Queen's University of Belfast, 1940)

Starr, Joseph P. 'The enforcing of law and order in eighteenth century Ireland: a study of Irish police and prisons from 1665 to 1800' (unpublished Ph.D. thesis, Dublin University, 1968)

Index

Lee, Israel, publican, 57
Lee, Susan, brothel keeper, 67
Leggatt (Ligget), George, night
    constable, 133
Leonard, John, day constable, 83
Lewis, David, police assailant, 113
Lewis, Samuel, 90
Limerick
    city, 3–4
    county, 3–4
Lindsay, Alderman, 123
Lindsay, Thomas, chief day and night
    constable, 38, 48, 52, 84
Linn, Isaiah, constable, 125
London Metropolitan Police, 1, 2, 24
Long Bridge, 62
Loughran, Biddy, prostitute and
    thief, 48
Loughran, Letitia, child thief, 72
Lynass, Samuel, day constable, 128,
    129
Lyons, Constable, 114
Lyons, W.T.B., justice of the peace,
    115
Lyttle, John, mayor, 126–27, 137

McAnulty, Mary Jane, juvenile
    thief, 74–75
McAughtry, Sam, writer, 142
McAuley, Thomas, watchman, 38
McBride, John, constable, 39
McCafferty, Patrick, sub-constable,
    136
McCallum, John, repeat offender,
    85
McCance, James Law, resident
    magistrate, 121
McCance, Sarah Jane, repeat
    offender, 87
McCann, Peter, prize fighter, 109
McCarrol, Dan, watchman, 56
McCartney, James, juvenile robber,
    69
McChestney, Samuel, constable, 125
McClelland, John, constable, 130
McClenaghan, Constable, 52
McClure, John, juvenile thief, 71
McClure, Victor, constable, 38
McConaghy, Anne, child thief, 73
McCrea, Constable, 113

McDonnell, Rose, alias Liddy, thief,
    21
McGee, Dr William, mayor, 76
McGibbon, Constable, 85, 113
McGowan, Watchman, 46–47
McGuickan, Watchman, 56
McIlroy, Hugh, inspector, 38, 130
McIntyre, A., clergyman, 65, 104
McKenna, Watchman, 56
McKittrick, Chief Constable, 85,
    136, 138–39
McKnight, Constable, 33
McLarinon, Watchman, 48
McLaverty, Henry, constable, 36
McLoughlin, Bernard, juvenile
    thief, 71
McLoughlin, James, *Ulsterman*
    proprietor, 132
McLoughlin, John, child thief, 71
McManus, John, child thief, 72
McManus, Michael, watchman, 46
McMaster, Constable, 52
McMullan, Hugh, constable,
    130–31
McMullan, John, watchman, 34
McQuilty, William, day
    constable, 47
McTear, Thomas, 104
McVeigh, Hugh, prize fighter, 109
McWilliams, Day Constable, 34
McWilliams, Stewart, detective
    constable, 36
Macaulay, John, constable, 133
Mackay, Betty, prostitute, 85
Magheragall, Co. Antrim, 126
Magill, John, day constable, 24, 43
Mallon, Patrick, constable, 37
Mann, Charles, constable, 48
marine stores, 24, 77, 96
Marks, Archibald, disorderly
    prisoner, 139
Martin, Agnes, 'Lamp Post', repeat
    offender, 88
Martin, Edward, watchman, 34–35
Massereene, Viscount, 78
Massey, John, begging
    impostor, 85–86
Mateer, street preacher, 138
Mathew, Fr Theobald,
    temperance advocate, 82

The Irish Legal History Society

Established in 1988 to encourage the study and advance the knowledge of the history of Irish law, especially by the publication of original documents and of works relating to the history of Irish law, including its institutions, doctrines and personalities, and the reprinting or editing of works of sufficient rarity or importance.

PATRONS

The Hon. Mr Justice   Rt. Hon. Sir Robert Carswell
Liam Hamilton

LIFE MEMBERS

Rt. Hon.   The Hon.   Rt. Hon.
Lord Lowry   T.A. Finlay   Lord Hutton

COUNCIL, 1995

PRESIDENT

Daire Hogan, esq.

VICE-PRESIDENTS

Professor G.J. Hand   Professor D.S. Greer

SECRETARIES

Professor W.N. Osborough
Dr. A. Dowling

TREASURERS

R.D. Marshall, esq.
J. Leckey, esq.

ORDINARY MEMBERS

The Hon. Mr Justice Costello   J.F. Larkin, esq.

J.I. McGuire, esq.   J.A.L. McLean, esq., Q.C.

R. O'Hanlon, esq.   His Honour Judge Hart, Q.C.
(co-opted)